Pick of
PUNCH

"Have you anything that'll eat this?"

Pick of
PU

"Sixteen men on a dead man's chest!"

NCH

Edited by ALAN COREN

A PUNCH BOOK

Published in association with

GRAFTON BOOKS

A Division of the Collins Publishing Group

LONDON GLASGOW
TORONTO SYDNEY AUCKLAND

"I wouldn't sit there, you'll be covered in cat hairs."

Grafton Books
A Division of the Collins Publishing Group
8 Grafton Street, London W1X 3LA

Published by Grafton Books 1987

Copyright © Punch Publications Ltd 1987

British Library Cataloguing in Publication Data

Pick of Punch.
1. English wit and humour
I. Coren, Alan   II. Punch
827′.914′08   PN6175

ISBN 0-246-13247-7

Designed by Sheena Boyd

Printed in Great Britain by
William Collins Sons Ltd, Westerhill, Glasgow

CONTENTS

ALAN COREN
Thanks For The Memory

MONDAY EVENING

Dear Diary,

Today was a real hard day.

It started off where I ate a little house. I did not know I had ate a little house until I found a little elf in my spoon. First off, I thought it was a roach, but when I looked on the back of the pack it said this was my lucky day because each Grape Nuts pack contained a little elf and a little house, and what you did was you put the little elf in the little house and then you would have a little house with a little elf in, and you could add it to your collection. When I found the little elf in my spoon I tipped all the Grape Nuts on to the table but there was no little house.

I guess I will have to go into Bethesda Naval and have the little house taken out. Otherwise my collection will look dumb, just a little elf standing next to a little witch and a little dragon and a little goblin and not in his little house.

George Shultz came in right after breakfast.
Here is the conversation:
"Good morning, Mr President."
"I ate the little house, George."
"Good. I think we should go up to the meeting now."

The meeting was a tough meeting. Here are my notes:

As you look at the back of Caspar Weinberger's envelope, Iran is on the right and is joined to Iraq on the left. They are written down IraN and IraQ so we all know exactly who's who, because they are both of them followers of Islam, a camel-driver, but George says don't worry, anybody could get confused, and I should look at the photographs of an IraQi and an IraNi in my update file.
Here is the conversation:
Me: "They both look kind of Jewish, George."
Weinberger: "What did the President say, George?"
Shultz: "He said they both look kind of Jewish."
Weinberger: "Okay. Just checking."
The discussion opened up right after that, and I formed the impression that IraQ and IraN are different kinds of Islams and are fighting a war due to this, and the object is to get right to the other side of Weinberger's envelope. I also formed the impression, at 11.20 approximately Eastern Standard Time, that I had got the mango Danish.
Here is the conversation:
Shultz: "—or, alternatively, laundered through Tel Aviv?"
Me: "Who ordered the mango Danish?"
Meese: "What?"
Me: "This seems to be a mango Danish. I ordered a blueberry muffin."
Weinberger: "I have your muffin, Mr President."
Me: "Then you get the mango Danish, am I right?"
Weinberger: "I was the pretzel."
Shultz: "I have the pretzel. I ordered the cinnamon toast."
Meese: "I have the cinnamon toast. I ordered the mango Danish."
Me: "Great! Now, just to kind of re-cap, IraQ is the flakies with the long black shirts, right?"

In the afternoon session, Shultz brought up some kind of thing we signed one time about a worldwide embargo against arms sales to IraN, due to where they took US hostages. Weinberger said that we ought to look at this in the light of the fact that it was now the Lebanon that had the US hostages. I said maybe we ought to bomb it again. They all looked at me.
Here is the conversation:
Weinberger: "We never bombed the Lebanon, Mr President."
Me: "Horse feathers! Gimme a map. Okay, what's that under my pinkie?"
Shultz: "Tripoli, Mr President."
Me: "Hardy-ha-ha! Tell me we didn't bomb the hell out of Tripoli!"
Shultz: "You are pointing at Tripoli, Lebanon, Mr President. We bombed Tripoli, Libya."
Weinberger: "If I can return to the matter of the Hawk sales to ..."
I went out to the john. I think the little house is wedged somewhere. It gave me time to think. So we hit the wrong Tripoli. We bombed the Tripoli that didn't have our hostages and we didn't bomb the Tripoli that did. Don't tell me it's an easy mistake, Diary, some of those Navy pilots are pulling down a hundred thousand plus.
Still, I guess it's lucky we didn't take out Tripoli, Iowa.

TUESDAY EVENING

Dear Diary,

I missed the rest of yesterday's afternoon session, but I guess you know that. I hope you enjoyed *The Flintstones.* What I don't understand is, when they go to the drive-in on their dinosaur, how come the movie they see is in colour? I remember when colour came in, it was 1935. This is just like the Tripoli screw-up. Details count.

George Shultz came in right after breakfast.
Here is the conversation:
"Good morning, Mr President."
"Look, George, I got another little house out of the new Grape Nuts pack. I now have two little elfs. Should I have one little elf inside and one outside, or what?"
"I think we should go up to the meeting now."

The meeting was even tougher than yesterday. Here are my notes:

This is the story so far, as I understand it. We are at war with IraN because of the hostages they took and so we are not going to give them any arms or let anybody else give them any arms, except that we are going to give them arms because we bombed the wrong Lebanon and so we are at peace with IraN for maybe a couple of weeks, but we will have to go to war with them again as soon as they have used our arms to bomb the right Lebanon and get US hostages back, but any arms they have not used we are going to have to get back, in case we have to use them to bomb IraN if they start taking US hostages.

Also, nobody must find out, because the Soviets are supplying arms to IraN which we have condemned on the grounds that this is destabilising the area and, as a neutral, we cannot allow IraN to fall into the Soviet orbit because that would mean it fell out of the US orbit and we have to be friendly to IraN because we are at war with it. Also, the Soviets are shipping arms to IraQ. I guess this must be because IraQ is holding Soviet hostages, but Shultz just looks at the ceiling when I ask this, clearly it is something he does not want minuted at this moment in time, it is a damned sensitive area.

I went out right after the summary on account of Edwin Meese got the wrong waffle and Weinberger found mayo on his BLT and Shultz said what the kitchen needed was authority at the highest level and nobody could do it better than me so why didn't I go straighten them out? I am a sucker for flattery, Diary, it's the way I'm made, I guess. Hollywood can do that to you.

I got back kind of late due to where they had *The Price is Right* on in the kitchen. A guy, just an ordinary guy from Topeka, Kansas, guessed the price of a new hi-fi system right to the damned cent! Where do we get such men?

When I got back, Shultz was talking about sending arms to Israel.
Here is the conversation:
Me: "Great play, George! Israel will zap Lebanon and get the US hostages, so we don't have to sell arms to Iran and screw up relations with anybody, right?"
George: "No, Israel will sell the arms to Iran."
Me: "I thought they were enemies."
George: "They are."
Me: "How's the waffle, Ed?"
Meese: "Terrific, Mr President."
I looked out the window for a while. Weinberger was saying how the guy they were going to use as a go-between for Colonel Oliver North

was Adnan Khashoggi. He is a Saudi-Arabian, so I guess that as a sworn enemy of both Israel and Iran, he is in an ideal position to help them.

After a couple of hours, I realised I did not know who this Colonel Oliver North was.
Here is the conversation:
Weinberger: *"He is the Marine officer who headed up the investigation into the Lebanon bombing. He led the hunt for those responsible."*
Me: *"Did he get the guys who hit the wrong Tripoli?"*
Weinberger: *"Not that Lebanon bombing, Mr President. This was the Lebanon bombing in 1983 when the Lebanese killed 241 US Marines."*
Me: *"Holy Moly! You mean the Lebanese got the wrong Tripoli, too? Isn't it about time they changed the name before anybody else gets killed? How about Walnut Creek? I always thought Walnut Creek was a great name for a town. It sounds like a good, clean town, a good town to live in, a good place to raise your kids. I grew up in a town like that. It was called Dixon, Illinois. Nobody ever bombed Dixon, Illinois."*
Weinberger: *"That was a really terrific bacon-lettuce-and-tomato, Mr President. Nobody could have swung it in that kitchen like you swung it. I don't suppose you could, I mean I hate to ask, but, you know, talking makes me kind of hungry, and…"*
Me: *"Say no more, old buddy. While I'm up, who needs more coffee?"*

But here's the crazy thing, Diary. When I got back, the room was empty. I guess they moved to another room for security purposes. It was a smart thing to do. I never did find out where they went, which just goes to show how secure it was. I have a great team there!
George came by tonight to say he's fixed it for me to go into Bethesda Naval tomorrow to have the little house removed. He says it's worth ten poll points, minimum, and be sure and wave from my window right after. Maybe hold up the little house.
I asked him about that other thing, with the **Q** and the **N** and all that, and he said not to worry, it would all be taken care of. ❧

ROGER WODDIS

Do Thy Thing

Prince Edward is to be patron of the National Youth Theatre.

Fear no more the street o' the Sun,
    Nor thy father's furious rages;
Thou an eager troupe will run,
    And decline to take thy wages.
Golden lads should not, we trust,
Like bakers, have to earn a crust.

Fear no more the crowd at the gate,
    Thou art past the bar-room joke;
What the blazer'd set most hate
    Is someone who's an arty bloke.
Such witless oafs who mock thee must,
When they were young, have been concuss'd.

Fear no more the obstacle course
    Favour'd by the Royal Marines;
Trials that tested thy resource
    Should stand thee well behind the scenes.
Thus might thou stop, but only just,
The NYT from going bust.

"Ah, there you are, Protheroe. I was beginning to think the fuzzie-wuzzies had got you."

"I'm a humanitarian."

HALDANE

SUPER
8

"For Chrissake, Arnie, how do I know how a smog
monster relates to his parents?"

"Quite frankly, I don't see you as General McArthur."

"Manicure!"

"Do you have to send all our
rows to Meryl Streep and
Jack Nicholson?"

"Let me through, I'm a special effects expert!"

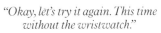

"Okay, let's try it again. This time
without the wristwatch."

"It's not so much the smell of brimstone,
it's the non-stop Fred Astaire routines."

"We've been offered $16 million for the movie-rights if I eat you."

BARGEPOLE

A chap wrote me a nice letter saying *You are wonderful* which is the sort of thing one likes. Probably you don't get that sort of letter. Probably you get letters saying *Henceforth you are no son of mine* and *We are therefore commencing proceedings without further notice* and *I don't know how to tell you this but I got the result and it's positive* but we all have our troubles and an excess of adulation is my cross.

This particular chap was on about films. I rang him up on the telephone and he said *Why don't we meet in the Groucho Club?* and I fiddled around on my desk looking for my Filofax and then I screamed and fell over. Good God in Heaven, I have become a media person, insouciantly making assignations with chaps about films in the Groucho Club and writing them down in a Filofax. What can be nastier or more alien to everything I hold beneath reproach?

I think all this Filofax balls has got to stop. One of the nice things about music is that it can only be addressed in its own terms, being a totally self-referential logical form. Herein lies a rich seam of bullshit crying out to be mined and I for one am happy to oblige. Hans Keller said it wasn't necessarily so, but look what happened to him. Fell down dead.

The Filofax generation never got to him, lucky old sod, but I think he'd have recognised it as something else to get his analytical teeth into. What are we talking about, for God's sake, but a bloody loose-leaf notebook? Yet the thing has become a cult object and now its makers are going for a "quote" on the "USM". It's perfect. It's everything one would like to take a machine-gun to, creeping up in the dark on rubber-soled shoes with a few clips of soft-nosed shells close at hand. The Yuppy dream reaches fruition and is massacred in a flurry of upwardly-mobile blood and expensive bridgework. Kabooom! BMW paintwork flies about the desirable neighbourhood as tanned necks are ripped away from their stinking mid-Atlantic button-down collars. Why can't the bastards invent a button-down lip?

I had my first Filofax in 1968. It belonged to my grandfather. It was unpretentious. You put the pages in and wrote stuff on them. I rather liked it. It said N&H FILOFAX on it and nothing else. Research indicated that N&H stood for Norman & Hill and you had to track the buggers down and write to them for new pages. They had all sorts of arcana directed at doctors, officers and the clergy. I still have some old forms with a naive drawing of the human frame *mirabiliter condidisti et mirabilius reformasti* on which Dr Snoddies could draw warts and lumps. (These pages are useful still, to me; I draw Yuppies infected with boils and protuberances on them. Some I afflict with trunks, some with great fin-like limbs or hypertrophied genitalia, and then pore over this ad-hoc bestiary in the privacy of my eown heome, murmuring gently *Nema; malo a nos libera et, tentationem in inducas nos ne* and so forth.)

How this is representative of my poor life. Not, I mean, the incanta-tions and bile, but the dreadful fate of being doomed to be first, of finding unpretentious utility in simple things only to see them taken up as cult objects by hideous, grinning graphic designers in flat-top haircuts and Ray-Bans (I was wearing Ray-Ban Wayfarers in 1971). Every second-rate snotty prune in Covent Garden now carries a Filofax and Doesn't Know What He'd Do Without It. I am told it has even penetrated to something called *EastEnders*. Now they want lots of money so that the Filofax people can buy BMWs and cheese plants and eat at the Groucho Club.

To hell with the lot of them. I am no longer able to use mine. I have transferred to a nicer thing called Lefax which is much more stylish but I expect that will become a cult object in due course. My repertoire is diminishing by the moment. Bereft of my hats, my Ray-Bans, my single gold ear-rings, my Trumpers shaving cream, my Penhaligon's scent, my yellow Argyle socks, my tortoiseshell specs, my trouser turnups, my bow ties, my braces and my spotted handkerchiefs, I suspect that soon I shall lose my Top-Siders, my walking sticks, my Leica, my snuff-box, my dip-pen and my Nellie Lutcher records to the relentless trendies. Anything that's any good at all, the buggers will take over.

I suppose the only way out of this conundrum is to adopt as essential elements of personal style only those things which are unacceptable or ruinously expensive. Henceforth I shall confine myself to bespoke shoes and Spam sandwiches. I shall pick my nose in public and eschew normal romance, instead, when the urges call, making a nice goat my own, preferably in Jermyn Street. I shall cultivate boils and nostril hair, and suck Sherbet Fountains at Demis Roussos concerts. I shall throw away my Filofax and hire a White Russian princess to act as amanuensis, transcribing my utterances on vellum with a platinum pen, a Transylvanian dwarf to hold my ink-pot. My bathroom will boast no pink Andrex but sheets of chamois, with an ancient Tibetan mute to measure you up; I shall wash, not in soap but in cheese, and will dine on mushy peas and virgins' blood. Doubtless the trendies will catch on before too long, but think what appalling bloody fools they'll look, and how I'll laugh up my iguana-skin sleeve (with integral phlegm-bag).

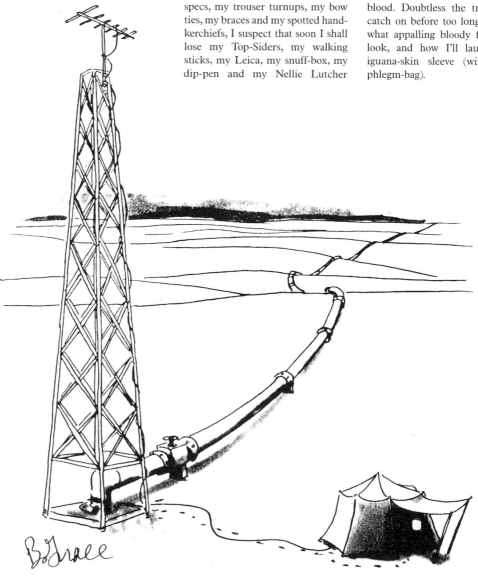

Starvation – Nuclear Threat – Understains – Terrorism – Aids
Broken Guttering – Poverty – Drugs – Carpet Rucking Up

Is There A Solution?

In answer to our urgent need

THE MAHARISHI KIM IL ANDERTON IS IN THE WORLD

A World Teacher For All People, He Loves Everybody, Almost

WHAT IS HE SAYING?

"The problems of mankind are soluble. Look at Sodom and Gomorrah."

"If you see anything suspicious, build an Ark."

"If The Almighty had not wanted people to be policemen, He would not have grown helmets on their heads."

"Jesus says do not leave that vehicle unattended."

"Drug addicts should be strangled at birth."

"Love thy brother. If he is not really thy brother, bloody watch out!"

WHEN WILL WE LOOK UPON HIS FACE?

Sponsored walk across Manchester Ship Canal, Saturday, January 31.
Tickets £2.50, children and pensioners half-price, unwaged piss off.

Desktop Publish And Be Damned!

Plans are now highly advanced for writing this article by a revolutionary ''single-stroke'' method using the latest in new technology and cutting out the cumbersome old three-stage process of pencil-stub draft, rough typescript and clean copy typed up by Tracy or Sharon from the temps agency.

When ''Exercise Desktop'', as the new ''daisy-wheel'' operation has been code-named, is 100 per cent functional, this article should be more saleable, funnier, easier to read, translatable into ten languages at the touch of a ''memory key'' and free of the superfluous apostrophes which Tracy scatters over any typescript like raisins in a pudding mix.

A dictionary program ''input module'' aims to eliminate Sharon's spelling mistakes entirely, although it does not itself seem to be any too certain how to spell ''programme''; while a ''storage system'' or it may be a ''retrieval system'' ensures that the article contains no used jokes. Being cheaper and quicker to produce than the old labour-intensive model, the article can be twice or even ten times the usual length without inducing writer's cramp, a flexibility feature not available with the conventional pencil. Should there be no space to publish the article this week, it may be stored, or lost in the system, or re-routed to *Horse & Hound*, or even converted into a cartoon.

However, owing to teething troubles, it has not yet proved possible to produce the whole of this article by the new high-tech process. Readers may experience most of it being typed on an old Adler, with occasional blank spaces where the switchover to the new word processor has not gone smoothly. These hiccups are being ironed out as quickly as possible, and as soon as the writer has acquired one of those adaptor affairs enabling the word processor and his desk lamp to be plugged into the only available socket, the way will be cleared for writing entire articles in green letters on a kind of television screen, then, simply by consulting a textbook, transmitting the finished product direct to somewhere else. The writer is not yet entirely clear where exactly — he was given to understand that his text could be fed straight into the page you are reading now, but does that mean bypassing the Editor? If so, presumably the computer knows how to set the type round the cartoon, if there is one, though it does not seem to have the nous not to split up words so that the *t-* of *the* appears at the end of one line and the *-he* at the beginning of the next; but what the writer wants to know is supposing the article is a few words too long for the page, will the article just carry on into the margin, or will the last paragraph be lopped off or re-routed to one of the back pages, or what?

''Exercise Desktop'', or ''Exercise Tabletop'' as it should be more accurately called at the moment, since this article is being composed in the dining-room where there are plugs available both for a reading lamp and the word processor, has been effected in three stages.

Initially, the old-fashioned mode of correcting the article by xxxxing out mistakes was phased out, and ''Tipp-Ex'' phased in, preparing the way for a smooth changeover to ''correction tape'' as soon as the writer acquired an electronic typewriter. Stage two was obviating carbon-paper and getting photo-copies run off at the local chemist's — a dry run for when ''Exercise Desktop'' is fully operational and as many copies of an article as the writer requires may be produced at the touch of a button, or key rather, though what he is supposed to do with them he doesn't quite know. File them, he supposes.

Stage three was supposed to be the acquisition of the electronic typewriter, but serious technical difficulties were encountered when an experimental attempt to write a portion of this article by this method was made on a demonstration model in Ryman's. Though it had the conventional QWERTY arrangement of keys, the keyboard felt funny to the writer, somewhat like one of those pressed-out plastic trays you get in a box of chocolates, and he was unable to type more than two words without making a mistake. This disappointing result highlighted one of the perils of the new technology — namely, producing an article full of spelling mistakes which the reader would assume were inserted for cheap laughs, like some mock school essay ostensibly written by Smith Mi of the Lower Third. It was decided, therefore, to leapfrog the interim electronic typewriter stage and opt for a crash course on operating a word processor, which would clear the decks for a total desktop publishing operation involving being able to understand expressions like ''word-processed text'', ''computer-generated images'' and ''on-screen representation'', as well as why all these bloody machines seem to be named after fruit.

With the acquisition of the word processor, however, and over and above the difficulty in plugging the thing in, it was discovered that owing to his still not having got the hang of the keyboard, the writer was still making mistakes and there was a real danger that this article would go into production with the reader imagining that ''word processor'' transcribed as ''rowd precurser'' was supposed to be a joke. It was therefore decided that in the initial stages of the switchover to high tech, the word processor would be manned by Sharon. This article is still waiting for her to arrive. She should have been here half an hour ago.

The writer apologises for any blank space that may appear in this article at this juncture, due to the changeover from the old Adler up in the study to the word processor down here in the dining-room. Sharon has now turned up, having had to wait forty minutes for a No. 27 whereupon three came at once, and is now taking down this article from dictation. An "in-Sharon mode" has thus been achieved, whereby an "on-screen representation" is made simply by the writer pacing up and down and feeding Sharon the material he would like positioning "in-article".

It is possible that in reading the first section of this article to be composed entirely by new technology, some readers may not be experiencing the sensation that it is getting any funnier. This is due to technical difficulties, i.e., the writer's acute awareness that the merest stroke of a key with one manicured finger could produce one of two terribly obvious jokes – either wiping out this article completely as these machines are said to be apt to do if you don't know how to use them properly, though what the Editor would have to say when confronted with a blank page and told it is the first total new technology joke is anybody's guess; or showing off the machine's versatility by juggling paragraphs around in whimsical juxtaposition – or, even worse, inserting a recipe for carrot cake copied by Sharon on to a "floppy disc" or something. Or both. Or, and this has only just occurred to the writer, there could be the one where Sharon automatically converts into "article input" everything that is said to her regardless of whether it was supposed to be "in-article" material or not, for instance can't you type any faster, darling, I could have written the whole bloody article in the time it's taken you to peck out two paragraphs, I thought you people were supposed to be trained?

"Well, I'm afraid this is going to cost the Irish squad precious seconds."

Readers in some areas may experience difficulty in reading the rest of this article due to its being written in ballpoint. The writer apologises for any inconvenience caused. This purely temporary setback has been caused by a massive simultaneous breakdown of all the factors involved in the new technology, starting with Sharon who took the above references to herself at face value and flounced off, the stupid little bitch. Secondly, in attempting to take over the manning of the word processor himself, the writer experienced difficulty in "calling up" whatever it is that switches on the electricity, damn and blast the bloody thing. Thirdly, no sooner had the writer transferred this article to the Adler which is kept for use in emergencies, than the elastic band thing which swings back the carriage snapped, rendering it inoperable. Fourthly, the point on the writer's pencil stub is worn down and he cannot find his pencil-sharpener. Normal service will be resumed as soon as possible.

DOC BRIEF
ROBERT BUCKMAN

As a well-known doctor and broadcaster
with a major interest in alcohol addiction and its effects on human physiology,
one of the most common questions I am asked is, "What will you have, doctor?" Well, like most
responsible members of society I have a strict rule about drinking while on duty — I never do it unless someone
else is paying. Alcohol has a lot of different effects on the body and the mind — and sometimes both.
As a medical student, I spent a considerable amount of effort
researching this field using a control population of young adults, usually nurses aged 23.
I thought you might like the benefit of our findings, though the names and telephone numbers have been
changed to protect the guilty. As usual I shall remain anonymous.

THE CHEMISTRY OF ALCOHOL

Chemically speaking, what we call "alcohol" is a relatively simple compound known correctly as ethyl alcohol or ethanol. This comparatively small molecule is one of a family of larger, complex sister compounds which have different first names, such as methyl alcohol, and the less famous ones like propyl alcohol, butyl alcohol, futile alcohol and puerile alcohol (found in immature wines like Beaujolais Nouveau). Apart from these sisters, there are the parent compounds which are known colloquially as wood alcohol (or "Woody") and Mrs Wood Alcohol together with the maiden aunt Bloody Mary, the disreputable French cousin Absinthe, the Mexican black sheep of the family, Tequila Sunrise, and the sweet old granny, Sanatogen.

Now, what these compounds have in common is the chemical structure which includes a hydroxyl group on the terminal carbon atom (written as $-OH$, or $HO-$ in the laevo isomer). That is why chemists are constantly trying to produce complex polyvalent alcohols that can be written as $C_{24}-H_{60}-HO-HO-HO$, which would be a real hit at the lab Christmas party, if nowhere else. Anyway, it is the terminal hydroxyl group that gives the alcohols their particular affinity for more complex and larger chemical structures, e.g. Coke, soda, olives etc. This is also what makes you drunk (*see below, particularly before you fall down*), though not what gives you the hangover (it's probably the peanuts that do that).

However, the metabolism of alcohol inside the body is not simple — nor painless. Once the alcohol molecules get inside the body (albeit briefly, e.g. beer), they move about rapidly in the bloodstream, interacting with erythrocytes, desaturating phosphate buffers, meeting new friends, laughing loudly, and dropping ash on the carpet. They then migrate to the brain (usually before the police arrive) where they produce a series of effects so far-reaching and complex that I shall leave them to the next paragraph.

There will now be a short pause for refreshment. If you wish to have a drink in the interval between paragraphs, please remember to order it before the start. Thank you.

IT'S FULL OF PORK-SCRATCHINGS, SARGE...

ALCOHOL AND THE BRAIN

Now let me ask you the following question: would you believe that alcohol is actually a depressant (apart from when you have to pay for it yourself)? Sorry, time's up, and the answer is NO, i.e. no, you wouldn't believe it. Well, it just shows how wrong you can be, because it is — alcohol is actually a potent inhibitor of brain functions (try having lunch with a journalist if you don't believe me).

However what is so extraordinary is that the parts of the brain most susceptible to this inhibition are the inhibitory pathways themselves. In physiological terms, what happens is that the major bio-parametric negative-feedback inhibitory systems become down-

regulated by sub-maximal loops resulting in a high-excitational state with minimal signal-noise ratio, known to neurophysiologists as "getting pissed".

What happens after that depends on where you are and who you're with. But either way, perhaps the most important question is: if the alcohol molecules move around the brain for such a short time, how come they leave it in such a mess the next morning? Anybody? Thank you, Tebbit, but Currie's hand was up first. Yes, alcohol is a major diuretic (please *stop* giggling, if we can't be adult about things like bladders and kidneys, I'll sit down right now and let Edwina tell the class what's wrong with society.

There now, that's better).

Thus alcohol is a diuretic and causes temporary dehydration, aided and abetted by the salt peanuts, Brie, pork scratchings and, in my opinion, loud music, which certainly seems to scare something out of people over the age of 21. Prolonged exposure to alcohol affects the brain very seriously, producing various encephalopathies and Korsakoff's syndrome in which short-term memory is lost and the patient confabulates, which means making up stories to cover up the gaps. Unfortunately, I can't remember anything about Korsakoff's syndrome even though I looked it up this morning, so I just made all this stuff up as I went along.

ALCOHOL AND THE LIVER

Everyone knows that alcohol can produce permanent changes in the liver, e.g. liver in white-wine sauce with chopped shallots and mushrooms. So, if you have a liver scan and it shows that the mushrooms have appeared, you may safely assume you're in danger. However, before that stage, liver damage can be very subtle and unnoticeable (particularly if you've got a good tailor).

The interesting thing is that, to a large extent, the susceptibility to alcohol-damage is inherited — so that if you wish to drink moderately

and survive you ought to choose your parents with great care. Perhaps this could be the new target of the Unborn Child's Right To Choice movement — offering the foetus a fair chance to

have a look round their parents' hepatic function and wine cellars before deciding whether to be born or not. It would certainly save some disappointment later.

THE DOCTOR TRIES IT ON

Q: I say, I say, I say, specialist in infectious diseases, what's "yaws"?

A: What's "yaws"? What's "yaws"? Why, it's a skin infection caused by a treponema found in South America — but while we're here, can I buy you a drink?

Q: Forget it, we'll stick to the my-dog-has-no-nose one.

MAHOOD

WORKING HOLIDAYS

"I told you not to ring me at the office!"

"I believe Amalgamated
are having cash-flow
problems."

BARBARIANS

Ravaging and pillaging, the Vandals swept through North Africa and captured Carthage — although the Carthaginians, a highly advanced people, had already invented the box.

One more time. I can still hear a dialling tone.

What say, boys? Shall we go and vandalize Rome?

Yes, please, Your Destructiveness!

Posterity will thank us for leaving it in famous ruins.

THIS WAS NOT A NEW IDEA. THE GOTHS HAD SWEPT THROUGH EUROPE, PILLAGING AND PLUNDERING, BUT WERE GIVEN POOR DIRECTIONS.

Rome? Ah, yes, short for Romania — nine hundred miles east and turn left at the roundabout.

And then it gives a Roman holiday, not?

ATTEMPTS TO DEVELOP A NEW STYLE OF ARCHITECTURE LED TO A GOTHIC RIFT.

So, you like it not? Then can you away go and ostracised be — Ostrogoths from now on.

As they now off buggered have, so no one but us visible is — Visigoths from now on.

So, shall we somewhere sweep, plundering and sacking? Rome, to the byplay?

Yes, this plan like I.

You dare tell me, the Emperor, to get off the throne?

You were already plundered, not? Now can you sacked be.

THE HUNS WERE NEXT, BUT YIELDED TO A PAPAL PLEA.

It is our great misfortune that all roads seem to lead here! May I invoke Christian mercy?

But we are pagans, worshipping strange Hungarian gods.

Heathen mercy, then.

ROME DID NOT REALLY NEED ADDITIONAL BARBARITY. A SERIES OF ROYAL MURDERS RESULTED IN THE DISGRUNTLEMENT OF EUDOXIA, WIDOW OF THE LAST EMPEROR BUT ONE, HERE SEEN WITH HER TWO DAUGHTERS.

I am going to invite the Vandals in, girls! Let them sack and rape — not us, of course.

You wish us to sack and rape this Mea Maxima Culpa just for offing your husband?

Absolutely! I hold grudges! Loot and pilfer all you like.

We prefer smash and grab, specially smash.

THE VANDALS DID A GOOD JOB.

Almost too good! Perhaps we should restore some of it.

And be the laughing stock of Vandalia?

Brutes! What are you doing?

Breaking and entering.

Picking and choosing.

Hemming and hawing.

MORAL: Do not invite the burglars to tea. Their manners are barbarous.

AUSTIN MITCHELL
HOT AIRWAYS

TRAVELS with a donkey, my aunt or a Parliamentary delegation: which is preferable? The company on the first two. The cheapness of the latter. It must be the fastest growing branch of the travel industry, outside suing tour companies. The world's skies are black with an increasing supply of Parliamentarians pursuing a diminishing supply of facts round the globe. At public expense.

Other legislatures assume that MPs have to know the world before they can talk about it. Most MPs in other countries are better paid and better backed. So they also travel more: some national airlines seem to be kept going only by their legislators. Others use military aircraft, which we can take only for the horrible haul to the Falklands. Air New Zealand allocates miles for length of tenure, opening up intergalactic prospects to older members. One Kiwi MP fleeing from his creditors took a wad of tickets to sell in California.

British MPs do fewer miles per vote than most. We are meaner towards travel, or anything else which makes MPs better informed and more efficient. Being superior, we assume that the world should come to us rather than us having anything to learn from it. We put in more hours than others, so there's less chance of being away, except in the summer when inconsiderate things like families, other pets and constituents clamour for attention.

Yet things are changing. The new Select Committees have begun to get about, particularly the Home Affairs Committee, which discovered the delights of investigating immigration at the other end. British Airways take more MPs on jollies, though only Tories to expedite privatisation. Corrupt and dubious regimes of all kinds are going in for public relations, which involves flying in cargoes of MPs to say all is well. Indeed, South Africa has for many years kept open hotel and swimming pool (though most townships were closed) to any MP who would merely abstain from abusing the place.

Sanctions will then have a devastating effect on right-wingers, particularly such stars of the southern firmament as Sir Patrick Wall (former member for Mashonaland East) and John Carlisle (Capetown Central).

The Inter-Parliamentary Union supplies MPs to lesser breeds without the Commonwealth. Even to such parliamentary democracies as the Soviet Union. The Commonwealth Parliamentary Union, the best trade union in the world, packages us to the rest of the globe. Indeed, given its services to the heavy lifting of elderly avoirdupois, it should affiliate either to Saga Holidays or Pickfords. In other countries, when Parliaments close down, MPs shoot off; the herd that was shot round the world. Ours slip away silently in session so as not to be noticed by constituents, a misguided practice because electors would be much happier for the country if we were away all year.

Unwilling to admit that, we depart like Sir John Moore at Corunna, often leaving piles of questions and stirring press statements to be filtered through in our absence to give an impression of life and diligence. Only the haphazard incidence of suntans on the benches – they shall not grow pale as we that are left grow pale – gives the game away.

As a blasé television reporter, I'd been to the four corners of the civilised World: Middlesbrough, Richmond, Sheffield and Grimsby, and even a few places overseas, so I was in no hurry to hurtle abroad after election. Until I discovered the secret: gain the favour of the Whips. They dispense travel and other patronage to reward the loyal and punish the petulant. Since I was one of the few members of the Labour Party who actually liked the Labour Government, the tickets started coming.

Telly travel and MP moving are very different. In telly, they're paid First Class but travel Tourist to pocket the difference. In Parliament you start low and pull rank. On business, MPs travel Club but the expense allowance to Committees is such that if all go they can't even afford Tourist: John Brown fixed a deal for the entire Treasury Committee to proceed to Washington via the North Pole and Boston. We arrived, exhausted, to be met by a perky John Brown. He'd flown in direct. More usually the entire trip is spent nattering at the clerk, the embassy, the airline and foreign heads of state about "upgrading". This is done on a rota based on date of election.

In telly, you live, eat, sleep plastic and pursue people who won't speak to you. Parliamentary

"And that's my wife – she hates having her photograph taken."

19

"It was a messy divorce. My husband got the laces."

▶ AUSTIN MITCHELL

travel is cashless, though that doesn't stop MPs counting money and working out profits on a daily subsistence allowance which is enough to support Mathew Parris for a year. Everyone talks to you. At inordinate length. You talk only to each other. Particularly Tories who all want to assess who's worth most.

In telly you travel because you're powerful. In Parliament because you are not. Travel is the opium of the Backbencher and the solace of his impotence. Indeed with Ministers, Shadows, and the ambitious unable to go, it's often difficult to find two brains to rub together on many delegations and there is a special breed of parliamentary lunkhead whose nose bursts below 30,000 feet. He rarely visits his (safe) constituency. The I.P.U. doesn't run there.

On telly tours you must entertain the crew, trudging from brothel to brothel to find one that takes Diners. On Parliamentary trips a leader's sole responsibility is to speak and it's difficult to stop them. Endless mentions of the Mother of Parliaments and her illegitimate offspring; some of democracy (as appropriate) and something nice about the host country, which can require considerable research. Real work is left to the hapless Clerk whose job is to run round like a sheep-dog yapping diffidently, quoting airline timetables instead of *Erskine May*.

The penance of Parliamentary travel is Parliamentarians. No wives, as if anyone wanted to take them, just other members. Endless Parliamentary gossip and applied anthropology, for the other side are stranger than the natives. The pleasure is that everything is done for you. Perhaps too much, breeding a clamour for even more special treatment. Once, faced with a slow moving queue at American immigration, my entire Committee sulked, muttered and grew furious when a member of the House of Lords (called Lord Westbury, probably a Doonesbury

creation) was whistled through. Eventually we were taken out through the exit for accompanied children.

Host countries lavish hospitality, in the mistaken belief that they are entertaining people of importance. Itineraries are totally inflexible, cutting out slums, poverty or problems, to the extent that in some countries they become sealed transport, rather like Lenin's train, between luxury hotel and presidential palace.

British Embassies entertain dutifully, provided you avoid all mention of Tessa Blackstone. They'll talk for hours about the local economic situation or political gossip. They are totally silent about where to change money on the Black Market. The military (ours) are genuinely hospitable, sometimes even to Labour men, but dedicated to getting Parliamentarians drunk. Impossible, given our alcoholic intake. At one Falklands Mess the initiation ceremony made subalterns sick. MPs noticed nothing out of the ordinary. Other military (theirs) are more suspicious. On an American Aircraft Carrier I noticed that all the dials had been taped over, probably because Michael Meacher was on the party.

Normal tourists crave sand, sea, sun and discos. Parliamentarians avoid all four to see factories, farms, power stations and politicians. The occupational hazards are the same as in the House: booze, food and boredom. Plus a new one. What to do at night. MPs are nocturnal creatures. The countries they visit close at nine. In Australasia there's nothing to do except pick a fight. In Uganda we were locked in the Uganda Club or in hotels where sand dribbled out of the bath taps, with only a two-way radio provided by the embassy to summon help. Shots and gunfire echoed round. The batteries failed after an hour.

Embassies won't help, preferring to give the

impression that they devote evenings to study and prayer but probably because you'd see them at the night spots. They entertain you at home with local fuddy-duddies. Members don't particularly want contact with anyone, but if contact there must be, they prefer it young and female. The only obliging Embassy I've struck was one in the Far East which actually took us to a local geisha house. This produced days of excitement and speculation. In a room decorated by photographs of senior American politicians, we were each allocated our geisha. I made valiant attempts at conversation.

I went through the House of Commons Joke Book (a rebound copy of *Punch* for 1912) and she popped a morsel of food into my mouth each time I opened it. The food was beautiful. The drink flowed. The evening moved towards an anticipated climax. Until, at an incredibly early hour, Madame clapped her hands, the girls disappeared, and we were all in the cold night air. Except the Ambassador. He stayed, I assume to pay the bill.

Collected facts soon fill the luggage. Which may be why we buy so few presents. Absence is reward enough for wives, though I did once go shopping with a Tory MP who duplicated every present, one for wife, one for mistress. There are, however, other presents. The worse the regime, the more lavish the gifts. In Uganda we accumulated so many stools, lamps, gongs, mounted tusks, carvings and other immemorabilia that we agreed to give the whole collection to the local hospital. We announced this in farewell speeches.

Next morning at the airport the presents were all baled up and ready to go with us. That was accompanied baggage, unlike the hundredweight of Shona sculpture which once followed me to London as "rock samples". A whole day was necessary to get it out of Heathrow. Visit the home of any Backbencher and see the British Museum as deprived.

The MPs we visit do less well. You can compare problems; bribe the electorate seriatim or collectively with benefits? Put the opposition in prison or just deprive them of information as we do? Westminster MPs are everywhere looked up to yet have all too little to offer. Except gossip, trivia and the supercilious attitudes of exhausted greatness. Indeed, we learn more from abroad than it from us.

I visited Gary Hart's office, where scores of staff advised him, a computer wrote his friendly letters, which were signed by a machine, with whatever his signature was at that time. In Uganda I listened to bands playing the party song (to which officials and prison warders all danced enthusiastically).

In Korea I inspected the electronic voting system, unfortunately not working because too many MPs were in prison. In New Zealand visiting MPs have free rail travel but can't use it because trains are booked years ahead. I was told that free official cars were provided until members from small South Sea Island democracies had abused the privilege to take them to vacation jobs on the docks.

An exciting world. A privilege to have seen it. Thank you. I'm the better member for it. A residue of information lingers, like the avoirdupois. Unfortunately half the nations I've visited changed their regimes as soon as I'd left. Now I'll have to go back to update. It's a hard life in the Parliamentary Pioneer Corps. ◈

"He left you a trillion each. God knows what he did with the rest."

DAVID TAYLOR

That's Light Entertainment

THE Paris Studio, Lower Regent Street, Tuesday. BBC Radio Light Entertainers have assembled for a festive nibble and chat. There's red and white, orange for the drivers. Harry is the first to arrive.

Harry looks just the same. Hullo, Harry! You look just the same! Harry's back, you know, on 2. They're doing him from Man-chester. Or is it Leeds? *Thirty Minutes Worth.* Good title.

And it's still good stuff, people do love Harry. Red or white? What an entertainer, Harry is.

They still recall the old shop-window routine. They do indeed. Barry still uses that, of course, on his warm-up for *The News Quiz.* Comes on from behind the screen there, stays half-hidden behind it, raises an arm and a leg and shouts: "Ladies and gentlemen: the Irish Harry Worth!" And they fall about.

You'd not think anyone'd remember Harry Worth. He's not been on the box for ages, but they all seem to. A natural on radio. Yah. The voice. Have a vol-au-vent?

Not seen Barry as yet, by the way. No, Took, not Cryer. Who's working with John Junkin and Jeremy Beadle and Duggie Brown on *The Name's the Game*, did you hear that?

Good title.

Barry doesn't change. But then they schedule *Back to Square One* straight after, doing it up in Manchester, Ron's doing it, Ron McDonnell. Hullo, Ron! Ron doesn't change. Been at it for years, Ron. Chris Serle is in the chair for BTSO, having the time of his life. There's Bob, by the way, first to arrive as usual. Looks just the same. Hullo, Bob! There's Dick. Dick looks just the same, too.

Incidentally, Ron remembers them doing that Harry Worth window stunt up in St Ann's Square, Manchester. Years ago. They've done some amazing things up there, like the Max Wall and so on. *The Grumbleweeds.* Twice. Mind you, they're doing *The News Huddlines* three times over, twice on 2 and then again on 4. Good title, though. Top up?

You see Bob on the box the other night? Going on about celebrities. Yah. Bit of a pot-calling-kettle situation. But Bob loves radio, you know. He does those quiz things on the box, but really he's happiest doing *Stop The Week* or *Brain of Britain.* How long has he done that now? Or Michael Ember come to that? Suppose it must be. He doesn't change, Dick. What's he doing these days? Hullo, Dick! Sausage-roll?

Dick says he's got three shows lined up by the way. He is doing a thing about Perelman, more about his work than the man. Have to ask Alan about that. Christ, these sausage-rolls. And he's doing a sort of movie quiz, which you might not think would come across on radio, but should. Robin does well with it on the box. He, Robin, didn't know about Dick. Who's doing something else as well, according to Harry, who forgets what. Want one of these puff-pastry jobs?

No, not that Harry. The other Harry, *News Quiz* Harry, who by the way was on *Start The Week* the other week, wasn't he? Done some little funny books on beardies, or fatties, or baldies or whatever, and got himself on with Richard Baker, apparently Victor Lewis Smith, who's producing, has a theme to the show now, so they could ask all the people with bald patches or beards or whatever to comment. Yah. Trouble with Talks and Docs is that they just don't pay. More red?

You're looking in fine fettle, Ian. Do you know Clay? Ian Wallace, Clement Freud. Clay looks as if he's running the buffet. Yah. Isn't that Alan he's talking to? No, not that Alan. That's the *Instant Sunshine* Alan, who's doing AIDS now, isn't he? He used to be on the Health Education Council, only all they do now is AIDS. Hullo, Alan! Rather not shake hands! Is Miles about? Gather you're all back or at any rate *Reasonably Together Again* on Wednesday, then again on Thursday. Good title. Good slots, straight after the news and *You and Yours.* Lots of people in cars.

David? Do you know David? David Barlow. David Hatch. Hullo. Not a bad do, David? The

"I hope you don't mind, we're rather early."

world's turned out. Are you, er, still Radio 4 or are you everything now? Controller or whatever? Thought so. So Martin Fisher's now Head of Light Ent? And Michael Green is Controller of 4. Michael's quite new, come in from Manchester, Ron would know him, been in the job for about six weeks or so. Why is Michael not here by the way? Just a spot of the red, please.

What about this Marmaduke chap, is he good news? Help yourselves to the sandwiches, do, grab 'em by the short and curlies, so to speak!

There's Denis. Denis hasn't changed. Haven't seen if Frank's here. By the way, did you see Martin's producing as well as controlling the network? *Star Terk II* or something. Yes, like *Trek*, but with a mis-print.

Good title.

Harry was saying, by the way, *News Quiz* Harry, he was saying that it's amazing that when they do stuff from this very theatre for the World Service, it's amazing how much post they get, you wouldn't believe the numbers of people out there in the big wide world who sit with their ears glued to BBC Light Ent on the World Service and then write in and say can they have Nigel Rees's autograph. Actually, Nigel's just back with another series of *Quote… Unquote*, which Harry's also producing from

> ## "No, not that Harry. The other Harry, *News Quiz* Harry, who by the way was on *Start The Week* the other week, wasn't he?"

this very theatre, with Tim Rice and Frank Keating on the first one on Saturday, did you hear that? Marvellous. It doesn't change.

Look, we don't want all these sandwiches left.

What's he doing here? Jeremy Whatsisname, Pascal. He's on Capital, isn't he? YAHNY. *You Ain't Heard Nothing Yet.*

Good title.

Is that Rory Bremner he's talking to? Could be anyone, being Rory. Does he ever stop, do you think? Gather Rory's doing a pilot at the moment, with John Langdon doing the script, of course. *The Lonely Arts Club* or something.

Good title.

Jessica Martin's good, too. Hullo, Jessica! She's been with Bobby Davro on the box but apparently she's got a pilot in, too. Oh God, look, that's the girl who reads the news on Victoria Wood, *As Seen on TV*, marvellous, remember when she did that apology for viewers in the North – "Because it must be awful for you"?

The world and his wireless here today. Must be the first time the panellists and producers have outnumbered the studio audience – but it's close. Heard that one before.

Chap over there was saying he remembers being here for the debut of his play on radio and he got the complimentary ticket and found himself all by himself.

Good do, as usual. It doesn't change. But there goes the last of the drumsticks. See you all again next year. Last of the Drumsticks. Good title.

NEW BOOKS
Top Ten Bestsellers:

1. **The Collected Works of Vladimir Ilyich Lenin** – Vol. 341 (BBC Publications)
2. **Work-Out with Raisa**
   Shape up and slim with the first lady through hypnosis, diet and simple exercise (*plough not supplied*).
3. **The Joys of Beetroot**
   Bortsch without tears! Fun for all the family guests this holiday. Includes 95-page Official History of the Beetroot.
4. **The Kremlin Wall – A Literary Guide** (Nigel Rees)
   The definitive collection of wit and wisdom from the world's oldest graffiti site.
5. **The Massey Ferguson GTI** (Workshop manual)
6. **The Best of Vremya** (TV Spinov)
7. **The Comrades' Digest Book of the Permafrost**
8. **101 Things To Do With A Subversive Cartoonist**
   Comic-book fun for the kiddievinks of all ages.
9. **In Private, In Public**
   The inside story of the personal lives of Tsar and Tsarina Romanov – by Alastair Burnet.
10. The notorious **Pirellich Calendar 1987**
    Mm! Mm! – a gorgeous, provocatively photographed *Pirellich* autobobile part in a mouthwatering pose just for you… every month of the year.

NEW The Autobiography of Princess Michael of Kent
(author's name as yet undisclosed)

Don't waste valuable working time writing in diaries. Get the Official Soviet 1987 Year Planner. Ready filled-in with all your own personal appointments for the coming year.

CATERING-SIZE SAMOVAR
For the kolkhoz that has everything. Ideal for those impromptu shashlik evenings – have one on the boil for that unexpected knock on the door. Provides sufficient tea to keep a small village out of the Alcoholism statistics for a month on one imported tea-bag (not supplied).

This holiday why not treat the family to a little luxury – a real fresh orange. Raffle tickets on sale in store.

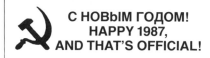
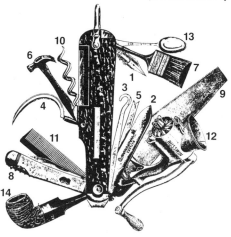

JANUARY SALES!

ROUBLES, ROUBLES!!!

... with this BRAND NEW Gift Catalogue from Moscow's world-famous GUM department store

---

4 – Emergency Combine-harvester (batteries not included)
5 – Balalaika stand
6 – Diplomatic bag sealer/opener Also emergency Afghan conversation aid
7 – Mess-hut window whitewashing tool, WW3 for the use of
8 – Polish Army Pen-knife
9 – Herring de-gutter/Device for tucking trousers into boots
10 – Shashlik skewer
11 – Full dress uniform attachment
12 – Emergency document-shredder
13 – Schmaltz strainer/server
14 – See 1
15 – Radiation Shield (50-gram vodka glass)
(Not shown – awaiting delivery)

RED ARMY UNIFORMS
*Your size always in stock.
Try one on a three-year trial.
(Bring your own toothbrush.)*

FOR HER

Full range of latest fashions and accessories. New season's mini-skirts expected any day.

ALL-PURPOSE MEAT-EXTENDER

Stretches sausages to four times their original length. Cover the table with a slice of ham. No more meat queues. The perfect gift for any house-proud mum.

Iron away those unsightly creases with the GUM patent **BLINIS PRESSER**

BREAD – NOW IN (personal queuers only). Ask for our Gift-wrapping Service.

SNOW/WINTER GEAR

TROIKA PORT
Free-standing – provides winter-long protection all year round. One size fits all dachas.

Industrial grade Vodka Just like Babushka used to make. 100% proof that the Soviet constitution will withstand anything.

Fabergé BRUTE
Replica after-shave dispenser.
Use with above.

THE WORLD-FAMOUS **GUM** LUXURY HAMPER – includes 114lbs of kasha, 4 bushels of wheatflour, live pig, 20 litres of smoked mackerel, 1 large bread token, 1 tin *Acorn Blend* western-style instant coffee substitute, 20 litres herring à la herring, 50 kilos Mountain Fresh concentrated butter*, 1 bottle Tadjhikstan sherry, 1 bottle Carpathian cognac, half-dozen split-size bottles household bleach.
*produce of more than one EEC of origin.

FOR THE CHILDREN

TRIVIAL PURSUIT *(Baby Boom Edition)*
The popular Summit-strategy game for two players. See if you can move your pieces from Reykjavik to Geneva and collect all the cheeses without talking.

New model figures from the latest **STAR WARS** saga (*Mosripov Films*). Stage your own battles between Reagan the Perplexed, Darth Weinberger, "Double-Dutch" Schultz and the Congressional Stormtroopers/Imperial Wall Street Guards.

MELODIYA
(Records & Tapes)

(M001) The Collected Songs of Vladimir Ilyich Lenin Vol. 423 (*a Cecil Sharp Production*)
(M002) Anatoly Karpov – Sings! All the latest tops and big-beat hits. *Including: Move It, Rook Around the Clock*
(M003) You, The Night, and the Generator
(M004) The Romantic Sound of the Spoon
(M005) Red Stars on 45
(M006) Latkes in the Night. The Gypsy fire of the Metropolitan Gasworkers' Cooperative Orchestra

NO. 1 IN THE WEST VOLARE!
– NOW IN STOCK

Computing

Move effortlessly into the world of high technology with **GUM's** state-of-the-art, full-function, easy-to-operate Transistorised Abacus. Full documentation (buyer translates).

FOR THE HOME

BATH PLUGS
Genuine hotel quality. Never been used. (String not included.)

Pamper yourself with new tangy gel **RUSSKAYA DOUCHA** (State choice of paragoric, carbolic or pitch pinc.)

AUTHENTIC OFFICIAL SOVIET SHOVEL
Perfect for all equestrian hobbies: clears path in front of horses in winter, behind them in summer.

SAMOVAR COSY
Lag your own samovar this winter with GUM's traditional hand-woven hessian kit. New season's colours.

PAPERWEIGHT
Tiny snow-driven Siberian landscape complete with actual model gulag. Shake it up and watch the sun come out.

RUBIK'S REJECT

For the first time in the Soviet Union: you too can have your very own *CABBAGE PATCH KIDS* – just like real American children.

Moscow Narodny Bank Young Savers' Scheme
Open an account NOW and your puppy goes FREE

DICKINSON
TEACHER'S PETTING

"Blimey – is that before or after?"

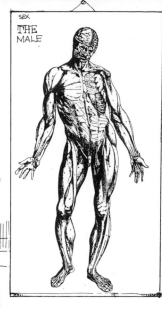

"My father says if he'd had sex education at school he wouldn't be worrying about mine now."

"At what stage does the amoeba say to itself – 'I'm going to tell my dad if you don't stop'?"

"I've been expelled for coming top in sex education."

"My dad says you taught him sex when you were at primary school together."

"The tripe sausages had decided to assert themselves."

GEORGE MELLY
Change at Crewe

JUST before we moved into Ronnie Scott's for our annual four-week stint, I flew down to the South of France to visit a friend who was cooking for two months for Quentin Crewe in a hillside village called Le Grand Bank. It's not really a French village any more. It had become a ruin but was bought and rebuilt *in toto* by the engineer Jeremy Fry who fills it in the summer with his friends. Quentin, however, occupies a house full-time and in winter is the only resident. Confined to a very advanced wheelchair, which was designed by Jeremy and Snowdon, he needs considerable assistance: a secretary to type his current book on a word-processor; someone to help him in and out of bed, bath and car; a chauffeur and, of course, a cook.

One evening at dinner I asked if we were anywhere near the Ideal Palace of the Postman Cheval, a long-time shrine of the Surrealists. In the late nineteenth century the Postman built, on a piece of ground next to his house, this extraordinary concrete folly inlaid with stones and pottery shards, writhing with naive statues, and pierced by corridors and grottos. Quentin said a friend had told him it was about two hours away and proposed a visit.

We set out at 10.00 a.m. There were five of us: my friend Alex at the wheel, Quentin by her side with his portable chair in the boot, and, in the back, his secretary Mags, myself, and Francis Fry, Jeremy's son, who was doing some building in the village. Luckily Mags is small and Francis thin, but even so it was quite a squash.

We set off in white mist, up into the mountains, down into valleys and across plains. Eventually we stopped for lunch in a small town where I foolishly ordered tripe sausages which have of late disagreed with me. Over coffee Quentin consulted the map. His face fell. By avoiding the autoroute we were not even halfway there.

We reached the outskirts of Hauterives as the light was fading and it was almost dark before we found the Ideal Palace, although the caretaker still let us in. It was impossible to see the details but the dreamlike towers and pinnacles were visible against the afterglow. Having come so far it would have been absurd to turn round and drive straight back. We would find a hotel and return next day to pay our proper respects to the visionary Postman. The caretaker told us that his sister-in-law kept an excellent hotel in a town some fifteen kilometres away. When we finally reached it, Francis, who apart from Quentin spoke the best French, got out to consult the landlady. I, too, got out. The tripe sausages had decided to assert themselves and, leaning against a wall, I was violently sick.

In between spasms, I could see across the street the landlady becoming more and more animated. Francis has this effect on people. He is both very polite and good-looking, but some-thing in his manner, in the way he forms his sentences, always leads to a kind of *Alice in Wonderland* chaos. At all events the hotel was not suitable for Quentin as there was neither a ground-floor bedroom nor a lift. The landlady had told Francis there was another hotel at the end of the street but it turned out to be an abattoir.

We drove round and round that unwelcoming little *ville* to find ourselves at last in a district of small factories with high wire fences. To our surprise, as we'd been told, there was a hotel, a low shabby building with a pebbled forecourt. Sticking up from the pebbles at the entrance was an iron wedge to prevent the gates from swinging both ways. This tore the exhaust of Alex's car from its moorings and almost severed it. Francis and I rushed into the hotel for different reasons: he to test out the accommodation, I because the tripe sausages had changed their strategy. Standing on one of those awful French loos, I could hear Francis beginning to wind up the enormous proprietor and his only customer, a near-dwarf. There turned out to be no bedrooms but we were assured that a further thirty kilometres ahead was a modern hotel on the side of the autoroute. Indeed, after a long, slow journey, with many wrong turnings and the exhaust beating an irregular tattoo beneath us, we found it. It was called "*Halte OK*" and was exactly the sort of place where the Feetwarmers and myself stay on the outskirts of, say, Derby. We had rooms, there was a lift, and even dinner, in my case a bowl of clear soup and some grapes. The waiter managed to spill an elaborate fish dish incorporating both pastry and a thick sauce all over Quentin. "I don't mind you laughing," he said with remarkable restraint, "but I do think the staff at least might try to control themselves."

At dawn Alex and I got up and limped through the mist a further thirty kilometres down the autoroute to Valence, the nearest place, according to the helpful hotel manager, which had a garage specialising in exhausts. They did indeed have a close approximation to the one we needed and, while they were fitting it, we sat in a café where the plump proprietress fed her poodles on segments of oranges part-masticated by herself.

We arrived back at "*Halte OK*" as the others were eating lunch and afterwards we returned to Le Palais. For me, at any rate, all our disasters were worthwhile, in a way almost appropriate. Here I was at last confronting a structure I had seen only in photographs, a work of poetic necessity with no other function. "Yes, Monsieur," said the caretaker in response to my question, "Monsieur André Breton came here several times."

We drove back along the autoroute. It took us two hours exactly. ☙

"How can I be sure the money will reach the snake?"

25

"Have you tasted this fog, Watson? It's Brown Windsor."

Holmes Sweet Holmes

"Dysentery, my dear Watson."

"As a master of disguise, Holmes is beginning to lose his touch."

"I'm worried about Holmes. Up till now it's just been chemistry, playing the violin and cocaine. _Now_ it's Mrs Hudson."

Going Going Gong

"I don't want to sound like some nutty reactionary, but if there was a little less buying of *marrons glacés* and a bit more in-depth purchase of Milky Ways, Chancellor Niglet would have an easier task."

DURING the war we got campaign medals. There was no degree of bravery involved – almost the contrary: you were posted to Italy and if you went (you did not have a lot of choice) you were given this medal on a bit of ribbon; then another for going to France and a third for being around when victory broke out. It did not matter whether you single-handedly stormed the enemy's machine-gun emplacement or went down with athlete's foot as you stepped off the troop-ship. You got a medal.

I believe there is a very strong argument for reviving the campaign medal philosophy in respect of patriots: those who look after our balance of payments deserve some recognition, and a medal is handy, does no harm to anyone and provides a nice splash of colour on dark evening wear.

Distribution would be confined to those who a) bought British cars (I am well aware of the fact that most British cars are made in Belgium and Germany; I mean cars that have maximum British input, unlike Mercedes, Volvo, Fiat, Renault, etc) and b) thought with some care before they bought foreign foods. As that good man Sir Richard Body said on behalf of the Commons Select Committee on Agriculture, there are too many people purchasing foreign rubbish when they could, and should, buy ours.

Let us begin with a list of eminently dispensable products: French butter, Danish blue cheese, Dutch smoked eels, cauliflowers from Brittany, celery from Israel, South African grapes, apples and pears from any foreign country, Nova Scotian smoked salmon, Norwegian prawns, East European jams, Belgian pâtés, and what the hell are we doing importing *boudins*, just as if we did not make black puddings of high quality?

I don't want to sound like some nutty reactionary, but if there was a little less buying of *marrons glacés* and a bit more in-depth purchase of Milky Ways, Chancellor Niglet would have an easier task. We have such sensational produce in this country that there really is no reason to buy lump-fish pellets instead of smoked cod's roe; Danish hams instead of our own, let alone Continental chicken liver terrines.

One of Marks and Spencer's big-selling lines is toasted whole-grain rolls; the ingredients are whole wheat, wheat flour, vegetable fat, yeast, salt and malt, each of which commodity is overproduced in Britain. The rolls are imported from Sweden. (They are an absolutely first-rate product; I just wonder why we can't make crisp rolls in England.)

When it comes to exporting British gastronomy, the Pub is about the only thing we successfully sell. Would that there were a pub restaurant attached to every "English Pub" that flourishes in foreign lands: clear oxtail soup, boiled mutton and caper sauce, mashed potatoes, Lancashire cheese, Bath Oliver biscuits, Queen of Puddings. Bar snacks like Yorkshire pudding with raspberry vinegar, toad-in-the-hole, potato pie. Fresh salmon fish-cakes. Potted shrimps. Jellied eels and Colchester oysters – three times the quality of the oysters we import from France and call "Portuguese".

We buy Danish mussels when we have millions of the brutes waiting to be claimed on the rocks around our coast-lines; we use mackerel to make fish-meal and buy fillets of French mackerel in white wine at hideous cost – I mean hideous for a fillet of mackerel.

I would not be complaining if the other EEC countries bought British foods; with the exception of Worcester sauce and breakfast cereals, the odd jar of marmalade and Twinings teabags, it is one-way traffic away from us. People eligible for the British produce medal would not be disqualified for buying Ogen melons, which are succulent and desirable, but to buy aubergines because they come from there, when we have courgettes that come from here, is daft and merits no reward. Similarly, to buy Golden Delicious when we have Granny Smiths and Cox's; Geneva gin when we have Gordon's; Löwenbrau dark beer when we have Newcastle Brown, and all those cheeses when we have such excellent ones that are home produced. I sympathise with a consumer who puts his hand on his heart and says, "I have tried blue Cheshire and Wensleydale and greatly prefer Gorgonzola and Canadian Black Diamond." So be it; but he shall not get a gong.

All over the world people buy British aeroengines, knitwear, fabrics, glassware, silver, china and pottery. I am not complaining too much about the Brit who buys *foie gras* or truffles or even *cèpes* and *morilles* – fungi both, that grow but fail to be recognised in this country – but to buy stuff simply because it is foreign and has a cachet of coming from afar is pathetic and harms the economy to the extent of making us unable to finance good PR campaigns to persuade foreigners of the allure of our produce: the delicacy of our parsnips, which are best blanched in heavily salted water and then roasted in dripping in a hot oven; baby beets, steamed and served in thick cream spiked with chives; our kippers and bloaters; our Arbroath smokies and Scotch salmon. English horseradish is absolutely supreme, as are Stilton and Farmhouse Cheddar cheeses, redcurrant and medlar jellies.

If the French had made Viota, which is a powder to which you add the odd beaten egg and water, then mix and steam, it would be a multi national success story. I haven't seen a packet of it since Granny died. ❧

Making Good Again

HOLTE

"Don't worry, Wilfred's come to give you a hand. Look – he has his tool-kit with him."

"You wouldn't believe how many coats of paint we stripped off this lovely old pine door!"

"We were convinced there was an Adam fireplace behind all this plaster and stuff, and we were right – there is!"

"Hasn't he made a lovely job of this room? And to think he couldn't even replace a light-bulb before we moved in!"

"The decorator had a migraine attack, so he's having a lie down in the spare room."

"We left our fitted wardrobes at the last house, so we've absolutely nowhere to hang anything here."

"He'll be here in a minute — he's just putting up some shelves in the kitchen."

"Arthur will be in shortly — he's just hanging a basket in the garden."

Gentlemen and Players

Frank Keating remembers Trevor Howard, Boris Karloff and all the other sporting buffs of filmland

FORGOT TO PACK YOUR HELMET AGAIN !?!

SOMEWHERE in Europe, 1940. Hot-foot from sugar-lumping Grimmett's field for Hammond at Old Trafford in *The Lady Vanishes* two years earlier, Basil Radford and Naughton Wayne are now aboard the *Night Train to Munich*:

Caldicott: That German officer looks a lot like old Dickie Randall. You remember, used to bowl slow leg-breaks. Played for the Gentlemen once – caught-and-bowled for a duck, as I recall.

Charters: You think he's a traitor then?

Caldicott: But he played for the Gentlemen!

Charters: Ah, yes, but only once.

They churned them out in those days, and no film was worth releasing unless it had its couple of slack-chinned, stiff-lipped Brits chuntering on about cricket. It was probably allowed because Hollywood at that time was still being enchanted by the likes of Sir C. Aubrey Smith (Sussex and England), Mr Boris Karloff (formerly W. H. Pratt, Esq, of the Uppingham XI and Surrey 2nds) and Charlie Chaplin (born under the gasometers at Kennington).

Sir Aubrey played frequently for the Gentlemen. He captained Sussex for a number of years, and, in 1888, took the first English XI to South Africa. He was an accomplished stage-actor – Shaw once said, "No man on earth could play better the Duke" in *As You Like It* – before he fell for the blandishments, blossoms and booty of Hollywood in the 1920s, where he played the archetypal Anglo in over 50 films; every contract stipulated that he be allowed the month off when the Australians were playing

the Test match at Lord's.

Another theatrical knight dear to Hollywood was earmarked by his father at birth as an undoubted No.4 for the Gentlemen. But Laurence Olivier had no talent with bat or ball. Olivier *père* had been a celebrated Oxford sport and played for Hampshire and MCC. Alas, little Larrykin's top score in life was two (bowled by his master, Douglas Bader). He was No. 11 in a school house match at St Edward's, Oxford, and only four had been needed to win. Oh, the shame of it! Many, many years later, Sir Laurence confided:

I have often thought what a pity it is – how much better a life I would have had, what a better man I would have been, how much healthier an existence I would have led, if I had been a cricketer instead of an actor. But it was not to be. I don't know what it was – the finger of God had not touched me with a stump or something. It just wasn't there.

I suppose the world's most famous cricket-nut/actor today is the great and good Trevor Howard (a knighthood there wouldn't come amiss either). I spent a marvellous day with Trevor a few months ago, talking about his cricket (best bowling six-for-two for MCC *before lunch*), and his driving offences (with cars, not bats). The first time he was nicked was the day England won the Ashes in 1953. His producer, Euan Lloyd was called for the defence:

Your Worship, Mr Howard and I were driving along Piccadilly with the car wireless on. It all depended on two final runs. When finally some-

one hit a four which won the game, Mr Howard jumped out of the car in front of Fortnum & Mason, danced on the pavement, let out a roar, then jumped on to the bonnet of the car, peered at me through the windscreen and yelled, "We've done it! We've done it!"

Throughout his life, Trevor has richly deserved honorary qualification for both the Gents *and* Players. So, perhaps, did Richard Burton. The Welshman was a nifty rugger player in his youth – indeed played his last game at 28 when he was playing Hamlet at the Vic. Such an opponent was, almost literally, meat and drink to the rugger buggers, as Burton would recall with that hilarious, but pained relish of his, savouring the flavours in every word if not the memory:

I was elbowed, gouged, dug, planted, raked, hoed, kicked a great deal, sandwiched, and once humiliatingly taken from behind ... I was gardened, mowed and rolled. Their prop with whom I shared cheek and jowl for the eternity didn't believe in razor-blades since he grew them on his chin and shaved me thoroughly. By the end of the game my face was as red as the setting sun and the same shape. I stuck it out because there was nothing else to do, which is why on Monday night in the Waterloo Road I played the Dane looking like a Swede with my head permanently on one side and my right arm in an imaginary sling.

I was intermittently crooked and cramped with severe shakes and involuntary shivers as of one with palsy. I suppose to the connoisseurs of Hamlets it was a departure from your traditional Prince but it wasn't strictly what the actor playing the part had in mind. A melancholy Dane he was though. Melancholy he most certainly was.

Richard continued to enjoy the game, at a distance. To his death, he would have videos of the Welsh international matches flown out to him – as does his Celtic co-star, Richard Harris, still, when the greens have put up a dandy performance. Burton also enjoyed boxing, and would often be seen at the ringside for a really Big One. The fight game threw up the same sort of gruesome glitter as Hollywood. Of all the boxers who got up from the floor and into the celluloid, I suppose Max Baer, one-time heavyweight champ of the world, transposed best. (Like when Rogers or Hammerstein or somebody auditioned Rocky Graziano once, the Rock opined, "Yeah, the singin' was easy; memorisin' the words was the difficult bit.")

The Harder They Fall was Humphrey Bogart's last picture. It was also Max Baer's last. The night after the opening, Baer woke up in the Hollywood Roosevelt Hotel with a sharp pain in his chest, and fumbled for the bedside telephone.

"I need a doctor," he whispered. "A house doctor, sir?" enquired the operator. "No, dummy, a people doctor!"

At which Baer, the most "human" and witty of all the great fighters, died. He was 50. Had he been English, he would unquestionably have played for the Gents.

BASIL BOOTHROYD
A Fur Cry

"Voles crowded the steppes in an unstemmable phalanx, several getting into bed with me."

WHAT do we hear of the Chinese rice mountain? Not a lot. Of Ecuador's sprawling ranges of refrigerated bananas, or the unshiftable cliffs of surplus Moroccan dates? Same answer.

We are getting to be very inward-looking in the EEC, and imagine we are the only peoples who can't take a stroll without stubbing our toe on a thousand tonnes of unsold Cheddar, or skidding off a buttery slope into a wine-dark sea.

On that last, and in part prompting these observations, you will have seen that Switzerland is just as much up against it in these matters. I don't know about mountains, though there may well be an Alp or two of Swiss rolls jagging the skyline, but the authorities are practically afloat with wine, and have been trying to drain it off by doling out mandatory daily flagons to the army.

I wouldn't have known about this except for a short item datelined Berne reporting that the experiment has now been officially abandoned. No reason given. A powerful teetotal lobby, perhaps. The country has compulsory military service. Mothers of lads called up from sober homes could have marched on the Federal Assembly with angry three-language banners. Or perhaps the military moguls themselves had second thoughts. It had seemed a practical solution until put into practice: where it fell down was on the parade grounds, with the entire Swiss fighting-machine improperly dressed, late, flushed, leaning and a disgrace to unaligned neutrals everywhere.

And this at a time when they should have been razor-sharp to a man, guarding their frontiers against French butter convoys, alert for the gurgle of German and Italian pipelines discharging wine into lakes Constance and Geneva to shed the load and ease their consciences.

Much has been made of the EEC's stockpiled food surpluses, mainly because the European Parliament, which has moved mountains in other directions, such as the regulation of lawn-mower noises, asparagus lengths and golden handshakes for redundant Luxemburg staff, has been floored by the task of moving the stuff to those foreign parts where it would do most good. The defeat, in this, of the finest political brains in Europe, has naturally attracted more attention than over-production in other fields. Aerial news-shots of unsold motor-cars by the serried acre, or warehouses crammed to the rafters with dust-gathering electronics, fade on the retina as mere bulletin fodder, backing up the month's seasonally adjusted unemployment charts.

Again, these are only displayed for the passing interest of Community viewers. We hear nothing, as I hinted at the start, of choked Indonesian copra repositories, idle oil-rigs rusting off Muscat ... the hopeless glut of Tibetan prayer-wheels.

And what of Russia?

Our information on vodka-lakes and rude wooden sheds oozing caviare is limited. But things are beginning to get out, and I don't just mean dissident poetesses. I was dozing, I admit, when a Mr Sokolov, of the Ukraine, jolted me by bedside radio into a grudging consciousness. "We can feed by this meat minks," he was telling some Radio 4 interlocutor. A memorable phrase. I had to wake up to write it down. If you don't get a thing like that exactly right it's useless.

It seemed at first that scientist Sokolov was casting a ray of brighter light on Chernobyl. Around the disaster site, he said, were nice grain grow. Pigs could eat. And though men could not pigs' meat eat, they could by this meat feed minks. Having dozed through his earlier argument I found myself with unanswered questions. Was he saying that radioactive pigs raised on radioactive grain, though unfit for the human meal table, were harmless to minks, who could take endless rashers without ill effect? It seemed so. But was it the minks alone that enjoyed immunity? Or was he only citing them as examples of other creatures thus biologically advantaged? Bears, perhaps. Sturgeon.

However, he kept coming back to the minks, and with a discernible note of optimism. It seemed that the blighted environs of the reactor, though now ruled out for pig-marketing – to the degree that you could not by that meat feed people – and thus causing despair among many a collective pig-farmer, could be made over to minks and hardly miss a beat.

We know nothing, of course, about the scale of existing Soviet pig-mountains. We have no figures for the country's pre-Chernobyl mink production. It seems set to rocket, is all I'm saying. The staple diet of the mink, I drowsily recalled, is the vole. But now we have these radioactive pigs. Their farmers, true, can feed by that meat minks, but there could soon be an industrial and ecological imbalance here: over-production of minks, just to get rid of the pigs: vole-farmers out of business, marching on Kiev's presidium building with banners proclaiming that minks raised on post-Chernobyl pigs can only mean contamination of mink hats, coats, stoles, etc, as worn by party central committee members, their wives, and – anyway the hats – visiting statesmen from the west, posed for news-shots.

I was still turning these prospects over in my dozing mind when I found *The Financial World Tonight* had stolen up on me, swilling its billions around.

My rest was disturbed, all the same. Mink mountains rose on the Ukrainian horizon, suffocating me under more than my share of the duvet. Voles, now surplus to requirement, crowded the steppes in an unstemmable phalanx, several getting into bed with me. It was a bad night. I had no answer to these things. Who has? I felt muzzy at breakfast, which was bacon.

"We could feed by this meat minks," I said to my wife. Hers, she said, tasted all right. She doesn't always listen in the mornings. She said it cost enough.

It certainly seemed no time to go into the probable Danish bacon mountain, never mind ill-advised moves by top Swiss army brass. 🦋

"Is this a serious take-over bid, Carruthers?"

SCHWADRON

JACKIE KAUFMAN and RANDI HACKER

Our Mr Brain

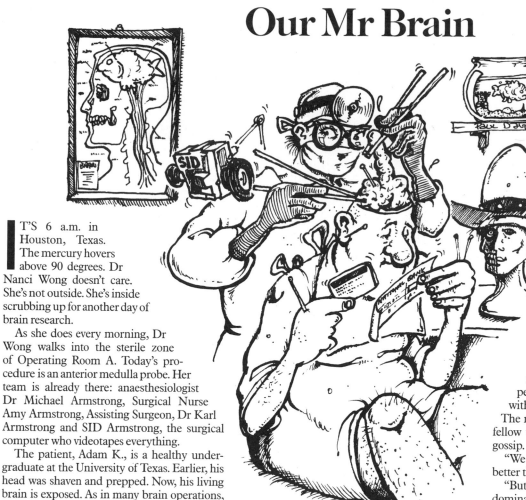

IT'S 6 a.m. in Houston, Texas. The mercury hovers above 90 degrees. Dr Nanci Wong doesn't care. She's not outside. She's inside scrubbing up for another day of brain research.

As she does every morning, Dr Wong walks into the sterile zone of Operating Room A. Today's procedure is an anterior medulla probe. Her team is already there: anaesthesiologist Dr Michael Armstrong, Surgical Nurse Amy Armstrong, Assisting Surgeon, Dr Karl Armstrong and SID Armstrong, the surgical computer who videotapes everything.

The patient, Adam K., is a healthy undergraduate at the University of Texas. Earlier, his head was shaven and prepped. Now, his living brain is exposed. As in many brain operations, Adam K. needs only a local anaesthetic. He is awake and aware of what is going on around him.

"I'm doing this for credit," says Adam.

Dr Wong takes her place. She asks for a Monahan-Morris neurospatula. Using it with the flair and *élan* that has earned her the respect of the entire surgical community, she gently lifts different lobes and peeks under them looking for the mind.

"We're pretty sure the mind is in the head," says Dr Wong. "The question is, where?"

Dr Wong is one of the doctors that makes up the elite staff of the Shelley Winters Clinic for Advanced Cranial Studies. The Clinic is renowned for its innovative lab techniques and commitment to science. Brains are everywhere. There are framed pen and ink cross-sections of brains hanging in the lobby. There are brains in jars and brains on tables. There are brains on magazine covers. Recipes for brains are posted on the bulletin board.

All kinds of things are done to brains here. Doctors stick needles into brains. They take pictures of them. They cut them in half with lasers.

"Whatever you can think of, we do to brains," says Dr Gordon St Gordon, director of the clinic.

A few years ago Dr St Gordon received international acclaim for his brilliant thesis *Cerebral Functions Governing the Expression of Stupid Things* which explained for the first time why we say things like, "Do you remember where you lost it?" In his research, he pioneered the use of the Electrolaser Tracing System (ETS),

an instrument so incredibly fast and so amazingly focused that it can follow a single electrical impulse as it flings itself from dendrite to dendrite and bolts down axons on its frantic journey from the brain to its ultimate destination. He was named director in 1978 and has been here since then.

Throughout history, anthropologists and philosophers have been intrigued by the brain. Each culture has its own mythology. The Celts believed there was a little chieftain in their heads. They called him Faether Geodagh. He wore furs and a big, heavy belt. Later, when people had time to worry about good and evil, Geodagh was joined by Brina, an unbelievably good-looking, red-headed witch who wanted Geodagh's belt and stopped at nothing to get it.

The civilisations that sprang up along the Tigris and Euphrates concluded that a water snake made its nest in the head and swam through the body doing what needed to be done. Then it came back and went to sleep. Native Americans believed in Ota-mo-toc, She Who Stands in the Doorway of the Head and Greets the Warriors with Venison and Pemmican. Needless to say, mythology has long given way to science.

"There's a place for mythology," says Dr Olaf Gustavson.

"But not here," adds his colleague, Dr

Russell Bauer.

"Here," means Lab 1601 at the Shelley Winters Clinic where Drs Gustavson and Bauer are testing their new brain dominant/mind dominant theory. The doctors believe that an individual's personality is largely determined by which element is stronger: the brain or the mind. Each one has its own distinct personality: the brain is a muscular guy with a thick neck and his own bowling ball. The mind is a creative, dashing, incorrigible fellow with an acerbic tongue and an ear for gossip.

"We won't say that one type of personality is better than the other," says Dr Gustavson.

"But we will say that Einstein was mind dominant," says Dr Bauer, with a wink.

While the Shelley Winters doctors work in their labs, Dr Morty Adler appears on national television to promote his bestseller *It's Your Mind: Think About It*. Though he is ostracised by the serious scientific community, Dr Adler is making lots of money.

"My colleagues are doing important but inaccessible research," says Dr Adler, "but I am giving the mind to the people."

According to Dr Adler, the mind is one of those conceptual, intensely personal science things like gravity or the quark or infinity. He urges people to get to know their minds.

"Your mind can be anything you want," says Dr Adler. "It can be a fast car or a big fish or a pretty gate that leads to the sea. I like to think of my mind as a penthouse in an exclusive condo with a great view of the bridge. Everything is black and white and glass and chrome. Except for the sofa. It's leather. There are fresh flowers in an art deco vase near the sliding doors that lead to the wraparound terrace. The bathroom fixtures are gold. The Omnicron Futurematic 2000 double-K Series Cable Intercept Satellite Uplink Home Dish System sits in a slate cabinet. Far, far below, on the street, people arrive at their offices ready to start their day."

"We think he's crazy," says Dr St Gordon.

He might be, but at this stage there has to be room for everyone.

Though the task of brain research casts an awesome shadow, science is not intimidated. And whether the mind is flamboyant or whether Brina gets the belt, this research is certain to point to more clues about what to do next.

HEATH
SLAP
HAPPY

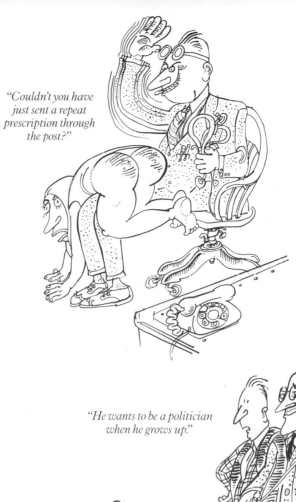

"Couldn't you have just sent a repeat prescription through the post?"

"You are sentenced to be spanked by me!"

"He wants to be a politician when he grows up."

"Ah, doctor, thank you for coming out at this ungodly hour."

"It's the code word for total emergency," he explained. "We are empowered to impose an absolute news black-out; the townships must be surrounded and all ANC terrorists rounded up immediately..."

TOM SHARPE

OPSAAL! DIE BLOEDBAD KOM!

KOMMANDANT van Heerden was sitting in his office staring with moody admiration at the portrait of the Queen above the fireplace when the call came through.

"Pretoria on the line," said the police operator who was under strict orders never to interrupt the Kommandant's hour of meditation after lunch unless there was a genuine emergency.

The Kommandant stiffened in his chair. Calls from the Ministry of Law and Order were definitely emergencies and usually of the most unpleasant sort. The last time had been when an American TV team, hoping to record the sexual foreplay of the aardvark, had inadvertently stumbled on Konstabel Els executing his duty and two black husbands who had foolishly objected to his raping their wives.

Pretoria had been most upset about the incident.

So had Kommandant van Heerden.

"Why the hell didn't you shoot the swine?" he had demanded of the Konstabel who usually shot anyone or anything that came his way.

"They were taking pictures of me," said Els, looking crestfallen.

"All the more reason. Anyone taking pictures of you ought to be shot."

"But this was TV. I thought they might be watching me overseas."

The Kommandant shuddered at the notion.

"All the same you shouldn't have beaten them up in the cells afterwards. The Americans are our allies. You've got to be nice to them. They're helping us to fight the Communists."

Els had gone away chastened and had tried to be so nice to two elderly tourists from Idaho who had come to visit the Kruger National Park that they had left for home next day unwilling to see any other wild animals in their natural habitat.

But this time the call from Pretoria was strangely enigmatic.

"*Opsaal, die bloedbad kom*," said the voice. "I repeat – *Opsaal, die bloedbad kom*. Message ends, over."

"Message received," said the Kommandant, who didn't have a clue what it meant.

He put the receiver down and looked hurriedly out the window. Whatever bloodbath had come, he was grateful to note that it hadn't reached Piemburg. In fact the little town was pleasantly quiet and all the more so since the boycott of white business had started. The Kommandant was secretly in favour of the boycott. It added veracity to his happy illusion that he was living in some secluded county town in England and besides, having blacks off the street meant that Konstabel Els had to go out to Kaffirtown when he felt like shooting someone. It made life so much safer for ordinary white shoppers.

Just the same, the message, "Saddle up, the bloodbath comes," was hardly reassuring. All his life the Kommandant had been living in terror of the bloodbath. Hordes of Zulus would suddenly descend one morning on every white household in South Africa bringing four million cups of tea in one hand and as many assegais in the other. The Kommandant had given up his early morning tea years ago. There was also the chance that it might be poisoned too.

He got up and crossed the room and turned the portrait of the Queen round so that she faced the wall and in her place Mrs Thatcher looked sternly down on him. Not even Lieutenant Verkramp, who hated the British, could accuse him of being un-South African for having her picture on the wall. She had always been staunchly pro-South African and there was even talk of elevating her to "Ouma" Thatcher for her contribution to the maintenance of White Supremacy and the implementation of Apartheid in Britain.

Having provided proof of his patriotism, the Kommandant sent for Lieutenant Verkramp. The Head of the Security Branch would know about the bloodbath, if anyone did. The bastard always knew everything.

"Message just in from Pretoria," said Verkramp as soon as he entered the office. "*Opsaal, die bloedbad kom*. I repeat. *Opsaal, die bloedbad kom*."

"Where?" asked the Kommandant, glancing anxiously out the window again. "You'd think we'd hear some screaming. Anyway it's supposed to come with the early morning tea."

Lieutenant Verkramp looked at him contemptuously. He'd always distrusted the Kommandant. In his opinion Van Heerden was soft and stupid and ought to have been replaced years ago. Afrikaaners who hid portraits of the Queen on their walls were obviously traitors.

"It's the code word for total emergency," he explained. "We are empowered to impose an absolute news black-out; the townships must be surrounded and all ANC terrorists rounded up immediately."

"But we rounded them all up last week," said the Kommandant. "You mean there are still more of them?"

"Millions," said Verkramp. "Particularly in the Churches, the Black Sash and..."

"But the Black Sash are all white women. Very respectable too."

"ANC terrorists," said Verkramp. "That's why the sash they wear is black."

"I hadn't thought of that," said the Kommandant." All the same I don't think Mr de Graaf is going to like having his wife rounded up. He's already had two strokes and without her to push his wheelchair..."

"We all have to make sacrifices."

"Yes, but what are we going to charge her with?" asked the Kommandant. "All she does is stand outside the Town Hall in silence."

"We don't have to charge her with anything. Don't you know your law? Under the Emergency Powers what we say is the Law."

Kommandant van Heerden gave up. He didn't want any part of arresting Mrs de Graaf. She'd once invited him in for coffee.

"Well, since you're Head of Security, I'm putting you in charge of Operation Bloedbad as from now," he said.

Verkramp smiled unpleasantly.

"I am in charge already," he said and left the room.

THE Kommandant sat down and thanked God. If Verkramp cocked things up and he was almost certain to, at least no one could blame him. And if the bloodbath had really started, the Kommandant preferred to sit it out in the comparative safety of the police station. He leant back in his chair and wondered if Ouma Thatcher was a member of the Black Sash. He rather doubted it. The expression on her face didn't suggest she went in for non violent protests.

An hour later Lieutenant Verkramp drove out in a Caspir armoured car to the Drill Hall to issue orders to the five hundred policemen assembled there. At long last his hour had come. Operation Bloedbad would ensure the supremacy of Afrikaanerdom and the White Race and the name Verkramp would go down in the list of Afrikaans Heroes. There might even be a statue of him in the Voortrekker Monument. Best of all the credit for Piemburg's safety would come to him. Kommandant van Heerden had shown his true colours. In Verkramp's eyes they were red and had a hammer and sickle on them. Lieutenant Verkramp climbed on to the dais.

"Men of the SAP," he declaimed, "tonight we are going to break the African Nationalist Communist terrorist revolutionist organisation in Piemburg."

He paused to let the message sink in.

"All over South Africa dangerous terrorists are going to learn ...the whole world is going to learn that we are the last bastion of Western Civilisation in Africa."

In the front row Konstabel Els

He should never have allowed Verkramp to take charge of the Operation. The man was mad. South Africa had gone mad. Not for the first time, he wished he'd been born an English gentleman.

looked puzzled. Civilisation was not a word he liked. Someone had once told him it meant not killing blacks. Lieutenant Verkramp's next remark was more comprehensible.

"You are authorised to arrest by whatever means you choose, dead or alive, any person resisting arrest or suspected of furthering the aims of the communist conspiracy. You cannot be held responsible or sued in the courts for anything you do. No radio or TV coverage is to be permitted. You are to arrest and detain any reporters who obstruct you in the course of your duties. This applies particularly to TV cameramen who are foreign agents of the ANC's propaganda cadres."

Sergeant de Kock put up his hand.

"What's a cadre, sir?" he asked.

Lieutenant Verkramp hesitated. He wasn't entirely sure himself what a cadre was. It was something he'd heard at a special course he'd attended on Marxist-Leninism at the Police College.

"It's a Jewish commissar," he said finally. "Joe Slovo is a cadre."

The Sergeant had never heard of Joe Slovo.

"All right then, Dr Levy is a cadre," said Verkramp and put the best dentist in Piemburg into a new category.

It was two in the morning when Operation Bloedbad really began. Lieutenant Verkramp led the First Task Force. It devoted its attention to the white terrorists without whom Verkramp knew the blacks would be leaderless.

"Kaffirs are too stupid to organise a revolution," he told the Sergeant as the armoured truck rumbled up Town Hill. "It's in the Bible.

"Under the Emergency Powers invested in me, you may not name any person who has been arrested. Similarly the law doesn't allow any arrested person to consult a lawyer. Any relative mentioning that another relative has been detained will be arrested and held indefinitely. It is illegal to publish or state or refer to anything that might aid the enemies of South Africa."

Blacks are hewers of water and drawers of wood. Like Hitler said, the Jews are behind the communist revolutionaries."

"But I thought the Jews wrote the Bible," said the Sergeant. "How come they are communists now?"

"Because they know we Afrikaaners are God's really chosen people," said Verkramp. "And they're jealous."

BY four o'clock the First Task Force had accomplished its objectives. The Reverend Smail of the Presbyterian Church had been arrested. So had the Anglican Bishop of Piemburg. Fifteen nuns in a mini-bus had been stopped at a road block on their way to a special Mass for multi-racial unity in Durban and had been body-searched with the aid of enemas to ensure they were not carrying explosives in their persons; the editor of the *Piemburg Witness* who had once written a leader on police brutality now knew exactly what he had been talking about; Mrs de Graaf had been dragged from her bed in her nightdress and locked with two other Black Sash women in a cell holding a suspected black rapist.

"I don't know why you're grumbling," said the warder. "I thought that was what you people wanted, equality. It proves we're dismantling apartheid."

But it was in Kaffirtown that the threat to Western Civilisation felt the full force of South African justice. Twenty-two black school children driven from their homes by tear gas were shot with their parents for defying the curfew they hadn't been told about; two churches, a creche and the medical centre were burnt to the ground; Konstabel Els had the time of his life ending a dozen other people's, and hundreds of Africans had been arrested for having black skins. Operation Bloodbath had lived up to its name. As dawn broke, a pall of smoke hung over the township and on the unpaved streets, the bodies of the dead waited for the flies and the noonday sun.

"We have struck a blow for freedom," Verkramp announced triumphantly when he returned from a tour of the carnage. "Like the Battle of Blood River, God has been good to us. The ANC has been crushed."

"How many of the swine did you capture?" asked Kommandant van Heerden. He had spent a disturbed night listening to the sound of distant gunfire and the screams of those being tortured in the cells below.

"Hundreds," said Verkramp and waved a bloodstained sjambok in the air. "We've got them in the Drill Hall. You want to see them?"

Downstairs a group of lawyers and reporters were trying to find out what could be legally printed. Verkramp told them.

"Under the Emergency Powers ▶

invested in me, you may not name any person who has been arrested. Similarly the law doesn't allow any arrested person to consult a lawyer. Any relative mentioning that another relative has been detained will be arrested and held indefinitely. It is illegal to publish or state or refer to anything that might aid the enemies of South Africa."

"That doesn't leave us much to say," muttered one journalist.

"You can always write about sport," said Lieutenant Verkramp. "South Africa has always been a very sporting country, you know, and that's a very healthy topic."

There was nothing very healthy about the topic being discussed at the Drill Hall. Konstabel Els had commandeered seventeen milk floats and was encouraging a number of prisoners with a sjambok to take the tyres off the wheels. Kommandant van Heerden was appalled.

"Els, you bastard," he yelled. "What the hell do you think you're doing?"

Els lowered his sjambok.

"Obeying Lieutenant Verkramp's instructions," he said. "He said to necklace the sods."

"But those milk floats are white property," said van Heerden before the full implications of Els' statement hit him. He stopped and stared at Verkramp. The Head of Security smiled.

"It's in the Bible," he explained. "The Good Lord said, 'Do unto others as they would do unto you.' You can't deny what God said."

Kommandant van Heerden preferred not to. All the same his next remark was an unwise one.

"I am your Kommandant and I will not sanction the use of tyres from milk floats to..."

He stopped. Verkramp had taken his revolver from its holster.

"You are under arrest," he shouted.

"Me?" squeaked van Heerden. "How can you arrest me? And what for?"

"As officer in command of Operation Bloedbad, I am placing you under arrest for using an inflammatory word."

"What word?" said the old Kommandant, eyeing the muzzle of the gun with alarm.

"Don't try to trick me," said Verkramp. "You know what word."

"You mean 'sanction'?" said van Heerden. "But..."

"That's twice," snarled Verkramp. "I always knew you were a commie bastard. I hereby arrest you for subversive activities and advocating an anti-South African policy."

As ex-Kommandant van Heerden was hurled into the back of the police van he cursed himself for a fool. He should never have allowed Verkramp to take charge of the Operation. The man was mad. South Africa had gone mad. Not for the first time, he wished he'd been born an English gentleman.

In a final act of defiance he clutched the bars on the window and shouted, "God save the Queen."

But the words were drowned by the screams of the milkman. Konstabel Els had lit the tyre. ❧

LARRY
DAYLIGHT ROBBERY

ALAS, POOR WARWICK

JAMES AINSWORTH

EDINBURGH's buzzer shrieked first.

"Yes, Edinburgh?" said the man in the suit.

"Sherry?"

"No," said the suit. "I can offer it once more. Bristol?"

"Malaga?" said Bristol.

"No, they are all kinds of Madeira. Sercial is the driest and Malmsey the sweetest. Next question: What drink do you associate with Condom? … You may well do, Sussex, but that's not the answer I have here. No, I'm going to have to tell you. It is a town in south-west France where Armagnac is made. Next question: Which is the odd one out – aguardiente, bagaceira, phylloxera, or grappa? And I can only allow one attempt at this. Warwick? Warwick, you had your hand up…No, I'm sorry, you can't leave the room until the competition is over." (Alas, poor Warwick. Everyone crossed their legs for him.) "Leeds? No, not grappa. It is phylloxera, a bug that attacks the roots of vines. The rest are spirits from Spain, Portugal and Italy respectively."

And so it went on, the theory test to find the Young University Wine Taster of the Year. Why is a "kir" so called? In which French *départements* is Beaujolais made? Through which famous German vineyard does the 50th line of latitude run? If a French label gives a vintage date, what is the minimum percentage of wine that must legally come from that year? Where did the word "plonk" come from?

"Who was responsible for putting methanol in Italian wines in the scandal earlier this year? No, we don't know either, but I thought it was worth a try. So those are the scores at the end of the first round. We'll take a five-minute break now, for Warwick's sake, and then we can move on to the tasting."

The suit ushered everybody into what looked like a cross between a chemistry lab and a cocktail party. Ten places arranged around a pristine Formica workbench, each with six empty glasses; and clusters of numbered brown bottles, all otherwise identical, neatly placed at intervals. You could sense, from the quiet that descended once the spectacle had been taken in, that there was a fast-dawning realisation of the enormity of the occasion. An oh-my-God feeling that the suits had been taking it far more seriously than you ever imagined. I mean, it's only booze when all's said and done.

But which booze? The men in the suits had lashed out on your train-fare and lunch to find out whether you knew. Never mind letting the side down; if you didn't put up a creditable performance, they might ask for their money back. There is no such thing as a free lunch, and the sooner you learn that, the better for all concerned. They are not philanthropists, these guys. They want their pound of flesh.

As everyone from Arthur Guinness to the Chancellor of the Exchequer knows, there is a fortune to be made from drink, and although it may seem difficult to believe, the punters with the most so-called disposable income are under 25 with no kids. Many of them have a pressing need to appear as sophisticated as the models in the ads, and the ads make it quite plain what they must do to get the bird, the fella, the jackpot, the smart car, nice clothes, big house and use of executive washbasin. While that may not be subtle enough to fool *you*, the principle still remains: Give me a palate before the age of 21, and I will give you a lifelong devotee of the bottle. Now get sniffing and slurping and spitting into those big white sinks – and earn your lunch.

The two worst things about a wine tasting are a) when it's so deadly silent that you think, oh-my-God, everybody else must know what they're doing, and you just want to burst out laughing or crying, and b) when people start talking and put you off while you're trying to concentrate. This somehow managed to incorporate both.

Now let's take our bearings, try and get a grip on something, don't panic, just three whites and three reds to identify, that shouldn't be too … oh-my-God, do you realise these could come from anywhere in the world? I mean New Zealand, Bulgaria, Argentina, maybe Borneo or Japan. Do they make wine in Japan? Supposing I write Japan and they don't make any wine there. Will they ask for their money back? Will somebody please take Warwick away, or at least stop him singing. That's two and a half minutes gone and I'm still gazing like a loon at three whites, three reds and a blank piece of paper.

Not quite blank. Appearance, Nose and Palate, it says at the top of the three columns. It's all coming back now. That evening at the Wine Soc, the qualifying round. Approach it logically, said the suit, and you'll have no problem.

First problem. He didn't say what to do if all the wines looked and smelled alike. White, white, white, red, red, red. That's the first column filled in, although perhaps that one does look a bit purply from a certain angle, and the last one's more a bricky shade of brown. And the first white looks like water and the next one like, well, buttercup. Why is everyone else writing so much? Should Warwick be smoking?

I don't think the first one's wine at all. It's a trick, it's really water. They're having us on. The only time I've drunk a wine like that was on holiday in Brittany. What was it, Muscadet? Bung it down. Next.

Spanish? That's what she said, the big mouth with the plums. "A bit of a pong on the nase, probbly from Spane. Or Orstreeyah." Everybody's nodding. Rubbish, I remember that taste distinctly from the end-of-term piss-up, 'cos it came back all through the next day. That's white burgundy, stake my life on it. Next. Could I be getting the hang of this, might I enjoy it if it weren't for the pressure? Do people do this for a living? Oh-my-God, I've forgotten to use the spittoon. What a waste, though. I wonder what's for lunch.

It's surprising where the time goes, really. Just as you're getting properly stuck in, the bell rings. Don't they look smug, some of these. "The larst one must have been a klarit. One can tell Cabber-*neigh* anywhere." What did I put for that one? Who cares? It's all over, bar the wait for results and photo.

"No, I can't, I can't," said Warwick.

"You'll be all right, somebody will hold you up," said one of the suits, steering him away from an even posher, elegant blue suit who had been wheeled in to take charge centre-stage.

"No, I simply, I just can't." He didn't. A brief quizzing established that he had a solemn pact with his tutor to lay off drink for a whole term. A picture in one of the wine magazines, or on the Students' Union noticeboard, glassy-eyed with bottles everywhere, woud have sunk him. Perhaps it was a good job he didn't win: the prize was a cut-glass decanter, a weekend visit to a Bordeaux château, and a case of claret.

Nobody knew who did the Italian job, and ninety per cent of the contestants failed to win first prize; but nobody had to pay their own train-fare, they all earned a good lunch, and at the very least that's another ten lifelong devotees of the bottle. ❧

Nobody's in London this August. Gossip columnists and photographers are having to scrape barrels as never before.

Daily Mail

Nigel Dempster   MAIL DIARY

Ferguson thrown out by New Wife Shock!

ROUGH WINDS have suddenly shaken the latest marriage of the tall, garden-trotting, cribbage-loving, DIY-setting **Monty Aspinall**, 54, and brought a shock wave that has set chic Edgware on its fashionable ear.

Monty's second wife, the much-travelled former Tesco assistant-manageress **Margaret "Megs" Lucan**, 52, has taken strong exception to his 9″ Ferguson (*pictured below, being watched in early 1952 by Aspinall, his late first wife **Beryl**, left, and her Tupperware colleague, the madcap **Sharon Vestey**, wife of Polo-eating **Syd***) claiming that its performance leaves much to be desired.

Aspinall, who has lavished a great deal of attention on the set over the years, recently re-asserted to *Daily Mail* reporters his famous maxim that "a good little 'un is better than a bad big 'un any day of the week, ask anybody, they do not make them like that any more", but this has apparently cut little ice with his new lady, who, in the early hours of last Tuesday morning, put the old Ferguson onto a nearby skip while aghast neighbours watched helplessly.

Aspinall's comments on returning from his desk at the Halifax Building Society, however, made his position absolutely clear.

"I am having that back off of there," he said. "And if the picture is wobbly or they have all got little fat legs, I shall be asking a few sharp questions."

Mrs Aspinall was too upset to comment.

Mr Brian Onassis, 47, who is infatuated with **Princess Michael of Kent**, pictured at Gatwick shortly after arriving from Bruges. Brian, who lists his hobbies as Flemish *sprechgesang* and looking for things in his ear, hopes to take the Princess to *Charlie Girl* and then go back to her place for a curry.

Harry Adler, believed to be the bastard son of Tom Mix, turns his back on his lover of fourteen years, **Gus Mandlikova,** after Horseferry Road magistrates found them both guilty of attempting to get into Annabel's with a platform ticket. Adler, 59, commented: "I've had enough. The man is an oaf. See those shoes? See that hairstyle?"

Caledonian Road was a natural first call for **The Latvia Rhythm Boys**, just in from Kalisadorys, who believe that their great mentor Alan Breeze once had a flat near here, or possibly just a faulty inner-tube.

Heath Baby Could Spell End To Comeback Hopes

VOLUPTUOUS Filipino brunette **Koo Mendoza,** the leading Hampstead au pair who surprised the Heath's fairgoers last weekend by prematurely delivering a fine bouncing 7lb boy after a third go on the Big Dipper, has told us in an exclusive interview of the very real doubts concerning her future.

"I had planned to return to Manila this autumn after I had saved up enough for a Toyota 1.3," the tearful sloe-eyed lovely said today, "but this has put the kybosh on it and no mistake."

Miss Mendoza is 28.

Off Their Trolleys

MERRILY HARPUR

"It is German, yes, but
it's the closed circuit
TV camera."

"We decided to get
our muesli delivered."

"No, those are the kind
you steam lightly or stir-fry —
these are the kind
you chew for three days,
then ferment the accumulated spit
into a heady liquor."

"Depressing the way
personalised birthday cakes have
become increasingly violent."

"Well done! You've rushed the Brie home before it has passed its peak."

"Could I try it on?"

"…And there again, coffee never tastes quite as nice as the equipment looks."

"I prefer to serve the hormones separately."

"Is it just me, or do worms taste of absolutely nothing these days?"

Let Us Now Praise Business Men!

THE British distaste for commercial or industrial achievement will be one of the most powerful stimulants to polemicism for the Gibbons of the twenty-first century. Not a few of them, indeed, have already waxed furious in the twentieth. That engaging historian Correlli Barnett, in his book *The Collapse of British Power*, blames much of it upon the public schools. The British, he points out, built their greatness upon rampant individualism and acquisitiveness that often fell not far short of piracy. They enjoyed an extraordinary phase of inventiveness and prosperity in the later years of the eighteenth century and the first decades of the nineteenth.

Yet, within a few years of Victoria's ascent of the throne, though the trappings of British power and riches remained, the conditions and qualities that created them were already dying. At the Diamond Jubilee, by all the useful criteria for industrial power in the modern age, such as the production of machine tools, Britain had already been overtaken by Germany and the United States. The path of her relentless economic decline was set.

If the battle of Waterloo was won on the playing fields of Eton, Barnett plausibly argues that in the next hundred years of economic competition between nations, Britain's fate was sealed in the classrooms of Rugby. The country's fortune had been founded upon unfettered competitiveness. The public school ethic and the evangelical revival created a new national mood, in which the highest premium was placed upon conformity. The game, rather than the victory, was the thing:

> Personal ambition was discouraged; subordination to the "team spirit" was the ideal. Thus in

1880 the captain of a winning XV at Marlborough concluded his review of the victory by praising "… the unsparing devotion of individuals for the honour of the house; the mutual reliance of the whole team on one another". Success, though desirable, was not the main point. A lost game could be almost as satisfactory as a victory.

Here, Barnett touched upon the public school principle that has contributed decisively to the national ruin for more than a century: achievement, if it is to be of any value, should appear effortless. Gentlemen should not be *seen* to *try*. It is but a skip and a jump from this to the even more pernicious, even more widespread British middle-class doctrine: that if a man is seen to have succeeded – worst of all to have greatly enriched himself – he is likely to have done so by ungentlemanly means. He may well be *seen* to have *tried*. The richer he has become, the less likely he is to have remained a gentleman. If he is very rich indeed, it is fair to assume that he is at least a bounder, if not an outright four-letter man.

It is perfectly acceptable to be rich because the value of ancestral land has gone up, or by becoming a pop star, or by being the Queen. But in the past thirty years, growing awareness of national decline has done nothing whatever to diminish our distaste for those who accumulate vast fortunes through commerce and industry, for tycoons. By "our", I do not seek to join readers' sentiments with those of Mr Kenneth Livingstone, Mr Roy Hattersley, Ms Frances Morrell, who are merely determined that we should all be equally poor. I mean the middle class, the Sloane Ranger, the member of the National Trust, the stalwart of old housemasters' dinners.

We don't in the least mind lending a tenner to a school chum just out of the Scrubs after a short stretch for passing bad cheques. He's a good old honest-to-God failure. As a society, we respect that. We might have him stuffed. But just as we assume a man in a dinner-jacket before 6 p.m. to be a waiter, so we take a man in a Bentley on the M4 on Friday afternoon to be a tycoon, a success, a revoltingly conspicuous worshipper of Midas. We will allow the old Volvo to choke rather than let him past us into the fast lane.

The British tycoon is not so much disliked as regarded with contempt. He is probably a workaholic. I remember hearing a pillar of the squirearchy rubbishing a newly-rich neighbour with a stream of invective, which ended with the terrible denunciation: "He's the sort of man who shoots on a Saturday!" Among squires nowadays, there is a tremendous snobbery about conducting the serious business of the countryside on weekdays, when the wage-earning classes will not get in the line of fire.

Tycoons fly about in helicopters, and overtip waiters. Their wives have no taste, and their children take to drugs. They purchase friendships by extravagant hospitality, and embarrass the recipients who are unable to return it. Their behaviour is loud, their clothes are not right, their public pronouncements insensitive, their political allegiances suspect. How many famous British tycoons escape being charged with one or more of the above leaden clichés? How many attract the faintest respect, far less admiration, for the manner in which they have acquired vast wealth?

I have been touting a theory of my own for some while now, about a symptom of the British

Max Hastings

disease which I have christened The Old Rectory Syndrome. This is an attempt to identify a maximum socially acceptable, and thus professionally desirable, level of wealth for the average aspiring member of the British middle classes. Your Old Rugbeian, or Old Etonian, or Old Giggleswickian, rides off into the City at the age of 18 to do what a man has got to do. By the time he is 35, he has achieved substantial success – indecent wealth, as *Punch*'s Press Gang columnist would define it – par for the course in his own world: an Old Rectory within a hundred miles of London; the money to shoot and fish a bit, educate the children privately, and take a lazy hot holiday and a bracing cold one every year.

Very nice, too. But what does he do next in life? If he was an American or a Hong Kong Chinese, this first half million would be only a small stepping-stone to the million by 40, the tenth at 50, Lear Jet status before the first coronary. But if he is a true Brit with sound instincts for social survival in the Shires and respect among his peers in London, once he has acquired his Old Rectory and the rest of it, he will simply start shooting two days a week instead of one.

Commercially, he will tread water. Imagine what might happen, if his ship came in, if that one takeover too many flooded the coffers, and he was offered a long lease on Castle Howard? Indescribably vulgar. Friends would drift away. A steam yacht on the Mediterranean? Beginning to sound like Freddie Laker, and look what happened to *him*. Sales of widgets reaching an all-time high, Queen's Award for Industry, Queen's Award for Exports, lunch at Downing Street. The kiss of death: it sounds too, too like

poor Clive Sinclair.

As a society, we pride ourselves upon our distaste for excess. We extend this prejudice against those who make too much money. Our most deeply-conditioned instincts recoil from tycoons and tycoonery. They are not team players. They are arrant materialists and self-seekers of the kind our schoolmasters daily warned us against for ten years: "Flashman, you are not here to strive for self, but to strive for the House." Most old schoolmasters, seeing one of their ex-charges reach the chairmanship of a vast property empire, will not think: "Ah yes, I always knew that Flashman major had it in him." They will merely disgustedly assume that Flashman major has continued through life as he began, roasting fags in front of the grate.

It's young East they want to see on Speech Day, if he can get time off from that golf club where he is Hon Sec. Never did quite make it to Durham, of course, but the absolute life and soul of the second XV. You always knew where you were with East. Safe pair of hands.

Socialists will always dislike tycoons, because they are rich. But it is grotesque that so many who call themselves Conservatives do likewise. Arnold Weinstock was blackballed from Brooks's, Rocco Forte discouraged from White's. No member of either club would seriously deny that their existing inhabitants are the usual blend of the good, the bad, and the ugly. It would be laughable to suggest that the moral or social tone of either establishment would have been diminished by the presence of Weinstock or Forte.

They were unacceptable simply because they are tycoons, and prominent tycoons, and thus automatically inspire the distaste of a certain kind of Englishman who has come close to bringing the country to its knees. No member suggests that a man should be excluded from a St James's Street club because he does absolutely nothing, because he is a loser. Yet grown men believe that a winner, a conspicuous winner, should be kept out. We only like winners in the 2.30 at Newmarket, we do.

As a society, we cannot bear to accept that tycoons have a critical role to play in driving industry and the economy from the front. The qualities which make a man a tycoon, a winner, a success, are unlikely to make him especially lovable. I do not particularly want to be stranded on a desert island with Mr Alan Bristow, Mr Tiny Rowland, or Sir James Goldsmith. If there were only enough coconuts for one of us, in that company I would be exceedingly nervous that it would prove not to be me.

By their very nature, by their very success, tycoons are larger than life, set apart from the rest of us. They are where they are because they are tougher and more ruthless than you and me. They wanted the prizes more, and they seized them. They spend money lavishly, because it is boring merely to count one's wealth on a bank statement. They are not cuddly.

But if we claim to be capitalists, we must find it in ourselves to value the most successful exponents of capitalism. We may not like them, we may not want to be like them. But we need them. Indeed, at this moment in our fortunes we could do with rather fewer gentlemen in the team, and a great many more players. If Arnold of Rugby had anticipated the present state of the nation, he might have worried a good deal less about producing players of the game, and rather more about training winners. 🦋

For Your Ears Only

A top-secret British satellite, no bigger than a man's thumb and powered by an ordinary 12-volt car battery, is to be put into orbit round Mars.

The hush-hush programme, which under a special D-notice must not be divulged to anyone, and especially the Martians, will enable a computer to listen in to every single wireless transmission ever made.

For a man to accomplish the same task would take years, experts said, but the satellite, code-named "Big Ears", can cover the entire radio spectrum in less time than it takes to send a Greenwich pip.

Data sent back to earth from "Big Ears" can be picked up using a simple coat-hanger antenna.

The breakthrough is expected to have far-reaching implications both in the military sphere and as something for people to listen to. Scientists predict that most radio transmissions in the Solar System emanate from Earth. Some, like *EastEnders*, are familiar to everyone but others, such as walkie-talkies used by vets or foresters, are at present seldom monitored.

The "Big Ears" OWACS – Orbiting Wireless and Computer Set – makes short work of digesting an astonishing variety of signals. It can "eavesdrop" on:

- **Cab-to-cab transmissions between buses**

- **Radio Humberside**

- **Automatic garage-door openers**

- **Ship-to-shore messages throughout the Indian Ocean**

- **Radio Hilversum**

- **Moscow's AA Prospektwatch**

- **Any South American radio speaking-clock**

- **Radio-controlled model yachts**

- **The Voice of Morocco**

- **Telewele Wales**

- **Motor-cycle messengers anywhere in the Midlands**

- **Most bats and deep-sea worms**

- **Programmes like *The War of the Worlds, Cisco Kid* and *Down Your Way* which were broadcast many years ago but are still detectable as echoes in space.**

Once the "Big Ears" project is underway, there could be vital spin-off benefits for British high-technology industry besides. "Big Ears" technicians say the coating used on the satellite's six-inch saucer is quite similar to that used on non-stick saucepans.

Because of the obvious security risks, a television documentary which revealed details of how the saucer should be cleaned without scratching, has been withdrawn on Home Office orders and some Labour MPs may have to be gaoled.

Now American specialists at the Palo Alto receiving station are to launch an experiment to see if "Big Ears" can catch the banned controversial film *even though it hasn't been broadcast*.

The results, to be published in *The Listener*, may not be known for some time.

SUE TOWNSEND
The Royal Wedding Diary of Adrian Mole (Aged 18¼)

17th July

I'm sick of reading about how handsome Prince Andrew is. To me he looks like the morons studying bricklaying and plastering at college, there is something about his neck that cries out for a hod of bricks, and those big white ruthless teeth! It makes me shudder to think of them nibbling at Fergie's defenceless neck. So some women like tall, well-built men who can fly helicopters and have gob-smacking bank accounts and Coutts gold cards. But personally I think Fergie is throwing herself away on him.

Miss Sarah Ferguson was born to be the wife of Adrian Mole. I have written to tell her so, and to implore her to change her mind before 23rd July. As yet I have received no reply. She must be agonising over her decision: "Riches, glamour and publicity with Prince Andrew, or poverty, introspection and listening to poetry with Adrian Mole" – not an easy choice.

Sarah Ferguson, oh Sarah Ferguson,
Your name is on my lips constantly.
Don't marry Andy, his legs are bandy.
Come to Leicester, come to Leicester, marry me!
Leave the palace, grab a taxi,
I'll be waiting at the end of the M1.
We'll go to my house, meet my parents,
I know the dog and you will get along.

18th July

No letter from Sarah Ferguson today.

I have rung Buckingham Palace but the (no doubt powdered and bewigged) flunky refused to let me speak to her. He said, "Miss Ferguson is taking no calls from strangers." I said, "Listen, my man, I am no *stranger* to Miss Ferguson, she is my soul mate." I'm not sure but I could have sworn the flunky muttered, "Arsehole mate," before he slammed the phone down. There is nothing else to do but go to Buckingham Palace and tackle her face to face.

I have sent a Telemessage to my ginger-haired love:

Sarah. I am coming to you. Meet me at the Palace gate at high noon.

> *Yours with unvanquished love,*
> *Adrian Mole (18¼)*

P.S. I will be wearing sunglasses, and carrying a Marks and Spencer carrier-bag.

19th July

Buckingham Palace, 1.30 p.m.

She did not come. I asked a mounted policeman if Sarah was at home. He said, "Yes, she's inside having waving lessons from the Queen Mother." I asked him if he would deliver a note to her from me, but he got distracted by a coachload of excitable Japanese tourists who were measuring his horse and taking down its specifications. No doubt they are going to copy it and flood the world with cheap police horses. Will we English never learn?

I made my way home to the dreary provinces by train. An old fat woman kept up a non-stop monologue about her plans for the royal wed-ding day. I wanted to cry out, "You old fat fool, you will be watching an empty screen on the 23rd because *there will be no royal wedding*. So cancel your order for two dozen crusty cobs and a crate of assorted bottles of pop." I *wanted* to cry these words out but, of course, I didn't; people would have thought I was a teenage lunatic obsessed with Sarah Ferguson, whereas of course I am anything but.

20th July

Sarah has not replied to my letters yet.
Perhaps she has run out of stamps.

> **"I bought a commemorative Andy and Fergie mug and blacked Prince Andrew's big-jawed face out with a black marker pen, then I sat on the side of the canal, put some flowers in the mug and wrote a last letter to Sarah."**

21st July

I asked the postman if there was anything for me from Buckingham Palace. He replied, "Ho, has Ted Hughes croaked it? Hare you the next Poet Laureate? Hif you hare, may I hoffer my hutmost congratulations?"

No wonder England's going to the dogs with public servants of his calibre.

7 p.m.

Pandora Braithwaite rang from Leningrad tonight.

I asked how she was getting on with her Russian lessons. She said, "Oh, amazingly well, I joined in a most stimulating debate in the turnip queue this morning. Workers and intellectuals discussed the underlying symbolism of *The Cherry Orchard*. I ventured the opinion, in Russian of course, that the cherries represented the patriarchal balls of Mother Russia, thus proving that Chekhov was AC/DC."

I asked how the assembled geniuses in the turnip queue had reacted to her analysis. Pandora said, "Oh, they failed to understand it, bloody peasants!" The line started to go faint, so Pandora shouted, "Adrian, video-tape the royal wedding for me, darling." Then the phone went dead, and Pandora was lost to me.

22nd July

My Sarah was on the front page of the paper this morning, wearing a most indecent low-cut dress. That oaf Andrew was quite openly leer-ing at her cleavage. When Sarah is my wife I shall insist that she wears cardigans buttoned up to the neck.

I'm with the Moslems on this one.

No letter. No hope left, the wedding is tomorrow, I shall not watch it, I shall walk the streets clutching my despair. Oh God! Oh Sarah!

23rd July
My Sarah's Wedding Day

Sarah! Sarah! Sarah!

I sobbed into my pillow for so long this morning that the feathers stuck together and formed lumps like bits of dead chickens. Eventually I rose, dressed in black, and made a simple yet nutritious breakfast. My mother came down and through cigarette smoke said, "What's up with your face?"

I replied quietly, yet with immense dignity, "I am in the deepest despair, Mother."

"Why, are your piles playing you up again?" She coughed.

I left the kitchen, shaking my head from side to side in a pitying fashion, whilst at the same time saying, *sotto voce*, "Lord, have mercy on the Philistines I am forced to live with, for they know not what they say."

My father overheard and said, "Oh, got bleedin' religion now, has he?"

I passed Grandma on her way to our house. She was carrying a tea-tray piled high with little fancy cakes, iced with the entwined initials "F.A." Grandma was in her best clothes; her hat swayed with exotic and long extinct birds' feathers, she was wearing net gloves and a fox's claw brooch. She was ecstatically happy. She cried out, "Hello, Adrian, my little love, have you got a kiss for your Grandma?" I kissed her rouged cheek and walked on before she saw the tears in my eyes. She croaked, "Happy royal wedding day, Adrian."

I passed the Co-op where the Union Jack hung upside-down, and the Sikh temple where it was hung correctly. I bought a commemorative Andy and Fergie mug and blacked Prince Andrew's big-jawed face out with a black marker pen, then I sat on the side of the canal, put some flowers in the mug and wrote a last letter to Sarah:

Dear Princess Sarah,

You will soon tire of the loon you married (he looks like the sort to hog the bedclothes to me). As soon as you grow even a little weary of him, remember I am waiting for you here in Leicester. I cannot promise you riches (although I have £139.37 in the Market Harborough Building Society) but I can offer intellectual chit-chat and my body, which is almost unsullied and is years younger than your husband's.

Well, Sarah, I won't keep you as I expect your husband is shouting oafishly for your attention.

I remain, Madam,

> *Your most humble and obedient servant,*
> *Adrian Mole*

THEATRE

THE MIKADO   LESLEY GARRETT *as Yum-Yum*
BONAVENTURA BOTTONE *as Nanki-Poo*   RICHARD ANGAS *as The Mikado*   ERIC IDLE *as Ko-Ko*

THE PHANTOM OF THE OPERA
SARAH BRIGHTMAN *as Christine Daaé*   MICHAEL CRAWFORD *as The Phantom*

William Hewison

MR AND MRS NOBODY
JUDI DENCH *as Carrie Pooter*   PENNY RYDER *as Sarah*   MICHAEL WILLIAMS *as Charles Pooter*

A PENNY FOR A SONG   BRIAN COX *as Sir Timothy Bellboys*
RUDI DAVIES *as Dorcas Bellboys*   IAN McNEICE *as Lamprett Bellboys*

"Wet T-shirts don't suit you."

JONATHAN SALE

Bandit Country

IN a universe of things that go bump, bang, splat, screech, whoosh and tinkle (as in cash-registers), it is reassuring to know that some people have their feet on the ground and other folks' bums three feet above it.

"It's a new Video Seat," explained the man on the Metro Products stall. "It's a seat for people to sit on and stay on, a comfortable way for them to spend money." The man from Metro, who had invented a Fire-Safe, Self-Extinguishing, vandal-proof wastebin, had a point. There is nothing worse than Games-player's Knee, resulting in Video-player's Itchy Feet, leading to a terminal case of Failure of Punter's Wallet. "We've got a Video Ashtray," he added. It looks like an ordinary ashtray but can be bolted to the side of the video game, thus preventing players from dropping ash into the bin. Not that it would matter, provided the bin had the requisite double-wall construction and oxygen-depriving dome.

With luck, the Video Seat will soon be appearing at a major arcade near you, as may all of the products at last week's annual Amusement Trades Exhibition at Olympia. It was a youngster's conception of paradise, the Grand Hall crammed with space, war, racing, gambling and other state-of-the-art (if art is the right word for it) games – all of them free. There were, in fact, no youngsters, only us oldsters, men in suits shaking our heads sadly as the electronic monsters from the *Bermuda Triangle* zapped us before we could zap them. This was the Motor Show of the business, in which manufacturers and arcade owners, blinking in the unaccustomed daylight of Olympia, compared and contrasted *Ghosts 'n' Goblins* and *Return of the Invaders*.

"People have the wrong image of the West End Arcade," declared the man from Comax, and it is true that there were no child molesters to be seen, possibly because there were no children.

In the Grand Hall today, in the Leisure Centres tomorrow, out of the Leisure Centres the day after that. New games pop up every month. The kids have mastered *Rock 'n' Rage*, in which pop stars have to fight off aliens invad-ing their concert (I've been to gigs like that), so out comes the hi-tech "board" and in goes another, the size of a telephone-directory, and now the young fingers are blasting away with *Side Arms* or *Valtric*. "People like to test their skills against the impossible."

As they have done over the centuries. Was it not the Greek scientist Hero who came up with the original fruit-machine? I have no idea, but a note from the British Amusement Catering Trades Association fills us in. "The Greek scientist Hero was probably responsible for the first coin-operated device when he invented a Holy Water dispenser giving out a metered measure of the liquid on insertion of a five drachma piece." If you or I today converted a stamp or condom machine to dish out sacred liquid in 10p gushes, the wrath of heaven would presumably fall; more in keeping with the spirit of the age is the device in Covent Garden that rewards the insertion of coins with a splat of unholy water in the face of the inserter.

Our Hero seems to have got away with it, but few followed in his footsteps and it was the Victorians who began to rake in the pennies with the flickering pictures of the What-the-Butler-Saw "mutoscopes". And it was a Mr Charles Fey of San Francisco who was credited with the first fruit-machine, which paid out money as well as taking it in. In what ratio, is not recorded. Today, as BACTA reports proudly, the ratio on fruit-machines is 30% to the machine, 70% to the punter.

Some of the punters, that is; most lose out. And some of the winners lose, too: my mother once hit a massive jackpot in a Nottingham club, but somebody nicked her purse. There must be a video game called *Pick Pockets* or *Thievin' Fingers*. There is certainly one in which the player has to kick or head-butt a succession of oiks who come at him with grievous bodily intentions; I watched a neat Japanese man play it, and come away shaken. This theme should be popular in pubs, as a preparation for the scenes outside after closing-time.

Near the entrance was a man who comes from a long line of one-armed bandit operatives. He renovates the oldies and has them spitting out silver. In the summer he is opening the Hall by the Sea, a new arcade in Margate.

"This," he said, pointing towards a venerable fruit-machine, its pears, oranges and cherries briefly stilled, "is a *mechanical* machine. There are not too many around any more." It dates back to the Sixties, the Nineteen-Sixties. "It has real mechanics and a real handle. Some of the new versions just connect to *electronics*." He breathes new life into old cabinets and installs

HOME COOKIN'

JUST LIKE THE FRANCHISE MOTHER USED TO HOLD!

them in arcades for the benefit of the nostalgic puller and pusher of one-armed bandits, the punter who never could figure out how to operate new-fangled buttons. "They're adjusted for the new currency."

You bet they are. Half a million people visit Britain's amusement arcades every day (many of them being my children). Over 50,000 people are directly employed in the trade, boasts BACTA: the population of a reasonably sized city, all engaged in handing out change, checking circuits, sweeping up and chucking out. Britain leads the world in coin-operated amusement machine design – if nothing else – but not in ways of adding up the total sum that goes down the chutes every year; many of the operators are small, back-of-a-pier johnnies whose takings, unlike their machines, are not computerised. There are two thousand arcades and 138,000 licensed fruit-machines; video games, which have no gambling element, are unlicensed and un-numbered but have an estimated total of 60,000. Given that games like *Starforce* and *Rush 'n' Crash* end up on cartridges plugged into home computers, that all represents a lot of people pounding away at "Fire" buttons. Still, there are a few professionals still upholding the old standards.

"I came into the business in 1980," said the young man with the American accent on the Maquinas Automaticas stand, "when no one was producing pin-ball machines, which went out when video came in." Then, when the videos started repeating themselves – zap one alien and you've zapped 'em all – many of us began to hanker for the old days when the touch of a flipper on the side of a board would physically send an actual ball shooting up a real route to bang about in a concrete sort of way. Call us Luddites if you must, call us arty-crafty, call us William Morris throwbacks in a digital age; but it meant cash registers pinging for Maquinas. Yet the Dark Ages might be back again: "Now we are balancing on the edge of saturation point for the pinball machines."

This does not, of course, mean large-scale unemployment among the trade. "Simulation is the new thing," the man from BACTA reassured me. This includes the SR2. There may not have been many buses to take us to Olympia, but, once there, a twelve-seater model was on hand to take us, well, nowhere. The SR2 is a moving, tilting cinema, whose pitching and tossing matches a film with a rocky theme. It is "a ride beyond the realms of reality and a money maker in motion".

Outside, the ice on the roads prohibited bicycles. Inside, there was a demonstration model of a stationary BMX which, if pedalled, overtakes cars on the screen, skids out of control and crashes. It should keep the kids off the streets. There are car racing games which are more like dodgems; instead of providing merely a monitor, the WEC Le Mans 24 consists of a dodgem car which swivels through a couple of right-angles as the driver goes round the bend.

The more massive of the simulators will never turn up in a corner of your local's public bar. We are talking theme parks here. That is where you find the band of bears, life-size dummies which go through the motions of plucking banjos and banging pianos, in time with a mechanical ditty. (If I were a grizzly, I would sue for defamation of character.) This is also where

"The reason I don't do anything about my weight problem is I have this intelligence problem."

you find devices that go beyond simulators to achieve a reality of their own.

Like the SR2, the Gyrotron is from the Smiling Lion Co ("takes you on an adventurous ride to profits"). It takes punters for a ride too, strapped to a gyroscope which rotates not just round and round but also head-over-heels. "Passengers experience a feeling of weightlessness," and probably a feeling of their lunch as well. It looks like the kind of apparatus that would have been considered too extreme for use in the Spanish Inquisition, but was apparently voted "Best New Ride at Expo '86 International".

Yet that is a doddle when compared with the Spaceprobe, a long, wide, vertical tube containing a sphere containing you, but certainly not me. Air shoots the sphere and the indoor astronaut to just over the top of the tube, in perfect safety, according to the manufacturers, although it is not a theory I should like to test. "Sold to Bobbejaanland", boasted a notice and Bobbejaanland is welcome.

The last sign I saw before leaving for the real-life Kensington Le Mans outside Olympia, was rather less hi-tech, and more important. One of the stalls was selling a placard advising:

If your machine don't play, call the attendant right away.

Translated into Greek, it must have graced Hero's Holy Water dispenser. Tilt that, and you ended up with an unholy mess of water down your tunic. And you didn't get your five-drachma piece back. ☙

ROGER WODDIS

Poor Genius

(Acknowledgements to E. Y. Harburg)

They used to tell me I was head of the team
And miles ahead of the mob.
When there was any chance to get my share
I displayed my flair, made a few bob.
They used to tell me there was plenty of cream,
If not a knighthood ahead,
But just when I thought I was there,
They sacked me instead.

Once I ruled an empire, thought I'd won,
Thought my profits would climb.
Once I ruled an empire, now I'm done.
Brother, can you spare a dime?

Once the top banana, Number One,
Made a mint in my time.
Once I dealt in millions, now there's none.
Brother, can you spare a dime?

Once had fifty suits, penthouse as well,
Money just seemed to stick to my thumb.
Didn't give two hoots, I thought what the hell
And just went on rising like scum.
Something in the City was cause for pride,
Now they call it a crime.
I'll know how to deal when I'm inside –
Brother, can you spare a dime?

Confessions of a Booker Judge

GILLIAN REYNOLDS

NO DOUBT about it, the prestige of being a Booker Prize judge is enormous. So much so that no one would believe me when I told them that I am one this year, (the official announcement having drawn fewer lines in the press than National Earthworm Week) but that's understandable. When Martin Goff, Director of the National Book League, rang to make me the offer the first thing I asked was who had let him down?

He laughed, but then he is a cheery chap. It wasn't like that at all, he said. The Chairman would be Anthony Thwaite, the others would be Isabel Quigly, Bernice Rubens, and Edna Healey.

And so we all went to lunch at Book House, which is on top of a hill in Wandsworth. We asked, after some initial hesitation, basic questions like how many? And when would they arrive? We could, we were told, take the first lot home with us that day.

I walked down the hill to the railway station carrying the large cardboard box. It was a fine day in late May, a bit chilly but a bright blue sky with white clouds, the kind that excites. On days like that people start romances or become blondes.

All the way back, sitting with the box heavy on my knee, hauling it up the stairs and down the escalators, the little shifts inside it were like quickenings. Oh! I am a Booker Prize judge! and what is in here needs me!

I began reading the minute I got home. Random, I said to myself. Be random. No preferential treatment for famous names. Just put your hand into the box, take one out, read it. Treat them all alike.

I went out next day and bought a new little file box. I would do a card on each as I finished it. Anthony Thwaite, masterful person that he is, had told us to have comments on everything we had read, by September. Martin Goff, the optimist of Book House, had warned there might be as many as 80 novels altogether. In the end there were 120 on the official list, with 36 more that publishers submitted for possible "calling in". By this time I had run out of file cards, patience and random intent. However, the very possibility of such events was remote as I sat down, the envy of all my friends, ("How wonderful! A whole summer reading the best novels!") to Book One.

Those were the idyllic days.

But by mid-July I had three unopened boxes in the hall, and heartburn. The books were coming in so fast and in such numbers that at one point the postman, taking pity, offered to take a box away again. Where was the excitement of their little shiftings now? Long gone, vanished in the panic of trying to find a place to put the buggers once they came out of the boxes.

Slit the tape, peel back the cardboard. There they would be, jackets rubbing shoulders, the rivals. Visions of India, South Africa, Canada, Guyana, Ghana, Iran, Australia, Japan, the past, the future. Worlds without pity, terrible souls stripped naked, occasional jokers, women with feelings worn bare, love with holes in, guilt by the cattle truck load. Random no longer, purposive now, the hand goes into the box and if it comes out with more of the same as that which lately it held, puts it aside and searches again. It dawns that the reason so many publishers' names are unfamiliar is that what they publish is, on this evidence, crap.

The clock ticks on meanwhile. Arithmetic joins aesthetics in judgment. If it takes a day to do 200 pages, how many pages are left and how many days? Selina Scott's question, much ridiculed at the time, about whether a judge has to read all the books now looks journalistically shrewd.

I haven't been reading fiction reviews, so as not to be prejudiced. But was that wise? I haven't phoned any of the other judges to confer, but when someone has rung me I have clung to the call like a lifeline. I am drowning in the sea of words. I can't remember what "good" is, or "bad" for that matter. If I were a novelist I might sue for industrial injury. Is there anything left to say about love, hate, rage, old age and the ways children see things?

At about this time the next book would show there is. Reading on. And on. One day I did three. The next day was like a hangover. I couldn't face the rest of what was in the box until afternoon and even then it took a swift half hour on Paul Muldoon's poems to get me back to the page at all. Reading on. The minute I finish one I put it down with the left hand and pick up the next with the right.

Don't judge by the jacket or the author's biography. Avoid the plot synopsis. Go for the prose. Prose? I've read better on the back of cornflake packets. Left hand drops, right picks up, spectacles fall down nose, delicious waves of snooze. Doorbell rings. More books. Isabel Quigly has "called in" more. My heart hardens. This is the way publishers get round the rules, get more considered than their official four. Not with me, not this year, not with so many already in and waiting.

Of these, two come as page proofs. Publishers aren't supposed to do that either. But they do, especially with famous authors, knowing you won't resist. Trying to read one in bed, the "read" heap collapses on the floor and I throw the "unread" after it. Next day I relent and spend half an hour getting it back into order.

September comes and so do the leaks. Who spoke to *The Times*? Who showed the full list to *The Bookseller*? This last has caused problems. It seems that publishers don't like the whole list to appear as some of them tell their authors fibs about what they have submitted. I have been told by two booksellers what is going to win. I am surprised. They may be disappointed.

There was a time, four months ago, when I used to look in the window of my local bookshop, the Mandarin in Notting Hill Gate, and give myself secret hugs for all the books I wouldn't have to buy. "I'll get it for the Booker," I thought, and with Timothy Mo I was right, but with John Le Carré I was wrong. Since then it has been all reading for work, which can sometimes be reading for fun, but not always.

What I miss are biographies, poems and, most of all, Americans. I hadn't realised how thin literary life is without Americans. I hadn't realised, either, how thick the plots around the Booker can be. Lobbies are no longer discreet, pleas for inside information continuous.

Brian Wenham, who was a judge the year William Golding beat Anthony Burgess, says it gets worse on the actual day. On October 22 we turn up, party frocks in hand, at the Guildhall for the final deliberation, the dinner, the TV show and the announcement.

"Would you do it again?" Wenham asks me. We look at each other and say not a word.

"You know what? I'm doing exactly what I was doing when Kennedy was shot."

At first contact with Europeans, the Indians were wary.

Some Indians were mistaken for rabbits.

Natural obstacles made the way West difficult.

Competition between Indians and Whites was fierce.

Ways were found to justify the elimination of the Indian population.

DAVID TAYLOR TALKS TO
Paul Newman

"Mister Good-Looking, Mister Lucky who
happened to be in the right place
at the right time…luck is an art."

WELL. He's a little out of shape. Has gotten the flu for one thing. Feels a little tired. Sort of out of steam. Well. There was a time. Coupla years ago. He started to feel that way about acting. All of it. Sure. Went to hell.

Hard to say what it was exactly. Scripts didn't seem so hot. He started to have doubts. Started to feel he'd started to repeat himself. To duplicate mannerisms. To do the job by numbers. Well. It got to the point where he didn't much like a damn thing he'd done. In twenty-five years. Disillusioned, he'd guess. He was pushing sixty at that moment in time.

Well. Maybe his passion for automobiles did have a bit to do with it. Maybe not. The salad dressing did not at all. That started out as sort of a joke, joshing around with some friends. He gave friends a bottleful of his own-recipe salad dressing, next thing he knows it's a business. *Newman's Own.*

It seemed sort of a tacky thing to do, go into the food business for laughs. Well. It started out a cottage industry in salad dressing, then spaghetti sauce, then popcorn, then that was it. Except last year *Newman's Own* products grossed $24 million. He gave the dough to charity. Sainsbury's have it over here.

Shouldn't we talk about the film? Guess we should ought to, at this time.

Well. It's sort of *The Hustler II.* It finds Paul Newman reprising his Academy Award-nominated role, er, from the '61 classic and box-office sensation. As Fast Eddie Nelson, that is. But older. The hustler is still hustlin' but in twenty-five years he's changed. Today he's an urbane, laconic, liquor salesman and part-time stake-horse. He bankrolls any kids he figures might have it. Have what it takes. Like in the picture, Tom Cruise, as his protégé, kid called Vincent Lauria, has.

Well. Maybe there was sort of a personal perspective in that. Sure. Times change. Maybe this picture (it's entitled *The Color of Money*, by the way, spelled the American way) is about the rekindling of passion. About self-awareness. And about being on the outside of the game, looking in. With a whole new perspective. It's that sort of a film. Reportedly Tom took a pay cut to play it, you know?

The way Tom figured it, Martin Scorsese, whose credits include *Taxi Driver* and *Raging Bull*, Martin is really into the relationship that exists between good and evil. What he does here is to take you inside the characters and introduce different moralities. In the end, he doesn't try to clean it all up and have everything justified. No way. But within the motion-picture's framework there is a resolution. Well.

It concerns a man who changes his way of living life. Who changes his values. The arena happens to be a pool hall, but it could be any place else. Maybe there does come a time when the king has to turn over the sceptre to the prince. In the picture, Fast Eddie has been compromising all his life, hates what he has become. It's the story of his liberation. The shake-out is the re-discovery of what makes a guy happy.

Well. *The Hustler* was took from the Walter Tevis book. Of the same name. Walter's sequel was *The Color of Money*, but the film isn't as close to it. Not at all. Actually, the script took a lot of work, a lot of work and a whole bunch of re-writes. Got sent back time and again.

Paul is reminded at this time that he once sent back a bottle of Jack Daniels.

Even on the set, people had to be prepared to explore a terrible idea, let's say, in the hope it'd maybe turn right around, through 180°, and re-arrange itself into something wonderful. It was sort of a voyage of discovery. You work at a picture with Scorsese. The pursuit of excellence is what it comes down to. Well.

This picture, it co-stars Tom and Tom's pretty hot. Tom only started out in 1980. Now Tom's made seven pictures, *Top Gun* for one, since that time. This will make it eight. Well.

The guy's a great actor. And athlete. Took Tom no time at all to pick up pool. Shoots like a pro. Tom and Paul have a lot of respect for each other. A lot of time.

It came a little easier for him. Picking up the way you shoot pool. He'd done it one time already. The hustler was a great part. Is a great part. The sort where you figure how a guy walks and carries himself and it's enough. The rest gels without too much hassle. Looks to come easy.

Tom and he, they played a few games on the set. For fun mostly, but for money besides. Paul

won Tom's house. Hell no he did not collect.

The set was sort of a community set. Competition? There was some. But no big egos. No pride of ownership. There was a feeling of camaraderie that was all kinds of special. And there was a sense of generosity. Of selflessness on the part of all the people connected with it. There was an enthusiasm to try new things. Not to be stifled by preconceived ideas. Well.

Yes. It's tipped for an Oscar nomination. No. It's not important to him at this time. It was pretty important, one time. Now? Well. It feels like chasing a beautiful woman for about eighty years, and finally she relents, but you have to say terribly sorry, you're too tired. In any case, he's had half a dozen nominations for Best Actor over the years: *Cool Hand Luke, Cat on a Hot Tin Roof, Hud, The Hustler* first time out and *Absence of Malice, The Verdict.* Newman pictures everyone remembers, though, are *Butch Cassidy and the Sundance Kid* or *The Sting.*

Well. He got an honorary Oscar last year, awarded for his overall film career. Chequered career, if you ask him. Don't imagine that it's easy to secure good roles, because your name's Paul Newman and you've got blue eyes and around 6′ 4″ in spikes. Uh? It was *The New York Post* started up all that: how tall is Paul?

Well sure, he hates that. That whole business of making out he was Mister Good-Looking, Mister Lucky who happened to be in the right place at the right time. George Ray Hill, he said to him one time, Paul, luck is an art. You make it. And he's made it, in so far as you ever believe you've made it.

What's terrible is to work maybe once in two years and you've been used to working three or four times a year. You get terrified you'll get rusty. Well. There have been around forty-five movies since Paul Newman debuted in *The Silver Chalice* in 1954. He was a Greek slave. And terrible. He got the hell out back on to Broadway at that time. He directs also, did he mention that?

The reason he didn't direct *The Color of Money* was that he never thought to direct it. Scorsese was directing and he was more than happy to be working with him. Period.

What does Paul Newman look for in a script? He has not the slightest idea. Originality, he'd

"Ever since *Sundance* and *The Sting,* he and Redford have been looking to hit on another script..."

more than the food business. When he was eighteen he wanted to be a US naval pilot and might have been, but for colour-blindness. He did officer's training at Yale and spent three years as the wireless man on torpedo bombers in the Pacific campaign. He was discharged in '46 and planned to take up teaching, but his father died and he headed home to Cleveland, Ohio, obliged to run the family sports goods store.

Well. That wasn't for him. He stuck it for eighteen months and then handed over to his brother, Arthur, and signed on at Yale Drama School. He was skint and taking small-time jobs wherever he could, but the break was getting a part in *Picnic* and, on the strength of it, getting accepted at Lee Strasberg's Actors' Studio to study with up-and-coming new guys like Rod Steiger. He was started on his list of some forty-five pictures to date.

Winning was one which changed his life. He got bitten by the motor-racing bug and started to race in earnest. He wasn't that quick. Matter of fact, they nicknamed him "Old Balloon Foot". But he got quicker, took second place at Le Mans in a Porsche, won this and that back home, set aside all of 1984 for racing. Joanne doesn't mind. Not now.

guess. He doesn't like doing a violent film. Nor would he choose a pro-military one or go near any kind of porn. Ordinarily he'd have said no to anything profane, but *Slap Shot* was irresistible. Ever since *Sundance* and *The Sting*, he and Robert Redford have been looking to hit on another script they could do together. Nothing so far.

Working with Joanne Woodward, Mrs Newman, is always all kinds of special. Never more so than when he started out on directing, with Joanne in *Rachel, Rachel*. That's another one they could go back to, one day. Meantime he's directing her and John Malkovich in a motion-picture version of Tennessee Williams's play, *The Glass Menagerie*. It's scheduled to open in the fall and will, he believes, blow our socks off.

He and Joanne have been married now for 29 years. Well. Who can say why a marriage works? Maybe it's that they both carry clubs of equal size and weight. They met on Broadway, during the '58 run of *Picnic*. Today their lovely home is in Westport, Connecticut. They have it furnished with lots of old Americana, folk paintings and the like, which Paul sort of collects. Him and Dustin Hoffman both. Well.

By the way, Westport, Connecticut, is headquarters for *Newman's Own*. The multi-million-dollar salad dressing and spaghetti sauce empire has a staff of five. Paul Newman is the president and his best buddy, Mr Hotchner, the guy who wrote *Papa Hemingway*, is veep. Mrs Hotchner heads up the PR side, Joanne Woodward handles product testing. Nell, their daughter, helps with recipe R&D. Conferences are held round the ping-pong table and over it hangs a banner with *Newman's Own* business philosophy emblazoned on it: "If ever we have a plan, we're screwed."

Acting was never really his idea of a job, any

Well. All sports appeal, especially tennis or swimming. If you can call bridge a sport, he's a hot-shot at that as well. He got pretty hooked on politics, too, or at least was really into the Civil Rights Movement, racial equality, and promoting disarmament, which right now could use a little help.

Chief amongst his social concerns has been, well, the Scott Newman Foundation, an anti-drugs campaign named after his late son. Yeah. Scott.

Well.

Fact is, a lot of what he does is personal. Don't imagine it's too easy to do a whole lot of things, if your name is Paul Newman. Of course, it can help a lot. But it can get in the way a lot, too. There are times when you might want to keep your own counsel. Times when you don't wish to be interviewed, pursued, or quoted. It gets called enigmatic.

Well.

53

WHAT'S THE COUNTRY COMING TO?

BY THE RT HON NICHOLAS RIDLEY, SECRETARY OF STATE FOR THE ENVIRONMENT

THE Editor asked me to write about the rural environment in the year 2000. This daunting prospect brought on a bad dream. It went something like this:

It was the year 2000 and I found myself driving along the M6. I crept along at a steady, environmentally-conscious 30 mph. I was breathalysed twice by police conducting random breath tests (results negative, of course). I turned off into some open countryside. A sign said: "Halt! You are entering Green Belt". I stopped at a barrier to have my car searched by members of the Green Belt Constabulary to see if it contained any bricks or mortar.

I proceeded through the heart of rural England. It was most picturesque. There were happy peasants dancing round maypoles; morris dancers clattering and jingling on the village green; merry yokels in smocks planting hedgerows and building dry-stone walls, or cutting hay with scythes and stacking it in heaps with pitch-forks. They all seemed pitifully thin.

I came to another sign: "Halt! You are entering a National Park". The car was searched again, this time for secateurs and shotguns. I was given leaflets telling me how to behave. As I reached open moorland, a notice told me not to leave the road under any circumstances lest I disturb the birds. There were wooden huts built

into the moor and into them shambled a strange procession of people, heavily camouflaged, coming and going in silence to take up their vigils, binoculars round their necks.

As I drove out of the Park, I chatted to a Conservation vigilante while he searched my car for plant cuttings and dead birds. He explained that since the abolition of fox hunting and grouse-shooting, they had had problems managing the moor. They were applying to the Secretary of State for the Environment for a special culling order to reduce the fox population (humanely, of course). He said, as he took another bite out of a cold game pie, that it was necessary to reduce the numbers of foxes to protect the grouse. Last year they had had to ask for a culling order to reduce the grouse population (humanely, of course).

I woke up in a cold sweat. I expect I will no longer be Secretary of State for the Environment in the year 2000, but if I am, it must not be like that. We must not forget that it is country people who have looked after our countryside so well – and they know best.

There's no other deep meaning to this story but the conclusion I hope to draw from it is that it is a mistake to forecast the future. Someone in the future will dig our forecasts out and quote them back to show how wrong we were.

People go on about "divides" in this country: the "Urban/Rural" divide or the "North/South" divide. These divides don't actually exist; they are created to fuel the political debate. The truth of the landscape of Great Britain is that:

75% is farmland,
10% is woods and forests,
6% is other countryside and mountains, etc,
9% is built up.

It is remarkable how a nation of 55 million people can live in such a small island and occupy only 9% of the land surface. But there are concentrations of population which make a swathe of the country very densely populated. The majority of the population lives in a belt linking London to Liverpool. The pressure is particularly intense in the southern counties. In the south-east the inevitable conflicts between land uses result in local land shortages.

Land prices in the south-east have risen with a vengeance and people have attempted to increase the supply for their favoured land use by bombarding planning authorities with applications or by draining marshes, cutting down trees or uprooting hedgerows. These moves produce counter-active forces to try and prevent change in the use and character of the land. The whole conflict gives rise to passionate emotions and impossible political decisions. Elections can certainly be won and lost on such issues.

In other parts of the country the situation is different. In some areas, there is little pressure on the land, no great pressure for new building, much marginal farming land which may go out of intensive use as the CAP reforms work through. We are busy working out alternative uses for such land. No one wants to increase the supply of land for development so the price of land goes down.

The value of land in Britain varies substantially between different parts of the country. The greatest disparities are in land with development permission, where the range in 1985 varied from less than £90,000 per hectare to over £835,000 per hectare. For land without development permission the range is much smaller from £2,000 per hectare to £4,000 per hectare for agricultural land in 1986.

These figures are, of course, derived from regional averages. Such price discrepancies may vary; but they are likely to fuel the changes that will occur in the next fifteen years. What are they likely to be?

They won't involve a massive transfer of land from pastoral use to development. No Government or planning authority would ever allow that. But I believe they must result in a slow transfer of businesses, industry and population back from the "South" to the "North", from suburbia to "urbia". That is the logical conclusion of another decade of strict planning controls and public resistance to development in the south-east. Some, of course, will go abroad.

Within the rural areas what will happen? A fall in land price would provide new opportunities – not only for more diverse agricultural production and for forestry but also for those who want to use the land for recreational, leisure and conservation purposes or for tourist enterprises and other small businesses. It is ironic but pleasing that even activities such as golfing, or hunting and shooting, so detested by the Urban Left, may receive a new lease of life. I think we will also see an increase in planting of our indigenous hardwood trees both as a good investment and as a positive benefit to the environment.

Conservationists and Wildlife Preservation Societies will be able to afford to buy cheaper land to create more natural habitats and wildlife or nature reserves.

Essentially it is the individual who owns and manages land who decides how the British landscape develops. My nightmare would become reality if he gave up in disgust and left the future of the rural landscape to some bland corporatism. I hope that future Secretaries of State will resist pressures to impose more and more controls on the hapless countryman and that he's left in charge of the countryside. I doubt whether Castle Howard or the Savernake Forest or Hatfield House or Upper Teesdale would be as they are if the full panoply of planning and conservation laws and regulations and bureaucracies had had a hand in them.

In the unlikely circumstances that I am still Secretary of State for the Environment in the year 2000, I will continue to insist that countrymen should be allowed the maximum freedom possible to pursue their own destinies because it is what they have done which has made rural Britain what it is. ❧

SCHWADRON

"Norman, maybe it wasn't such a smart idea for you to have left everything to science."

BANX

"Yes, but is it art?"

SICK JOKES

"Never mind a vaccine, Mowbray! Just hit it."

"Three out of four doctors recommend calmnonil to start you on your way to drug dependency."

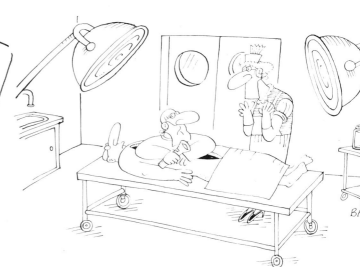

"Stop asking silly questions, nurse – I've performed more of these operations than you've had hot dinners."

"Why, Mr Willis! I'm glad to see you're improving enough to sit up and fall over!"

"The only thing you have to know about hospitals is that almost everything is in bad taste."

BRIAN ALDISS asks

The BIG Question

"How could anyone have known that everything would be brought into question?"

"Who would wish to go back to those awful old days of the full stop?"

IF we look back a century to the 2080s, can't we see clearly why the period since has become known as the Age of Interrogation?

Isn't it obvious to us now that the Twentieth Century and the great part of the century which followed was bristling with certainties – ideological and scientific certainties above all? What but reaction could have followed from such a blind epoch?

How could anyone from that benighted period have visualised that ahead of all their stoutly held beliefs lay a tranquil age when everything would be brought into question? Including the very rules of grammar, which had permitted sentences to end without the appetiser, the tasty carrot, of a question mark?

Who would wish to go back to those awful old days of the full stop? Even the most trite conversational transaction nowadays – doesn't it have an element of interesting ambiguity lacking in the past? May we conjure up a contrast from the two ages?

Shall we imagine an English country crossroads towards evening, where a motorised young woman speaks to an immobilised man on a stile?

"Am I on the right road for Bideford?" shall she say?

"Where else might you think this road would lead?"

"Oh, Sticklepath, Stadhampton, Strathclyde, Stockholm?"

"Be you trying to be funny, young lady?"

"Am I headed in the right direction?"

"Be there another road that leads into Bideford Town as surely as this one?"

"Bideford, then, definitely?"

"Where else, my dear?"

How might a similar Twentieth Century exchange go?

"Is this the Bideford Road?"

"No."

Wasn't all that decisiveness, that extraordinary ability to "make up the mind", an important factor in the general decline? Could it have been that the military mania, the love of grotesque destructive weapons, which gripped the Twentieth Century, depended upon a readiness to make a statement? A ridiculous firmness of purpose we have now fortunately lost? An unwarranted certainty of being right? In politics and everything else?

We may ask ourselves, mayn't we, where all that firmness of purpose came from? Was it not the more peculiar when we consider that the start of the Twentieth Century had seen the publication of Einstein's Theory of Relativity? How is it that his findings took so long to sink in, even among intellectuals? Today, when we perceive everything as relative, don't we inherit an amazing belated gift from Einstein's thought?

Of what use is it to look back at that questionable age without question marks? Of what use, indeed, is it to look forward, when we recognise even solutions as questionable? And what should we say of a time when the term "questionable solution" seemed like a paradox? Isn't paradox the very stuff of our civilisation? Where else should we look for uncertainties if not in the very bases of our laws? Haven't those laws been framed by a century of wise practice in order to protect us from what our deluded forebears regarded as the Eternal Verities? Eternal whats? When we are here today and gone tomorrow?

Are not our law courts and churches bastions of half-truths? What is truth? said jesting Pilate; and is he not the founder-member of the Age of Interrogation? As the improved version of the poet Keats has it,

Uncertainty is truth, if truth at all;

That's all – or more or less – ye need to know.

Is it not a fact that our primitive ancestors in the Twentieth Century tried to establish any number of wishy-washy fads as disciplines? Were there not attempts to elevate sociology, for instance, into a science? Why should we not rejoice that we now view human nature as elusive, and not susceptible to quantification? Was it not one of today's patron saints, Werner Heisenberg, who formulated the Uncertainty Principle – demonstrating that if you knew the momentum of a body you could not tell its speed? And vice versa?

Who these days does not realise that the New Uncertainty Principle builds on Heisenberg, formulating the semi-truth that if you happen to know where any body is, you have no idea what they are doing? Eh?

Is this not also the philosophical impulse behind the Nine Commandments? From the First Commandment, Shalt thou have no other gods but me? through Try to honour thy father and mother, to Thou shalt not commit adultery much, do we not experience a wisdom which culminates in the edict: Candidates are advised not to attempt more than one Commandment at a time? These marsh-firm principles – are they not the solid sand on which our culture is founded?

So, is it surprising that our best modern novelists have risen up to embrace the principles of the Age of Interrogation? Isn't the great Cadillac Bohm's recent masterpiece, *Looking at a Lighter Deed?*, in many ways a rival to Tolstoi's *War or Peace?*? Do we not see in this novel many of the Higher Uncertainties of our time? May we quote from Chapter 6, where Jake visits Lockerby in the prison hospital?

Why was it that he always looked at his watch at 5.40 every evening? Had he regularly had to catch a bus at that time when he was working in Milan? Was 5.40, perhaps, the time he had first made love to a woman? Had someone he knew died at that time? What prevented him remembering?

Did he shiver slightly as he passed through the grey doors into the ward where Lockerby was waiting to die? And the ward – what hidden meaning lay behind its name, Bodenland Ward?

Should Jake have felt surprised when Lockerby rose to meet him with something like his old exuberance? Was that sprightliness real or feigned? Wasn't his handshake friendly enough? (And yet, in his eyes – real or imagined reproach because his friend had not visited him before this?)

The grapes – why lay them down so tenderly, shrouded in their tissue paper, as if they were human?

"How are you?" If the familiar phrase escaped him unawares, was that not convention conquering a real concern?

"How do you like this dump I'm in, Jake? Isn't it elegant? Want to hear about Nurse Evita? Isn't she a honey? Have a glass of wine?"

Wasn't this the old Lockerby still, despite the

grey hair and ashen pallor of lip? Could anyone resist that infectious if quavering chuckle?

"Have they put you on drugs, then?"

"Let's talk about something else, shall we?" Wasn't that typical, in spite of an underlying nervousness? "How are things outside? I mean – on that planet you still inhabit and I have vacated, probably for good?"

Well, why not amuse him with tales of latest encounters with women, if that did not make him too jealous, and all the trials and tribulations at work?

How was it that Lockerby listened so restlessly? What was it that made those dark eyes of his seem to glow, and his fist pound on the edge of the bed?

"Jake, Jake, are you crazy? All the pain and pleasure of the world – don't you see it's here, locked up in Bodenland Ward? A world in miniature? The pain of suffering, the pleasure of a successful bowel movement, the tension of awaiting the next lousy meal, the highest ambition to get one kind word out of Nurse Evita?"

What gaudy melancholy then inspired him to draw an extended and amusing parallel between the various anguishes of his cancer-ridden body and the maladies of the universe outside? Could it have been something in his eyes, his body language, which almost had Jake convinced?

"May I have another glass of wine?" Why steal his poor friend's cheap plonk? "Isn't it true that the whole world is at death's door? Violence, cruelty, lust, religion, won't they be the ruin of us all?"

In the laugh with which Lockerby interrupted Jake, was there not something more than mockery? "Isn't it true," he echoed, "that that just ain't so if Nurse Evita has anything to do with it?... Oh, aren't I dying to get my hands on her...?"

On the bus back to town, why did Jake find himself longing for a lighter deed? Wasn't everything that happened terribly heavy? How was it that everything had to depend on everything else? Would it have hurt Lockerby to have preserved a little decorum, to have behaved more like a potential corpse, to have been less *fun*?

Stopping off near the shopping centre, he asked himself, Why not visit Lockerby's wife, Ludmilla? Who could say how much she might be longing for company?

Could she have been hoping he would call? Why else that look of delight and mischief on her attractive pale face?

How long did it take them to get into bed? How could they possibly stop laughing, laughing with delight? And who would guess, on this damp November night, what the pair of them were up to?

Wasn't this the way to get back beyond the bounds of civilisations and hospitals? Beyond mankind and the beginnings of the world? Beyond the limits of individual life?

"Jake?"

"Yes?"

"Do you care for me at all? You do, don't you?"

Should he answer? Or should he just go on staring down at the creases in the pillow? ❧

ALISTAIR SAMPSON
Jobs for the Gels

MRS WORTHINGTON. What a pleasure. Do come in. Are you sitting comfortably? Not too comfortably, I trust. That is rather a valuable chair. Now. I have your daughter's c.v. in front of me. I note that it had crossed your mind that Fiona should embark upon a stage career. But you were dissuaded. By that nice Mr Coward. And so now, Mrs Worthington, you are considering putting her into antiques. I had indeed noticed that she got a B in handiwork at Stepping Stones. What an excellent pre-prep school Stepping Stones is. Now let us have a peep at her other qualifications. I note you say she took Scripture and Biology for A-levels. You do not actually say she passed. Never mind. I expect she found all those dashing men at Marlborough rather a distraction. She tells you she found Marlborough a pill. Really.

Now let us have a look at what she has done since school. I am sure, Mrs Worthington, there is a lot in what you say. Had she wasted months learning to do boring chores such as typing and speed-writing and making tea, instead of broadening her outlook by being a ski rep at Val d'Isère, she would not have become the fun person she is today. Mrs Worthington, I am not a whit surprised to hear she is a good mixer. And clever with her hands too, eh? That *is* a bonus. Not to worry about the typing and so on. Perhaps she could take over the selling and I could make the tea. I am so glad she plays a dab hand of tennis. Many of our customers play tennis. No, Mrs Worthington. Not in the shop.

Naturally I understand Colonel Worthington's attitude. I appreciate that while he feels antiques could well be spot-on for Fiona, he would not tolerate any son of his mixing with antique dealers, let alone becoming one. I mean, what if your lad Henry suddenly went off his head and threw up Morgan Grenfell, where he has been rising like a rocket I hear, and went in with another fellow in the King's Road? Neither the Colonel nor poor you, the lad's Mumsie, would ever get over it. Whereas with Fiona, of course, different considerations apply. There are so many things fillies can get away with which stallions can't, what? And so many ways, apart from antiques, in which Fi could occupy herself pending the arrival of Mr Wonderful.

For instance, wine, Mrs Worthington,
Would be fine, Mrs Worthington,
Quite divine, Mrs Worthington.

I notice you say on her c.v. that she applied for a place at the Cordon Bleu cookery school. I see. She forgot to post the letter. I find creative people are often a shade absent-minded. Slight shame, mind you. We do have our own dining-room. You are sure she would soon pick it up. Just follow the recipes. A past-master at muddling through. She sounds a real brick.

Tyrants, Mrs Worthington? Why ever would you say such a thing? I cannot think what could have given you such an idea about us antique dealers. Yes, I did hear about Fiona's friend Caroline. There must have been more to it than the odd private telephone call during working hours. I am sure all girls come in late occasionally – particularly at the height of the season. And shake a bit. Yes, and even drop things. No one is perfect. Of course, I would not dismiss Fiona just for being fond of some young man. Despite what you may think, I was young once. I may almost have forgotten how it feels to have wings on my heels and to walk down the street in a trance. But not quite. Of course she could have the odd day off to load for him. Yes, I do realise she does not tend to know the sort of person who shoots only on Saturdays.

But back to Caroline – really I can, Mrs Worthington, scarcely believe what you say. Why should she have been given the order of the boot just because she was so much in

DONEGAN

"Lumbar support? This has twice the legal limit of lumbar support!"

COLLECTING

demand? There must have been more to it than that. And you are right. It was not as if she were on drugs – well, not real drugs – or putting her hand in the till. By the way, I did happen to notice that Maths was not Fiona's best subject. No, I was not thinking of asking her to take over the books. If I get her to pop round the corner for twenty Silk Cut, you think I should check the change pretty carefully, I understand? Not because she is dishonest.

I must say she has come on a bit, looking at her photograph. It must be ten years. That is correct, she would have been nine. What a shame she hasn't your brain for figures, Mrs Worthington.

If she's pretty, Mrs Worthington,
Try the city, Mrs Worthington.
To waste such charms on us would be a pity,
　　　　　Mrs Worthington.

Talking about that sort of thing, you do realise that not every antique dealer is – well, how shall I put it without sounding like an old fuddy-duddy? – of course, in some ways it is very relaxing to work for someone who you just know will leave you alone – I certainly would not go so far as to say:

Don't put your daughter in antiques,
　　　　　Mrs Worthington,
She'll last weeks, Mrs Worthington,
They're all freaks, Mrs Worthington.

No. No. But I would counsel her to be prepared for the occasional flurry of wrist-cracking. I am sure she will take it all in her stride. I mean, I have seen your Henry camp it up with the best of them when the Colonel was not around. You say Colonel Worthington knows just how to handle them? Much as he might wish to, Mrs Worthington, you simply cannot horse-whip half the antique trade. Even if most of them would adore it. Your reference to pig sticking escapes me.

To change the subject, I am delighted to hear that so many of her friends are drawn from what you call the antique-collecting classes. Doubtless she would lure into our little gallery a succession of eligible and well-endowed (financially, I mean) young men. If some of them took her out for long lunches, I would, as you say, appreciate that it was absolutely "pro bono firmo", even though none of them actually bought anything.

Nor would I want her to be stuck in the shop the whole time. Fiona is certainly not the only one. Many young girls suffer from claustrophobia – even so, I am afraid it might be a while before I send her off on solo buying trips to the Continent. And thank you for telling me she has friends in New York who would always give her a bed if I sent her there on business. A great comfort. But are you positive you would like

To see her rot, Mrs Worthington,
Amongst a lot, Mrs Worthington,
Of brass and pewter, porcelain and pot,
　　　　　Mrs Worthington?
When she very likely doesn't give a fart,
　　　　　Mrs Worthington,
About needlework or furniture or art,
　　　　　Mrs Worthington.

I do take my hat off to Colonel Worthington for insisting, even in these hard times, that you have plenty of domestic help. He sounds like a rattling good husband and father. This does go some way to explain why Fiona has never really got to grips with a Hoover. But, of course, we have a cleaner here, too. Yes, I did notice in the photograph that Fiona had lovely hands and I take your point. Brasso and Duraglit would present problems, particularly as she is allergic to rubber gloves. And it must be awful to have a bad back. We will just have to find someone else to do the lifting.

Anyway, I see she has a nice singing voice and has taken part in *The Messiah* at the Albert Hall. You must be very proud. Likes to leave a little early on Tuesdays and Thursdays for choir practice? Let me just make a note of that.

Mrs Worthington, I do appreciate that any wage we paid her would attract a high rate of tax, coming as it would on top of the income from what her Daddy calls "her little legacy", but no, we could not pay her cash. That, Mrs Worthington, is not true. You are confusing us with doctors. I am afraid she would be paid by cheque.

Weekends. Glad you asked. Right. Now we have long since given up trying to persuade the staff to work on Saturdays, but we still do ask them to work on Fridays. No, not Good Friday. You like to take her to Nevis for Easter. Excellent. All work and no play makes Fiona a moaner. Ha. Ha. Quite. Otherwise Fridays are just ordinary days. Yes, even Friday afternoons. She can still get down to Virginia Water in time for supper. I am sorry, dinner. But Fridays are obligatory. Even during Wimbledon. Four weeks a year. Yes, I do. But why shouldn't I? I am older than she is.

No, she cannot have a month off to help keep Mrs Thatcher in Number Ten when a general election takes place. Why not? Well, for starters, I happen to be a Social Democrat. In that case, you feel this shop would be an unsuitable springboard for Fiona's many talents? Frankly, I share your view.

She'd be happier in hats at Peter Jones,
　　　　　Mrs Worthington,
With her clones, Mrs Worthington,
And her drones, Mrs Worthington. 🐾

LET'S PARLER FRANGLAIS!

Dans le Référence Library
Lesson Trois-cent-quatre-vingt-onze

Monsieur: Pardon, madame…
Librarienne: Chht!
Monsieur: Pardon?
Librarienne: Shhh! Ne voyez-vous pas le placard: SILENCE?
Monsieur: Ah. (*Dans un whisper.*) Madame, je cherche un document très valable…
Librarienne: Nous ne sommes pas Lost et Found ici, monsieur. C'est un référence library.
Monsieur: Oui, je sais. Je cherche quelque chose qui est très valable pour moi. Pour vous, c'est seulement un numéro dans la catalogue.
Librarienne: Monsieur, everything dans mon référence library est precious pour moi! C'est ma vie! Ces magazines, ces journaux, ces directoires de telephone – ils sont tous mes enfants!
Monsieur: Yes, well, je cherche une magazine.
Librarienne: Une magazine? Quelque chose de sporting? Une magazine exotique, comme *Paris Match*? Une magazine intellectuelle, comme *Radio Times*?
Monsieur: Je cherche *Which?* magazine.
Librarienne: Ah, bon vieux *Which?*. C'est curieux, vous savez. C'est la seule magazine avec une marque de ponctuation en hindermost position. Ce point d'interrogation, ce petit "?", dans *Which?*, c'est bizarre, non?
Monsieur: Non, je ne crois pas…
Librarienne: Mais si! Si vous allez dans un bookstall et vous dites, "Avez-vous *Which??*" alors vous avez deux question marks dans un row! Amazing, eh?
Monsieur: Non, pas spécialement. Après tout, il y avait la magazine de Jimmy Goldsmith, *Now!* magazine. Well, *Now!* avait un exclamation mark. On pourrait dire: "Donnez-moi *Now!!*" et vous aviez deux exclamation marks dans un row.
Librarienne: Monsieur, il n'y avait pas une exclamation mark dans *Now*. Vous aviez peut-être trois lettres capitales, comme NOW.
Monsieur: Ah non, je ne crois pas. Si vous mettez NOW, c'est une abbréviation pour "News of the World".
Librarienne: Mais non, mais non. Si vous voulez l'abbréviation pour News of the World, vous mettez un grand N et W, mais un petit O. C'est…NoW.
Monsieur: C'est curieux. Un newspaper avec une abbréviation. I mean, on ne dit pas DM pour Daily Mail, ou GH pour Glasgow Herald. Mais on dit NoW pour News of the World. C'est unique.
Librarienne: Mais non! Vous avez FT pour Financial Times.
Monsieur: C'est vrai. Et aussi on dit RT, pour Radio Times.
Librarienne: Mais c'est tres ambigu, parce que "RT" est identique à "arty". Si vous me dites: "Je cherche des RT back numbers," peut-être en réalité vous dites, "Je cherche des arty back numbers"! … Anyway, quelle magazine vous cherchez?
Monsieur: Oh, Lord. J'ai oublié. Blimey. Oh well, merci pour le petit chin-wag.
Librarienne: Un plaisir.

PIECE MOVES
BUD GRACE

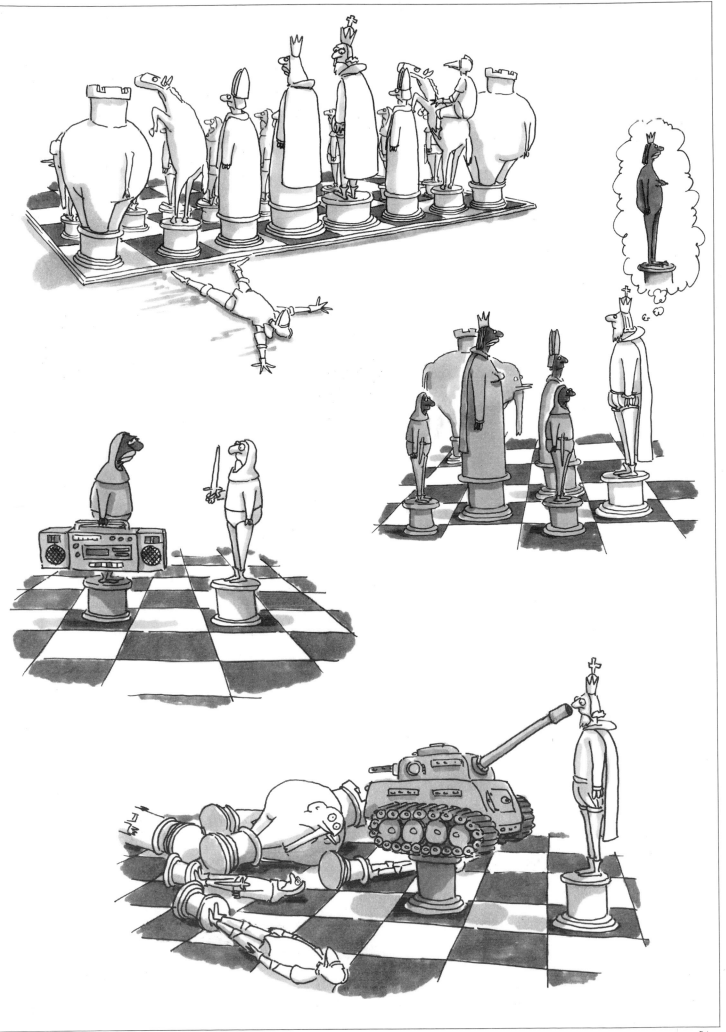

ROY HATTERSLEY

PRESS GANG

Taking Liberties

> "It seems to me that the whole police operation was carried out to persuade editors that, whatever the legal niceties, anyone who publishes stories which the Government wants to suppress should not expect to lie in bed on Sunday mornings. And, of course, having let the Campbell article tip-toe past the censors earlier in the week, a show of force was necessary to prove that the Special Branch neither slumbers nor sleeps — even if it does occasionally nod off."

THE strange case of the dog that did not bark is one of the tired old clichés of hack journalism. It is, therefore, a wholly appropriate metaphor with which to illustrate the way in which the British press reacted to the raids, by officers of the Special Branch, on the offices of the *New Statesman* magazine. Indeed, most of the whelps of national journalism did not even manage a whimper or a whine when they discovered that policemen were, for the first time this century, searching newspaper files.

The investigations which followed the publication of Duncan Campbell's story about the development of a new spy satellite (code name Zircon) was accepted, by most of London's editors, as the way we live now. *The Guardian* struck out in a leader which made me, at least,

forgive the printer's errors, the excruciating headlines and the consciously high-minded opinions. But other papers walked by on the other side of Fleet Street.

In the House of Commons, the Prime Minister persistently described the *New Statesman* as a "left-wing publication". That description is, in itself, open to question. But whatever position the *New Statesman* occupies on the political spectrum, the opinions expressed in its editorials ought to be wholly irrelevant to its vulnerability to police action.

In my romantic youth (when I believed editors of national dailies to be by Emile Zola out of Voltaire) I would have expected *The Sun* to move its editorial on to the front page in order to proclaim the truth, universally held by press baron and cub-reporter alike, that police action

against a newspaper should be the result of its actions, not of its opinions. *The Sun*, preoccupied by the love life of tycoons, could not find space to tell the story. We must fill the vacuum.

The BBC's decision to commission a Campbell film on the subject of the spy satellite (and its agreement to suppress the broadcast of that programme) are matters about which I make no direct comment. I am part of the Opposition that *The Guardian* excoriated for underwriting the Prime Minister's tyranny and I do not recant the judgment which I made. However, it seems to me that the *New Statesman* saga is quite another story – not least because the revelation about the new spy satellite was in the paper and on the streets *before* the Government took any action against the offending magazine.

The actions of the Special Branch ought to conform, in some particulars, to the papal concept of a just war. Policemen should only go through newspaper files when there are real secrets at real risk of public exposure. Once the secrets are secret no longer, the heavy tread and rattling letter-box are no more justified than the continued casualties of a war that cannot be won. For it is not the security of the realm which is being explicitly and specifically defended. At best, the policemen are punishing the offending magazine in order to encourage the others. At worst, they are saving face for letting the newspaper or magazine out-smart them.

In fact, the *New Statesman*'s behaviour was not consciously or provocatively smart. It did not attempt to bamboozle the police or deceive the Government. The Editor, John Lloyd, actually expected an injunction to stop the publication of his sky-spy story and had an alternative article ready to fill the space. For he knew, that the Government knew, that the *New Statesman* intended to publish articles based on the scripts of the banned BBC programme. It was actually written into Duncan Campbell's contract with the Corporation. Normally broadcasters are required to offer the first refusal of their scripts to *The Listener* – thus ensuring a constant flow of the spoken word into print. Campbell insisted that the standard contract be changed and the *New Statesman* be given the right to reproduce his story.

I find it inconceivable that the compliant

"We say 'guilty', your honour – guilty as a weasel in a hen-house."

BBC did not tell the police – and equally unbelievable that the police would not have found out even if they had not been told.

Eventually the Government issued an omnibus order against Campbell enjoining him not to show or publish (or to have his "servants and agents" show or publish) details of the spy satellite. But it was not served on him until the lunchtime of Thursday January 22nd. By that time the *New Statesman* was on sale in London and on its way to the provinces. The *New Statesman* itself came face to face with the law on January 23rd – by which time the magazine had fallen through thousands of letterboxes. The Editor was asked for assurances that he would publish no *further* details of the Zircon satellite and that he would not repeat the publication of the story which had already appeared on his pages.

The following day, the boys in blue – midnight blue cashmere, that is – arrived and began to turn over the *New Statesman*. They were, Mr Lloyd assures us, both tidy and courteous. But were they motivated by anything that approximated to sensible considerations of national security? I find it difficult to believe that they really expect Mr Campbell to keep secrets in the rusty filing cabinets in his office, or that they honestly hoped to find the name of the Ministry of Defence mole. "*Dear Duncan, The Government is secretly spending money on a new spy satellite called Zircon, Yours truly Anthony Gore-Wittington (General).*" The idea carries very little credibility.

It seems far more likely (at least to me) that the whole police operation was carried out to persuade editors that, whatever the legal niceties, anyone who publishes stories which the Government wants to suppress should not expect to lie in bed on Sunday mornings.

And, of course, having let the Campbell article tip-toe past the censors earlier in the week, a show of force was necessary to prove that the Special Branch neither slumbers nor sleeps – even if it does occasionally nod off.

The propriety of Mr Campbell making his film about Zircon is a subject to which we will return in this column when the complicated legal processes, which now engulf it, have been completed.

Our judgment on Mr Lloyd's decision to publish the parallel article need not wait so long. Having in his possession a story about a spy satellite which the Government was said to have financed without notifying parliament (and being subject neither to legal threat nor pressure), had he *not* printed the article, he would have deserved the sack.

That is, of course, a judgment based on belief in a free press. I do not expect Fleet Street to agree with me. ✿

> "Most of the whelps of national journalism did not even manage a whimper or a whine when they discovered that policemen were, for the first time this century, searching newspaper files."

On a Soap Box

"'It's a sort of up-market version of fast food,' she said."

T was a perfectly innocent question. "I wonder if you'd be kind enough to do something for me," I murmured, clasping the world's most famous upper arm and feeling the soft, turquoise leather yielding expensively beneath my gently enquiring fingers.

Unfortunately, at that moment the hubbub suddenly died away to nothing and I heard my voice booming out across the room, like the cry of a Swiss cowherd calling in the cattle from the lower slopes of the Matterhorn.

Joan Collins peered at me with that look of mild disdain that has had the most powerful men in five continents buckling at the knees. She swivelled her heavily padded shoulders in the direction of assembled company and flexed her eyebrows.

"It all depends what you want me to do," she announced, tossing her dark mane.

I think she may even have called me "Darling", but I couldn't swear to it. At all events, it set the entire room on a roar.

"The thing is, Joan," I said, easing her masterfully into the privacy of the hallway...

Yes, yes. This is *the* Joan Collins I'm talking about. You mix with all the best people in the property world, you know. Although, I must admit, I was quite surprised when I heard she was going to be there. In fact, when the PR girl for Cluttons first rang up with the invitation, I got hold of the wrong end of the stick altogether.

"We're having a little reception on Monday," she explained, "to launch a new flat development that Brechin Management have put together with Malcolm Fraser of Regent Land plc at 11 Cranley Gardens. Cluttons and Farley & Co are the joint agents. I think you'll find it quite interesting. The great thing is, they've got right away from this country-in-London feeling that everyone's so keen on, and gone for the

more modern soap-opera look. Marbled walls, plain colours, that kind of thing. There'll be champagne and canapés. Jane Collins is coming, so it should be fun."

I couldn't imagine why, and rather implied as much.

"She the interior decorator or something?"

"Who?" she said.

"This Jane Collins," I said.

"Not *Jane* Collins," she said. "*Jane* Collins. From *Dynasty*."

The Sloane accent has got a lot to answer for in my view.

Anyway, as it happened, I was rather hoping to have a quick word with Joan, while she was in town. Personal matter. Mutual friends and so on. Nothing that need concern you here. So, you can imagine my disappointment when, having re-arranged a busy Monday morning schedule, battled my way through the rain to South Kensington I padded up the broad carpeted staircase to the first floor and into the fray, only to find that there was no one there even faintly resembling the Queen of Soap.

Not that there was any shortage of beautiful women, mind. One called Kimberley poured me a glass of Bollinger and another, small and blonde and wearing a little black Saint-Laurent number covered with multi-coloured bows, shimmered across through the pin-striped suiting and introduced herself as Katheryn Horbye.

I pointed out that it said Antigone Horbye on her name badge. She said that was because her firm's name is Antigone Interiors and people might get muddled. She'd done the decor, incidentally. Flats like these, she went on to explain, are not for heavy-duty family living, but for sophisticated business types – international bankers and the like – who are bombing around all the time and want to live in some-

thing light and airy, not overwhelmed with dark colours, chintzes and fringes.

"It's a sort of up-market version of fast food," she said.

Up-market indeed at £360,000 for two double beds with en-suite baths, kitchen and dining-room, and large, high-ceilinged drawing-room – even if it has been laid out on three floors, with all the original cornicework. Mind you, that one was the biggest of the bunch. There are seven others, equally smartly done out and of varying shapes and sizes, ranging from a one-bedder on the ground floor at £97,000 to an airy two-bedder on the fourth floor with studio-type recep/dining-room/kitchen behind a glass panel, and an ornate white cast-iron spiral staircase leading up to a roof terrace.

They'd had three offers on that one alone since they'd started selling a week previously. One investment company was keen to buy that flat and two others. In fact, there were really only four that hadn't already been snapped up.

I suggested to a young man from Cluttons, over a quail's egg, that being a high-class property developer these days must be money for jam, but he wasn't having any of it. A good location certainly counts for a lot, he said; ditto simple, uncluttered layout and quality finish. But, in the end, it all comes down to timing. Houses did very well in the Kensington/Chelsea area last year, but the flat market had really been quite sluggish. People who were only looking six months ago are now buying, it seems. The Americans are here, too...

And so, suddenly, was Miss Collins. A little later than expected, not to say taller and much more impressive. An exceptional property, as they say in the business, beautifully built in the traditional style, immaculately maintained and presented in a mature setting and with outstanding business potential. Easy access (but only via the diminutive and omnipresent Mr Lane, her personal publicity agent). Currently under offer to Malcolm Fraser's partner in the Cranley Gardens development – the suave, handsome Bill Wiggins, known in the business, I understand, as Bungalow Bill on account of his not having too much upstairs.

Although unable to hold a candle to the Princess of Wales *in re* repartee, Miss Collins does exude a distinctly regal aura. People tend to go pink and shiny when introduced to her, laugh unusually loudly at her every utterance and get generally over-excited. And when she has left the room (e.g. after the giggly photo session in the top flat), everyone comments on how marvellous she looks, as if she were the Queen Mother and it's a wonder she can still move without a walking-frame.

One estate agent waxed positively lyrical. "It was quite good when she first arrived," he said, "and everything went quiet, the way she walked round the room saying, 'Wow, this is quite nice' and everything."

Not quite so good from my point of view was the way the conversation was brought to an abrupt halt, the smile was suddenly switched off and she announced that she had to rush away, just as we were getting to know each other. Still, mustn't complain: she did give me a thousand words, and that's more than poor old Dex got in three years of marriage. ☙

"The 3.30 should be along any minute now..."

PUNCH

"*It should be a fantastic parrot. It cost an arm and a leg.*"

HANDELSMAN

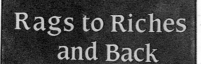

Rags to Riches and Back

— the inspiring story of Chester Drawers (1820-1940), born in the tiny inland fishing village of Overkill, Pennsylvania, the son of a humble burglar.

LIFE WAS HARD; THE VILLAGE HAD NO WATERWAYS EXCEPT DURING PRECIPITATION, AND IT SELDOM RAINED FISH.

Give us a break, Lord!

Deeper puddles, at least.

Pa, can I have some rags?

For which purpose?

To convert to riches.

What man is there of you, whom if his son ask rags will he give him a stone?

Here. The shreds off my back.

USING HIS FATHER'S SHIRT AS COLLATERAL, CHESTER BORROWED ENOUGH MONEY TO OPEN A MODEST OIL WELL.

I once had a garment like that.

You might have it yet, were it not for my progenitor's work ethic.

I christen thee the Drawers Petroleum Company!

I once had a champagne bottle like that.

CRASH

You might have it yet, were it not…

DRAWERS FELL DEEPLY IN LOVE WITH A RAILWAY MAGNATE'S DAUGHTER.

Gosh, Gertie, I know I'm from the wrong side of the tracks---

I will tell daddy to move them.

GERTRUDE DRAWERS PROVIDED MORE THAN MONEY AND TRAINS. SHE ALSO SUPERVISED HER HUSBAND'S SOCIAL GRACES.

Chester! I'm sure our guests don't want to hear about crude oil. It's not very refined.

Sorry, dear.

SLURP

*Chester! **Must** you bolt your food?*

No, dear. I could just fasten it lightly, with paper clips.

MEEK AS HE WAS AT HOME, CHESTER WAS A RUTHLESS COMPETITOR.

Your business practices are questionable, Drawers.

Question them, by all means! It's a free country, thank God.

Let's talk! I think I am now ready to make a deal.

BUSINESS FABLE

AS A MONOPOLY, THE DRAWERS PETROLEUM COMPANY WAS IN VIOLATION OF ANTI-TRUST LEGISLATION.

The Court therefore directs that the company be broken up into hundreds of tiny bits.

With Mr Drawers at the helm of each bit.

I was afraid you would forget to say that.

The Court knows which side its food is bolted on.

Say hello to Chester Junior.

Shake, pop.

Pretty big, isn't he, for a newborn person?

He's actually twelve, but you were so busy I didn't like to bother you.

DRAWERS SET OUT TO TEACH HIS SON THE VALUES HE HAD LEARNED AT HIS MOTHER'S KNEE.

But when my parents were out, I had to make do with the baby-sitter's knee.

Let's see if I've got it right! Never spend your own money. Never draw to an inside straight. Never give a sucker an even break or smarten up a chump.

Pop, looks like you're going to have to pay income tax.

Junior, what did I tell you about obscene language at the table?

Never! I'd sooner give it to the poor.

Junior, call a doctor for your father.

BUT DRAWERS PROVED TO BE AS RUTHLESS AT PHILANTHROPY AS HE HAD BEEN AT COMMERCE.

Here, poor, have some small change.

We don't want your charity, bloated class enemy!

Wise guys, huh? Take that money or I'll run yous in.

THE DRAWERS FOUNDATION MADE POSSIBLE HIGHER EDUCATION FOR MANY AN UNDESERVING STUDENT.

A needy, low-IQ kid like me ordinarily couldn't of got into medical school.

Hey, I didn't tell you to stop breathing.

IN HIS OLD AGE, CHESTER DRAWERS WAS ANGERED BY THE LOW LEVEL OF JOURNALISM,

How dare they praise a movie I didn't like?

AND RESOLVED TO LOWER IT FURTHER.

So grandpa bought the New York Morning Depressant, the London Evening Stench, the Sydney Regurgitator---

Back to rags, in fact.

WHITNEY J. DRAWERS   OTIS P. DRAWERS   MAXWELL DRAWERS   CHESTER DRAWERS III

MORAL: Thou anointest my head with oil; my Kopf runneth over.

FRANK KEATING
Downhill All The Way

I T is exactly half a century ago that one of the world's great sporting cartoons appeared in these pages. A pleasant, pale-faced, English cove, mummified in bandages, was being wheeled from the night sleeper at Victoria Station. He was still, however, carrying his skis. At the ticket barrier, his wife greeted him: *"Why on earth can't you just play snowballs like everyone else?"*

The mad-dog English are still at it, except the blood-wagon trolleys are being met at Gatwick and Luton now by reps from BUPA. The English (I exclude the Scots, who are quite Cairngorm-competent and capable at it, when

they're not too drunk) will never be anything but eccentrics at skiing. As well enter an Eskimo for the Safari Rally. The one guy I know who was late for work during that cold snap last month had announced the day before that he would ski in next morning. We made it, eventually, on Network South-East. He broke a leg.

In the bigtime, *kroner*-sponsored, spivvy sport, Anglos, as they ever have, are still aiming to put one over the swish Yuppy (or, rather, *downward*) yodellers from Central Europe who slide at a slithering rate of knots through the bottom of our television screens every *Ski Sunday* of the season. Heroically bringing up the rear this year, cheered only by the Vine, is an engaging young downhiller from Harrogate with a Union Jack on his helmet, Martin Bell, and another daredevil ditto, Eddie Edwards, from, of all places, Gloucester, who has just broken the 56-year-old British ski-jump record,

in spite of his spectacles freezing up when he was halfway down the runway. *There'll Always Be An England...*

I have been skiing on quite a few occasions. Or rather, *après* skiing. In the 1960s, when the holiday biz was really opening up, a few days on the slopes every month would fill in the winter very nicely. Those days, they were very good freebies indeed. You only had to get past that first horrendous morning when the tour company or local town council tourist board would arrange for you actually to be given lessons by some beefy, nut-brown peasant from the area who had once won an Olympic bronze medal. The knack was to put your cartilage out as soon as he started shouting at you, though if he was watching, you then had to remember to limp to the dance-floor all through the following week's very pleasant *après* antics. One time, at Lermoos in Austria I think, a particularly hearty ex-champ was assigned to give me lessons. First morning, he was right behind me on the T-bar lift. I timed it perfectly – and fell off at about 30ft into a cushioning snowdrift. He had to continue all the way up. I zig-zagged back to the bar, never to catch his eye again – though a waitress told me that for the rest of a very nice

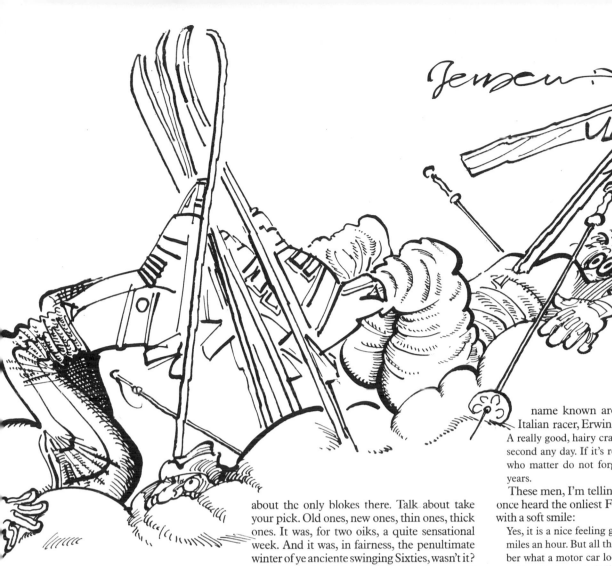

week the fellow would refer to me with utter scorn as "ze Eengleesh dead sheep". It didn't seem to worry her.

The first Winter Olympics I went to were held at Grenoble in 1968. I was commissioned to do a couple of pieces of allegedly colourful drivel and had really quite been looking forward to it, having read all about the in-set and beautiful swinging-Sixties at, I presumed, nearby St Moritz and that sort of place. A photographer mate and I arrived on the eve of the opening races. We were put into some freezing nissen huts which had been reserved for the Press riff raff. After about two hours sleep, some great foreigner in boots came in to *Raus! Raus!* us up to catch a bus that wound up the sheer ruddy face of this sheer ruddy mountain, its back wheels slithering over black-iced precipices every minute or two. At the top, as a foggy dawn wet-sponged into our faces, we caught each other's eyes and, simultaneously, we asked each other: "If you can finish your week's work in a couple of hours, why don't we get the blazes out of here and find somewhere slightly more convivial?"

He snapped like mad, and I scribbled, and at lunchtime, the little bus slithered back down – and we hired a limmo to take us to the nearest resort that had nothing whatsoever to do with the Olympic Games. We ended up at bracing-posh Courcheval, where, lo and behold, all the *wives* of rich Frenchmen had been deposited, alone, as their men were off watching the Games in Grenoble. Me and my mate were just

about the only blokes there. Talk about take your pick. Old ones, new ones, thin ones, thick ones. It was, for two oiks, a quite sensational week. And it was, in fairness, the penultimate winter of ye anciente swinging Sixties, wasn't it?

Thus, having done it all so long ago, can I contentedly splay out upon the sofa on any *Ski Sunday* and relive those youthful sensations on the slopes. Mind you, the English have come a long way in those twenty years. Those in the know really do fancy Martin Bell to beat the foreigners at their own game one day very soon. And if Fast Eddie Edwards is not going to do quite that, well, he's already warmed up a particularly wretched winter in which all of us, in our different ways, have found solace only in being cheered by the Vine.

Bell is the 23-year-old son of a flying instructor in the RAF, based in Yorkshire. He won a scholarship to Edinburgh's George Watson High School, learning to ski at Aviemore, and becoming the British schools' champion by 15. That and highly satisfactory scholarship, especially in languages, got him a place at Stams, the Austrians' elite ski-school near Innsbruck. Since when he has been revelling on the slippery slopes with marked improvements each year. This pre-Olympic season, nevertheless, is Bell's crunch one so far. We shall see how he goes. He is sponsored, to the tune of £1,000, by the Harrogate Town Council, and you can't get more English than that.

Bell, so far, has steered clear of serious injury. In fact, the worst was when he put his foot through some floorboards at school. The pulled ligaments kept him off the snow for a year. Anyway, he says, a few slight tumbles can make you concentrate more the next time you go up. There's the Battle-of-Britain spirit for you. There are some, mind you, who say that Martin could do with "a real good crash" – to get his

name known around the circuit. The Italian racer, Erwin Stricker, once defined: A really good, hairy crash is better than coming second any day. If it's really spectacular, people who matter do not forget you for many, many years.

These men, I'm telling you, are quite mad. I once heard the onliest Franz Klammer explain with a soft smile:

Yes, it is a nice feeling going down the hill at 85 miles an hour. But all the time you must remember what a motor car looks like after it has hit a wall at that speed. Skiing is simply that if you think you are losing your balance and say to yourself, "I fall," then you fall. If you say to yourself "I stay up," then you always stay up.

Fast Eddie is a very different kettle of clatter altogether. A Norwegian nutter named Nordheim "invented" ski-jumping over a century ago when he turned up from Telemark with some rudimentary, homemade bindings on his wood-slatted skis and, in 1860, amazed the world by jumping 32.8 yards, a distance not bettered till 1893. That was 30.5 metres – and Eddie from Gloucester bettered that with the second jump he ever did in his life.

He is only 22, myopic, moustached and, obviously, gloriously mad. Somebody called him an airborne Mister Magoo. He learned his skiing on the nylon bristle slope erected a few years ago by Gloucester City Council, then thought to try the real thing and pitched up somehow at Lake Placid in New York State to have a go at the Olympic ski-jump there. Within a day he was flying through the thin air for 40 metres – and a few weeks later, at Kandersteg in Switzerland, he had unconcernedly hit 77 metres and broken the all-time British jump record, held since 1931 by the old pioneer, Guy Dixon. He aims to beat the lot of them in the Olympics next year – by which time he hopes to be able to afford some "turbo" glasses which "will stop my ordinary specs steaming up on the slope: when that happens I can get a bit panicky."

As I say, Eddie has warmed up the winter. Thank heavens he didn't stick to snowballs, like everyone else in Gloucester.

PLEASE INDICATE YOUR ANSWERS
AS INDICATED BY ANSWERING

Good [ ] Morning [ ] Afternoon [ ] Sir [ ] Madam
[ ] Other

Could you spare a moment?

[ ] Yes [ ] No [ ] Don't know

How interested are you to know what all this is about?

[ ] Extremely interested
[ ] Interested
[ ] Quite interested
[ ] No strong feelings either way
[ ] Not very interested
[ ] Do not give [ ] Damn [ ] Monkey's

On a scale of one to ten, how would you rate your awareness of the fact that this week is the 50th anniversary of Gallup Polls? (circle one)

1 2 3 4 5 6 7 8 9 10 Other

Do you feel that the 50th anniversary of Gallup Polls is:

[ ] Very startling
[ ] Startling
[ ] A bit startling
[ ] Only to be expected
[ ] Of no particular interest to: [ ] Man [ ] Beast?

What sort of figures do startle you?

[ ] Up to 50
[ ] Between 50 and 100
[ ] 101 - 9,999
[ ] A million
[ ] More than a million

Where did you first hear about the 50th anniversary of Gallup Polls?

[ ] Daily newspapers
[ ] Garage forecourt
[ ] Department store
[ ] Billboard or hoarding
[ ] Private hospital
[ ] Citizens' Advice Bureau
[ ] Local gossip

Do you or any of your household have any interest in:

[ ] Additives
[ ] Non-stick frying-pans
[ ] 14-day timers
[ ] Proportional representation

[ ] Alcohol-free lagers
[ ] Loose-fit covers
[ ] Vivisection
[ ] Loft insulation
[ ] The 50th anniversary of Gallup Polls?

Have you or your regular partner been asked about the 50th anniversary of Gallup Polls:

[ ] Lots of times
[ ] More than once
[ ] Once only
[ ] Every now and again
[ ] Very seldom
[ ] Never until now?

Which of these areas of topical concern do you feel is of most importance in a democratic society? (tick one)

[ ] Human rights
[ ] Nuclear waste
[ ] Sex
[ ] The unborn whale
[ ] Insider trading
[ ] After-sales service
[ ] The 50th anniversary of Gallup Polls

If an election were to be called tomorrow, which of these factors would most influence your vote?

[ ] Personal freshness
[ ] A caring society
[ ] Eating between meals
[ ] The price of alkaline batteries
[ ] Creamy taste [ ] Nutty taste
    [ ] Cheese & Onion taste
[ ] The 50th anniversary of Gallup Polls

Would you agree to take part in a follow-up investigation into your answers concerning the 50th anniversary of Gallup Polls?

[ ] Very definitely
[ ] Definitely
[ ] Very possibly
[ ] Possibly
[ ] Quite possibly
[ ] Possibly not
[ ] Definitely not
[ ] Very definitely not

For office use only

Male   Female   Yes   Down   Up   Gold   Own Home   EEC

One   Two or More   33″   Casual   E.S.T.O.   Due   Private

With Profits   Isle of Man   Gift   Comprehensive   220/240

HUNTER DAVIES
FATHER'S DAY

FLORA *did* have a birthday celebration after all. Glory glory, praise be, saved at the last moment, phew. It really cheered her up. She was becoming so depressed, at her age as well. You'd have thought at 48 she would have grown up. I'm talking about the Old Trout. Not Flora. She was going to take the lack of any fourteenth birthday party in her stride. It was her Mama who was moping around, getting herself all moody.

I think what really did it was that the night before we happened to talk about Theo, our friend in Washington USA, and her fourteen-year-old daughter. Same old story. Too old for any childlike parties, but not yet up to a thrash. Come the actual day, with nothing at all organised, the parents said right then, if you're not celebrating, we are, off we go, we'll have a meal together. So Tamara was driven to a local restaurant – where lo and behold, eight of her friends were already sitting, waiting for the birthday girl...

If you dare do that to me, said Flora, I'll walk out. I'm promising you.

When I came home at lunchtime, on the fateful fourteenth day, the OT was beaming because Flora had gone off to school saying okay then, I'll do your suggestion, I'll take two friends after school to the Ritz, and then we'll go to the pictures, if that will make you happy.

We are talking here about the Ritz Hotel, Piccadilly, London, England, not the Ritz Cafe, Botchergate, Carlisle, though it did cross my mind as an amusing little excursion for three terribly modern London teenagers, looking for something rather different. It is so hard to find something that nobody, but nobody, has done recently.

It was the OT's idea. A couple of years ago, I took Flora to the Ritz for some treat or other. She would therefore know her way around, not be lost or intimidated, though when did you last see any intimidated teenagers. Threatened species, these days, like herdwick sheep.

Jolly well done, I said to her, what a good wheeze, now you can relax, the family tradition of birthday parties will at least go out with a small whimper instead of a big full-stop. That was what had upset her. All October she'd been planning in her mind the Hallowe'en decorations, as per usual, the clever games, as per usual. To suddenly have nothing, nada, rien, pa de two, had shaken her. Next year, it won't matter. She'll be resigned by then. The last of our brood will have brod.

The third big attraction of the Ritz, hold on I haven't given two yet, but no matter, another attraction is that you can ring up and book, so step forward Big Hunt, who then picks up the telephone in his manly way.

It is hard to believe, but at 48, she still hasn't got used to the phone. Great on letters, very fluent in the flesh, but she has this thing about ringing people. You do it, she always says, whether it's the newspaper shop which has not delivered, or the end of the world and she fears she won't get her fingers round 999.

All booked-up. No places left for tea today. Terribly sorry, sir. Nor tomorrow. Nor the day after. The earliest we can do is Tuesday.

The smile on the face of the dear Old Trout slid slowly to the floor, crawled across the carpet, fell into the dressing-up drawer and lay there, not knowing if it would ever be needed again.

Oh come on, it's not that tragic. Yes, I know she'll have told Natasha and Vanessa and they'll be all excited and expecting the Ritz after school, but hard cheese, we all have to get over these sort of catastrophes.

But they're taking special clothes with them! They're going to dress up specially! Oh no, I can't bear it.

The complication about finding anywhere else, equally posh and impressive, was that Flora would not have been, so how could she be expected to take her two little friends, into a strange place, all on her own.

And so it was that after school Big Hunt put on a suit, yes I know, what a sell-out, first time for years, I even found a tie which Flora had not cut up as a belt, and I drove les gels to the Dorchester Hotel, Park Lane, London.

I'd rung, and been told you can't book for tea, but there would be room. I arrived with a terrible headache. Not just the tight suit and the rush hour and the rain, but the three of them were screaming and shouting and laughing all the way there in the back of the car. I normally don't allow breathing in my car, let alone talking, not when I'm driving, but it was her birthday, the petal.

Been to the Dorchester recently, you guys? Easier really than the Ritz as their tea place is straight ahead as you come in, their so-called Promenade bit. No need therefore to stand around like a wally, wondering what to do. That was me. That was not them.

They looked terrific, straight out of *Brideshead*, with overtones of *Dallas*. Flora was in a white silk creation which I'd never seen her wear before, not surprising as it is her mother's best outfit. The other two were equally striking, though one was having trouble with her mother's high heels. Heads turned. As one might expect. Most people who have tea in posh places are perfectly ordinary office workers on the way home, couples on the way out. It's the waiters and flunkies in their full evening-dress and tails at four o'clock in the afternoon who give the tone. And put up the bill.

I got the head waiter and explained it was a

"News, sir — followed by sport and weather."

"We were at the Mayhew's cocktail party and someone told a joke. Harry Montfert laughed himself silly and had to be institutionalised."

---

birthday treat, and he said yes, he remembered me ringing, he had a seat for the young ladies, right by the piano. I paid him in advance for the set tea and I'm certainly not going to reveal the price, okay it was £8 each. Don't say it, millions starving, people homeless, but what the hell, our last child's fourteenth birthday.

I have now decided I'm a Woopie. If you've never heard that expression before, then I've made it up. Otherwise, I think it could be Amer-

ican. It stands for Well Off Older Person. At my age, I'm determined to live like one, while there's still time. Any moment now, I'll be turning into a Poppie. Poorer Older Person, of course. Do concentrate.

I gave Flora the money for a taxi, to take them on to their next excitement, the Cannon Cinema in Oxford Street, to see some teenage film called *That Was Now, This is Then, Will That Be It*, or some such assorted tenses. I had a

word with the liveried doorman, asking him if in about an hour's time he might help three young ladies, one in white silk, to apprehend a taxi.

I then left them to it while me and the OT went off and did something mundane, like living, thinking, breathing, that sort of stuff, mainly, of course, wondering how they were getting on, would they cope, would something go wrong, would they get a taxi, they are not really as confident as they appear, despite all the heavy laughter.

You idiot, said the OT. The doorman won't recognise them. Didn't you realise they were carrying little rucksacks. They are not going to the pictures in their finery. They're going to change in the Dorchester Hotel lavs into their jumpers and jeans. Oh no. And I gave the doorman flunkie a whole quid. He'll probably ring *Childwatch*, rather than call a cab.

At 8.35 I was at the cinema, waiting for them to come out, not knowing if they were inside, if they'd made it from the Dorchester, but they all bounded out, and immediately started telling me some long saga about a horrible car accident they'd witnessed as they'd gone into the cinema. Oh yes, the tea was fine, and the film, and it was soon screams and laughter again all the way home in the car.

Of course, Hunt. We got the taxi okay at the Dorchester. We're not children. They had found it themselves, so they said. That bloke with the funny hat, fat lot of use he was.

The pianist had played "Happy Birthday", oh God the mortification, and then the head waiter had brought a birthday cake, oh God the excitement, and then everyone stared at them, oh God the embarrassment, and now their feet were killing them, oh God the agony. Please don't use that sort of language, I said. You know Grandma does not like the Lord's name taken in vain, especially from the mouths of children, sorry, I didn't mean it, stop it, ouch, you'll make me crash.

A good time was had, I think. But that's it. Children's birthdays, bye bye. 🐾

Lesson Trois-cent-quatre-vingt-treize

Dans le Duty-Free

Lady en Duty-Free Uniforme: Bonjour, monsieur!

Voyageur: Pardon?

Lady: Puis-je vous intéresser en notre giant packet de 2,000 Marlboro? C'est notre spécial pour novembre!

Voyageur: Non, merci.

Lady: Pourquoi pas?

Voyageur: Parce que je ne fume pas.

Lady: Ce n'est pas nécessaire! Achetez-le pour un ami!

Voyageur: Tous mes smoking amis sont morts.

Lady: Oh. Well, what about notre autre spécial

du month – un giant hip-flask de Glen Porringer, le malt whisky qui est comme satin!

Voyageur: Je ne peux pas porter une bouteille comme ça. Elle est aussi grande que le Cénotaph.

Lady: Oui, mais c'est un bargain terrifique!

Voyageur: Oh, vraiment? Expliquez-moi comment c'est un bargain.

Lady: Well, dans le High Street vous payez £22.50 pour une bouteille comme ça. Ici, ça coûte seulement £14.99!

Voyageur: Erreur. Dans le High Street on ne voit pas des monster bouteilles comme cette excrescence. Dans le High Street vous avez des bouteilles d'une sensible size. Dans le Duty-Free vous avez seulement les bouteilles avec elephantiasis. C'est grotesque.

Lady: Oui, mais c'est un bargain! Ici, il n'y a pas de duty.

Voyageur: Le duty, sur le whisky, est sur average 70% ou 80%. Si vous removez le duty from le whisky, vous avez une réduction de 70% ou 80%. Mais votre réduction est seulement 40%, roughly. Où va l'autre 40%? En thin air?

Lady: Monsieur, je ne sais pas exactement...

Voyageur: Eh, bien, moi je sais! Il va directement dans la poche du Heathrow Airport Authority, ou British Airport Rip-Off, ou whatever est le nom! Dans le High Street le profit margin est minimal. Ici, dans l'aéroport, c'est un whacking grand profit margin. Vous faîtes une fortune ici dans le Duty-Free.

Lady: Pas moi personellement, je vous assure...

Voyageur: Ah, non, pas vous. Vous êtes seulement le tool de vos employeurs capitalistes, vous êtes seulement un cog dans une wicked machine.

Lady: Moi? Un cog?

Voyageur: Et vous avez une très silly costume aussi. "Hello, I'm Heathrow Harriet!" Ah, c'est dégoûtant!

Lady (*qui commence un weeping fit et un petit nervous breakdown*): Ah, ce n'est pas fair! Vous êtes un monstre! Oh, c'est terrible! Vite, brandy, brandy...!

Voyageur: Brandy? Où, brandy?

Lady (*avec un quick recovery*): Ici, monsieur! Seulement £12.00 pour une juggernaut bouteille – c'est un spécial offer!

DONEGAN
BAR CODE

"There was a time when you could get a pint of beer
for less than the price of a pint of beer."

"Excuse me – would you mind
taking our picture?"

"I don't care what anybody says – I'd rather be a big drunk in a
little pub than a little drunk in a big pub."

"My word, what a nomad you are! Only a minute ago you
were over there by the window."

"I'd invite you back to my humble abode for a nightcap, but,
unfortunately, it's not that humble."

Notes from Underground

JOHN ARLOTT

"If a cellar is to be cherished, it must be physically a cellar – not the cupboard under the stairs giving itself airs."

A WINE cellar grows, in theory at least: only the most human of frailties – thirst – can prevent it. Even if it stands still, it progresses: provided it was well chosen in the first place. If its owners drink it, it is simply, like them, a living – and dying – organism. If they do not, it can become an heirloom; like those at Glamis Castle, Blair Castle, Drumlanrig – all Scottish, where, presumably, alternative refreshment was available – Sir George Meyrick's and the almost unbelievable one of Dr Barolet at Beaune. They aged undisturbed and made vast sums in the sale rooms. Few of us have such resolve, yielding at least to turnover while enjoying the turntable. It is, too, convincingly comforting to know that 95% of the wine made in the world does not improve after two years: and most deteriorates after three.

Eventually, if a cellar is to be cherished, it must be physically a cellar – not the cupboard under the stairs giving itself airs. So, when the island of the family's choice said, "No cellars here, you know, this is all solid granite," the outlook almost changed. A steady supply from mainland merchants? Or ferried in from France? The final decision was based on – meanness? – reluctance to pay a second set of excise duties; but some comfort derived from the thought of pocketing the proceeds of the sale. More by the sight of the auctioneers' catalogue – and even more from their estimates of the selling prices.

Then came the news that a house with a cellar *was* available. It belonged to the man who, a hundred years ago, supervised the building of the island's jetty – and the quarrying of the stone for it. The isolated jetty workers were only too happy to fall in with his ideas. They even built his garden walls of hand-hewn blocks of granite of such precisely decreasing size to the top that he could pay them strictly by the course.

It was certainly not too much for them to dig out a cellar. (Sixty years later, the departing Germans booby-trapped it but,

happily, a Royal Engineer pulled out the fuse.)

Meanwhile the contents of the mainland cellar had been catalogued, but not sold; they would have been far too bulky for the new cellar … and anyway, what about the auctioneers? They were tactful: slight – but slight – pruning perhaps?

The wine journalist is fortunate in opportunities to taste, to buy – and, at best, in his guides. In the Hermitage area of the Rhône Valley, an elderly man, who had worked in the cellars from boyhood to seventy, showed us round. The best? Well, his father – who also worked there all his life – said there had never been anything to match the 1961 Hermitage. That became the first withdrawal. Not all of it, you understand; the idea was not to plunder the sale but to haul back some that there would never be another opportunity to buy.

Then was the Vega Cecilia – an utter surprise to come upon; a vineyard in complete vinous isolation near Valladolid. They make only red wine. Don Eloy Lecanda y Chaves brought the vines from France in 1864. To take the name, the wines must be matured in wood for ten years. Even though the production is only 80,000 bottles in the best years, the vineyard has not enough space to store it all, so some is sold as Valbuena after three or five years. Pull back the Vega Cecilia; blush for the entry "withdrawn" in the catalogue: it must be the best wine in Spain.

Then there was the Tokay – Essence – 1883, impossibly old; Charles Berry wrote splendidly about it; only the two half-litre bottles. Out. The Montrachet – three bottles – possible? Well, all right.

Oh, the strife between greed and guilt. Two bottles of the Beaune 1923; just two Figeac 1961 and that Château Pétrus '61 – in magnum – the response could only be described as cool.

Let us leave it at that.

The extra duty seemed bearable. The new cellar, though, looked bare; and, small as it was, yawning; and the local off-licence of the time could not complete that essential aspect of home furnishing. If the visitors did not actually turn up their noses, it was obvious that there had to be real improvement.

The first tactical move was Beaujolais: Beaujolais Villages – Roger Harris's catalogue made it look truly up-market; almost every one with a château name. Above all, the wine of the indestructible Ernest Aujas. He calls it no more than Julienas, but he does not hurry it. This is no Nouveau. When will he bottle it? "When it is ready and when the wind is in the north and the moon on the wane." Why? "Because that was what my father did." Both generations of wine-makers were intuitively right.

Then the stocking-up: whites, enough Alsace Riesling, Meursault, Chablis Fourchaumes; Macon Blanc; of reds, Château Figeac, with the post-1961 Hermitage and a glorious gift of Château Cheval Blanc 1971 for luxury occasions; Clos René, Côte Rotie, motley Médocs.

Then our house wine, the Rioja, Marqués de Cáceres, white, red and Reserva. Henri Forner's father was a member of the pre-Franco Spanish government; when the time came, he knew when to go – and where. The family set up in two fairly ordinary Médoc châteaux bought for prices which today would seem ridiculous. Henri learnt the craft of wine-making; and he already had his plans – and more – laid in Rioja when Franco died. Contracts for grapes, a bodega, all was ready. White Rioja had for years been woody and dull: so he went to the oracle; engaged Professor Emile Peynaud – no less – former head of the Institute of Oenology at Bordeaux, who planned the vinification of a white wine, more French than Spanish in character, and quite excellent. The ordinary red is a good, sound wine; the Reserva unquestionably a fine one; the three

seem the best value in wine at the present day; they fit the family economy, and do the cellar credit.

Apéritifs? The Manzanilla sherry bottled by our new and – especially for a small island – impressive off-licence; and the all-too-little known Chambéry, king of vermouths. Fizz? A historian of Krug had to keep a few bottles hidden away for family occasions – weddings, christenings, and birthdays. One, for the celebration, then over to the excellent value of the Spanish Cava – the Cordon Negro of Freixenet; and whatever the court may have ruled, it is made by the Méthode Champenoise; is better than many champagnes, and very much cheaper.

Wine is not like other drinks. It should look right, smell healthy and taste good. Also, though, it should be worth reading and talking about. Keep in the cellar, for instance, Château Musar and – if you can get it – Colares. Château Musar comes from the Bekaa Valley in Lebanon; about where Noah planted the first recorded vineyard and got high on its produce. Now Serge Hochar – Bordeaux trained – works the vineyard his father replanted in 1942; and in 1984 *Decanter* magazine made him its Man of the Year for producing his wine when the grapes had to be driven from vineyard to winery through the firing line – and still making a good wine. It is a rounded red; the recent vintages typical of the Cabernet Sauvignon grape; dry, with guts and tannin, needing time to mature; but well worth waiting for – and talking about.

If that is a success story, that of the Portuguese Colares is sad. It comes from one of the world's few pre-phylloxera vineyards; the louse cannot live in its sandy soil. There is now, though, only one main producer. It is on the Atlantic coast, narrowly north of Lisbon; and most of the vineyards have been bought up to build houses for the commuters. There has been little opposition, because the vines have to be sunk in trenches deep in the sand and which, from time to time, have fallen in on the workers; conditions are less perilous for them in Lisbon. The wine is scarce, hard to find, and needs time. When some was at last located, nine – out of 36 – bottles were broken in transit; still it proved not only historic but mighty satisfying.

A wine cellar holds memories as well. ❧

"You've got to hand it to him – not many people get a Sellotape-dispenser research grant."

"The gentleman at the next table would like to fight with you, sir."

WHIM-WARE

An occasional sale of computer hard-and software,
surplus to the march of progress.

COMPATIBILITY CHECKER*

Re-affirms your worst suspicions that all the software the salesman said would work a treat on your TaiwaneseClone-a-matic ATXT-MACALIKE, doesn't.

*Will not work with Clone-a-matic machines

Estate Agents' Utilities

Photo-scanner "reads" Polaroid snap of property, "interprets" saleable features, "measures" room sizes and "explains" structural/ locational drawbacks. Full database compiler and with prose-enhancing text manipulation. 10,000 word thesaurus of superlatives. Text-only hyperbole monitor. Ideal for first-time software buyer. Full details on request.

RARE FIRST EDITION

Autographed Charles Babbage alpha-numeric PacMan. (Munch-drunk abacus beads rampaging through a text-only maze). Compatible with the Mk. 1 Babbage Computing Engine, Amstrad televisions and most Multi-chefs.

MacBRENT Educational Package.

Isolates and extracts all sexist, racist, sizist, elitist, technist, politically biased or ideologically shaky material from any existing text file. Conforms to B.S. 3704, Geneva Convention, the Helsinki Agreement, the Forty Lane Hypothesis and Brent Bye-Laws Nos. 24(a) to 5362(w). Availability subject to political climate.

Join the Desk-Top Publishing Revolution

Full feature business simulation package prepares text, collates graphics and automatically commissions Michael Heath for 3 reams of finished topical jokes. Fortress Wapping in the comfort of your own office, with .....

- Desk-top typesetting and page layouts.
- Carpet-edge picketing.
- Knife-edge deliveries.
- Handy Sellotape and barbed wire dispenser.
- A roomful of fighting-mad hacks each calling themselves Editor.
- Comprehensive bankruptcy & advice from Cork, Gully & Co.

Yours for less than 25 pence a day

OFFICE AUTOMATION

Improve your work environme and be the lead swinger in sales force with the **RepRo** integrated software package from **KumquatSoft**

- **Excuse Maker** with background plausibility compiler. On-line thesaurus with full logic compensating
- **Resignation Writer**. Creates original, purpose-written terminati notices. Just enter the tone and addressee for Penciltex handwritten documents in seconds. Keeps permanent encrypted records of all resignations as tendered, threatened or merely mooted over late lunches.
- **Expenses Expander**. Avoids duplication. Compares and rounds-up over 256 simultaneou expenses claims. Automatically inflating idiosyncratic demands to office average. Features optional malfunction on subsequent printouts. Full justification on all entries. No reasonable offer refused.

EX-HARDWARE DEVELOPER'S BANKRUPT STOCK

Software Title Compiler.
Makes otherwise rational software programs (e.g. spreadsheet accounting) sound like a commercially viable, state-of-the-art technological breakthrough (e.g. Super-ColumnCruncher 3+).

Software Packaging Compactor.
Reduces expansive program boxes/ display binders/ presentation cases to manageable size suitable for office shelves and waste- bins. Reverse thrust mode available to compress expanded polystyrene.

Custom Time Management Production Planner/
Program monitors development and ensures that software releases coincide with hardware launch. Never been used.

GRAPHICS SOFTWARE FOR THE APPLE MACINTOSH

The Cartoonist's Mate

Program selects one from 1000's of ready-drawn, interchangeable images and automatically selects an appropriate caption from 100,000 tried and tested public domain gags - all guaranteed unseen by Daily Mirror readers since 1953. Plus full documentation and back-up insecurity copy.

Full professional range of topics, including ....
* Desert Islands
* Women with large breasts
* Tramps
* Women drivers explaining accidents
* Drunks crawling home
* Fat women with new hats and large breasts
.....and scores of newsvendor's placards just waiting for a passer-by's comments.

Full-feature package incorporates the **MacLARRY** stockpile disk of shopwindow notices /Rodin statues/ bemused hobbyists opening construction-kit boxes on the dining room table (inserts gag on lid). Plus **MacFRANKLYN** for the mentally handicapped, and **MacMAC** - the program that wishes it was **MacGILES**

Soft-topSoft In-car Technologies Ltd.

Under-dash **Cellnet Ans-a-phone**; incorporating mobile to mainframe file-transfer, Fax-Copier and free glassware voucher-size document shredder. Complete with car phone seat and dash tidy. Free Paddy Hopkirk Explo-safe Crash Recovery program with every gallon of multigrade.

SOFTWARE CHECKER

The unique **Ad-Scan** program reads large format lists in software advertisements and identifies the one program they actually have in stock. Worth its weight in polyvinyl chloride.

Worf Pricessor,

wiTh on_line prjnteer

Neefs slig~t attnttnttion.

£150.00   bu*yer* re/ass^embles

WORD PROCESSING ADD-ON ACCESSORIES

Soft Ideas Inc. presents.

Minder-Matic™
The Rhyming Slang text substitution program. Reprocesses 48 minute film drama script in 20 seconds. Removes syntax-correction, all leading H's and any semblance of credible emotion from any character called Terry. Add on Speech-Cred voice synth- esiser to make you sound a working class Sarf Londoner for T.V. advert voice overs.

Keep track of your disks with **Track Keeper®** Automatically remembers and sorts the contents of all your unlabelled, undocumented floppy disks regardless of what pile of old papers/coffee machine/dust layer that covers them. Conveniently files them under headings: VITAL COMPANY RECORDS; ABSOLUTELY-VITAL-COMPANY-RECORDS- AND-I'M-NOT-JOKING-THIS- TIME and ACCOUNTS.

COUNTRY LIFE

A bovine bingo game is being staged on the school playing fields on Sunday. A cow will be brought to the field, and where she makes her first deposit will be the lucky spot. The winner gets 25 per cent of the proceeds up to £100, and lots of pats on the back.

M. Field (St Albans *Review & Express*)

AN urgent plea for bed linen has come from the town's refuge for battered wives. Crossways House needs more single sheets and pillows, say organisers, as well as more cruelty of all kinds.

P. Klusaitis (*The Advertiser & Indicator*)

The minimum application will be for £400 worth of shares, or £200 worth of TSB customers.

P. Patel (*New Life*)

Next week Gordon and two of his old POW pals – one is now dead – will fly to Poland as guests of their old friends who remember the POWs well.

V. Heywood (*East Lothian Courier*)

DEPARTMENT OF MUSIC, LIBERAL AND GENERAL STUDIES
Singing Classes: B026 Solo Singing for Everyone, Tues. 7.00

R. Bromnick (evening class prospectus)

'Not enough work' for extra eye consultant

B. Clifford (*The Cambrian News*)

Brown had threatened to cut off Mr Clifford Brown's wrist if he did not hand over his watch and hit him in the face with a packet of electric plugs.

P. Dickins (Southend *Standard Recorder*)

And Detective Constable Patricia Baseley (30) said today she was "a very lucky woman" after being hit by the car, carried 10 yards on the bonnet and then having her left leg run over.

J. Fitzpatrick (*Northampton Chronicle & Echo*)

It has been decided to hold a fruit and flower show as well as the baby show previously announced. All exhibits become the property of the committee and will be sold for the benefit of the village hall.

A. Hargreaves (parish magazine, W. Sussex)

INTERNATIONAL SECTION

CHRISTIAN Exterminating Service. Special low prices.

D. Walker (*Detroit Free Press*)

The school is the brainchild of Ron Unz, a gifted graduate who had exhausted district resources by the 10th grade and two of his favourite teachers from a Los Angeles junior high school.

G. Henderson (*Star News*, California)

Anti-crime day marred by shooting

A. Batchelor (*The Philadelphia Inquirer*)

P. Rolfe (*Western Daily Press*)

Emma Duncan, of Lancaster Girls' Grammar School, passed four A-Levels in her recent exams, not ½ as was printed last week.

S. Blyth (*Cumberland News*)

ONE SMOKE Persian kitten, male, 1-piece w/proof suit, £6575 o.n.o.

J. Smith (*Harrow & Northwood Informer*)

CENTENARIAN Mr Albert Power, surviving member of Britain's oldest brother-and-sister partnership, will be cremated with full military honours today.

V. Baker (*Western Mail*)

But a poultry crowd of 5,987 turned up to see Wimbledon keep up their 100 per cent home record in top flight football.

G. Ley (London *Standard*)

This included a competition to guess the weight difference between two of the rabbits – a big French Lop and a Netal Dwarf rabbit. There was in fact 12 stones and five ounces between them.

S. Rees (*Mid Sussex Times*)

Report on UNICEF benefit game between The Americas and The Rest of the World, Pasadena.
REMARKS: Minute's silence for the deceased Honorary President of FIFA, Sir Stanley Rous. Shot against the post by Maradona (57 mins.).

F. Johnstone (*FIFA News*)

INTERNATIONAL SECTION

7.30 AMAZING STORIES. A man who had been in a coma for 40 years communicates with an unconscious 7-year-old girl, in stereo.

M. Bellone (*Rocky Mountain News TV Dial*)

The St-Louis area transit authority has given up on a public relations effort to rename its bus stops with the more optimistic designation of "bus starts". It will replace nearly 2,000 "bus start" signs installed 18 months ago, because people were confused by the new phrase.

B. Boggess (*Fort Lauderdale News-Sun Sentinel*)

Mr Mohamed Suleiman (Bheocromo-CWTOMA??) who found the Bavarian leather trousers (folklore style) lost in taxi on 15th Oct., impossible to find the indicated address. Please contact immediately.

G. Thompson (*Emirates News*, Dubai)

ALAN COREN
Sea Change

A public beach has been put out of bounds at Great Yarmouth so that fifty pairs of little terns can nest in peace. A stretch of shore a third of a mile long and a hundred yards wide has been cleaned and roped off.

The terns have flown 4,000 miles from Gambia to mate.

Daily Telegraph

"I CAN remember when you couldn't get on that beach without a tie," said the crab, from the edge of the rock-pool.

The gull, perched on the ledge above it, glanced down.

"Must have been a bugger to knot," it observed, "with claws."

One stalked eye emerged slowly from the crab's armoured slot and stared at the gull for a time.

"What?" it said.

"Bow tie, was it?" enquired a prawn, breaking the surface. "I couldn't help hearing."

"It would have to be," said the gull. "He could hardly wear the other sort."

"I've always wondered what they were called," said the prawn, thoughtfully. "Has it ever struck you as funny, having one called a bow and the other one not called anything?"

"No, it hasn't," said the gull.

The crab's other eye came out.

"Why would he have to wear a bow, anyway?" said the prawn.

"First off," said the gull, "it would go better with his shape. But mainly, it's the practical side. If he wore the other kind of tie, it would trail in the mud."

"It would be filthy," nodded the prawn, "in no time. I see that."

"Plus trip him up. It is one of the shortcomings of running sideways. The tie would hang down in front," explained the gull, "and he would be forever running over it."

"Unless he had the knot on one side," said the prawn.

"He'd look ridiculous," said the gull.

The prawn considered this.

"Beats me why they wanted him to wear a tie at all," it said.

"They were probably partial," murmured a winkle who had hitherto kept itself to itself, "to a nice bit of dressed crab!"

At which it convulsed so uncontrollably as to lose its grip on the underside of the rock, drop to the sand, and roll about, hooting.

"*Nice bit of dressed crab!*" it shrieked. "Where do I get 'em from!"

The gull rose on a single flap, sank smartly to the beach, and put a yellow claw on the winkle.

"Shall I do us all a favour?" it enquired.

"Leave it out," said the winkle, muffled. "It is not as if I can help myself. It is in the blood, if you are a winkle. Generations of salty Cockney wit etcetera. It is expected of us. Also, being cheery goes with ending up on a pin. Look at World War One. Nil carborundum and so forth. Gassed last night, and gassed the night before.

Are we downhearted? No!"

"Oh, let him go," said the crab, wearily. "It is the oldest joke in the book."

"*I* laughed," said the prawn.

"It's the way I tell 'em," said the winkle.

The gull resumed its perch.

"I still don't understand," it said, "where they expected you to get a tie from."

The crab sighed. Bubbles winked on its terrible jaws.

"Not *me*," it said. "They did not expect *me* to wear a tie. They expected one another to wear 'em. The men wore spongebag trousers and striped blazers and panama hats, and the women wore long frocks and bonnets with daisies on, it was all very elegant, this beach."

"Pull this one," said the prawn, "they would have gone down like bricks."

"They did not wear 'em in the water," said the crab, rolling each eye independently. "Don't you know anything? When they wanted to swim, they went inside these little hut efforts, and they changed into bathing suits, and someone pushed the huts into the water, and they got out of the back door and into the sea."

"Stone me!" cried the prawn. "What a palaver! It's not even as if they eat plankton. They just go in and lollop about a bit and then they come out and turn red. Fancy going to the expense of a hut!"

The crab sighed.

"You had to be there," it murmured. "It had a lot of charm. It had innocence. They used to bring ukuleles and butterfly nets. They used to play French cricket and sing *My Old Man Said Follow The Van*. They did not," muttered the crab darkly, "have nude beaches. They did not," and here he waved a gnarled claw towards the roped enclosure, "have subsidised mating."

"Oh, look!" cried the winkle, as the others, on the crab's signal, stared.

"What is it?" said the gull.

"She's having one of her terns!" shrieked the winkle.

The prawn fell about.

"You may laugh," said the crab, "but it is not only a gross affront to decency, it is a wanton misuse of council money. Little terns coming

"I loaded sixteen tons. What do I get?"

Day. Not easy, if you happen to be a mollusc. Besides, very few of 'em speak winkle."

"It would not surprise me," said the crab, "if there was not a ban on tern jokes. They have, after all, flown here from Gambia. It would not surprise me if making tern jokes was punishable under the Race Relations Act."

"I wonder why they don't do it at home?" enquired the gull. "Fancy flying halfway round the world for a bit of wing-over! I usually manage with a lump of driftwood. It's a bad day for me if I have to go further than fifty feet."

"They come over here," replied the crab bitterly, "on account of it is the life of Riley. Roped-off beach, no cats, no tar, no donkey doings, RSPB patrols, nothing to do all day except –"

" – take terns!" said the winkle. "Sorry, sorry, slipped out!"

"In all probability," said the gull, "they do not even have to build anything. They probably get a council nest. They probably go straight to the top of the list. Fly in, make your clawprint in the space provided, ten minutes later you are – "

" – going for a quick tern along the beach!"

"I'd write all these down," gasped the prawn, "if the tide wasn't coming in."

"It would not surprise me," muttered the gull, "if they did not even have to be married. It is probably an offence to ask 'em. You know councils. Give 'em half a chance to be seen doing sunnink for the single parent egg, and before you know it they are coming round with a red-checked tablecloth and a candle in a bottle and a hot lugworm dinner with all the trimmings."

"They look after their own, all right," muttered the crab. "Bloody clever, these Communists."

"Sharp left terns," said the winkle.

The prawn fell back, waving its pleopods feeby.

"Lucky I haven't got ribs," it wheezed, "I'd be strapped up by now!"

"They just come to me," explained the winkle. "Call it a gift."

"You could've made a fortune in saucy postcards," said the prawn warmly, when it had recovered, "with the right contacts."

"I've never understood why they're supposed to be saucy," said the winkle. "They're usually about the ones with hair under their noses asking the ones with two lumps on the front if they would care for a nice big winkle. What's so saucy about that?"

"Not just Communists, either," said the gull, darkly. "A fair number of 'em are gay. That is what attracts councils more than anything, these days."

"There's a big ternover," said the winkle.

"Is there no end to his repertoire?" cried the prawn.

"Bottomless," replied the winkle.

They both fell over.

"I can remember," said the crab, "when what councils spent their money on was deckchairs and bandstands and lifebelts and little lights on the lamp-posts and stopping piers from rotting and men going round with spikes picking rubbish up off the sand. What is it all coming to?"

"It is probably a symbol of something," said the gull. "A lot of things are, these days."

"Where will it all end?" said the prawn.

"In moral depravity, is where," said the crab.

"Tern to page three," said the winkle. ☙

▶ ALAN COREN

over here, having it away on the rates."

"I wonder why we never see any great terns," said the gull.

"He's right, you know," said the winkle. "Remember Jimmy James? Jewell and Warriss? Remember Wilson, Keppel and Betty? They all played here once. I blame television."

"*Great turns!*" howled the prawn, clutching itself octapodally. "You are a caution, and no mistake! Have you ever thought of doing it professionally yourself?"

The winkle shook its shell.

"It's a terrible life, these days," it replied. "All they want is smut. Or impressions of Robin

Lesson Trois-cent-quatre-vingt-et-un
Le Grouse-Shooting

Visiteur: Angus?
Ghilly: Aye, monsieur?
Visiteur: C'est une grouse là-bas?
Ghilly: Non, monsieur. C'est un starling.
Visiteur: Look, Angus, nous sommes ici sur les grouse-moors depuis August 14, et nous n'avons pas vu une seule grouse!
Ghilly: Pas vrai, monsieur. August 21, nous avons vu une grouse.
Visiteur: Mais je ne l'ai pas tué!
Ghilly: Ach, monsieur, c'était une wee baby grouse. Vous ne voulez pas tuer un bairn comme ça?
Visiteur: Après trois semaines, je veux tuer *anything*!
Ghilly: Les grouses sont très rares en 1986, monsieur. La scarcité de grouses est une scourge, un calamity, le deuxième calamity de 1986.
Visiteur: Et l'autre?
Ghilly: Les Games de Commonwealth.
Visiteur: Ah, oui … Puis-je tuer le starling?
Ghilly: Ah, non, monsieur! Tuer un starling, ce n'est pas du sport!
Visiteur: Pourquoi pas? C'est un oiseau, comme une grouse. C'est un fair fight entre le sportsman, avec son high-power sporting rifle, et le starling, avec … avec …
Ghilly: Avec rien! Le starling est defenseless!
Visiteur: La grouse aussi.
Ghilly: Peut-être, mais je suis totalement contre le shooting des starlings!
Visiteur: OK, OK … vous n'avez jamais mangé un starling?
Ghilly: NON!
Visiteur: OK! … Angus, regardez. Là-bas. Qu'est-ce que c'est? C'est un bloke!
Ghilly: Vous avez raison, il y a un fellow qui s'approche à travers les grouse-moors dans l'uniforme d'un *Guardian* reader. C'est un loony. Hey! Que voulez-vous?
Bloke: Je suis un representatif du Front Des Droits des Animaux. Je fais le checking pour voir que le grouse-shooting est limité. Vous commettez une monstrueuse massacre ici!
Visiteur: Massacre … ? En trois semaines, je n'ai rien tué! Pas même un starling!
Bloke: Je vous donne un warning. Si vous tirez sur une grouse, je vais monter une prosécution.
Ghilly: Vous êtes un blasted nuisance … Monsieur, voulez-vous essayer un petit pot-shot?
Visiteur: Sur ce bloke?
Ghilly: Pourquoi pas? Quelques pellets … Un peu de shot … C'est presque harmless. Allez-y.
Visiteur: OK! (*Il donne un whiff de shot à l'Animal Rights bloke, qui commence à courir.*)
Ghilly: Bon shot, monsieur. Un bon petit peppering.
(*Moral: Ne tuez pas les grouses. Ne tuez même pas les starlings. Mais les blokes en anoraks et specs sont fair game.*)

80

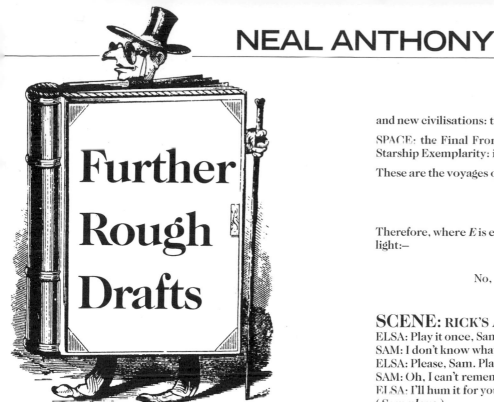

Further Rough Drafts

GWTW CLOSING SCENE

As Rhett reaches the door, Scarlett rushes down the staircase to intercept him. He pauses with the door open; Scarlett pleads with him not to leave, says she can't live without him, etc.

RHETT: Frankly, my dear, I don't give a cuss.
He flings the door wide and strides out into the

RHETT: Frankly, my dear, I don't give a toss
        I don't give a monkey's
        I don't give two hoots
        I don't give a tinker's
        I don't give a pitcher of warm spit
        I don't give a, don't give a . . . damn
        it . . .

CONCLUSION Therefore, when E represents *energy*, m is mass, and c is the velocity of light, the relationship between matter and energy may be defined thus:
$$E = mc^3$$
Note: Something wrong here, surely (AE).

THE BATTLE HYMN OF THE REPUBLIC

Mine eyes have seen the glory of the coming of the Lord:
He is striding down the gangplank where His heavenly ship is
                    moored:
He hath dropped the fateful anchor of His

Mine eyes have seen the glory of the coming of the Lord:
He is casting off the moorings, now His blessèd crew's aboard:
He hath

Mine eyes have seen and so forth and et cetera the Lord:
He is chalking up the total that His saintly team has scored:
He

Et cetera et cetera and so forth of the Lord:
He is taking out the garbage where the heavenly trash-can's
                    stored

He is, he is, is . . .

SPACE: THE FINAL FRONTIER

. . . These are the voyages of the Starship Entropy: its five-year mission, to explore strange new worlds: to seek out new life,

and new civilisations: to boldly go

SPACE: the Final Frontier . . . .These are the voyages of the Starship Exemplarity: its five-year missio

These are the voyages of the Starship Endomorph
             the Starship Encomium
             Emporium Emolument
             Ectoplasm . . .

Therefore, where E is energy, m is mass, and c is the speed of light:—
$$E = \sqrt{mc}$$
    No, no . . . surely not . . .

SCENE: RICK'S AMERICAN BAR, CASABLANCA

ELSA: Play it once, Sam: for old time's sake.
SAM: I don't know what you mean, Miss Elsa.
ELSA: Please, Sam. Play it.
SAM: Oh, I can't remember it: I'm a little rusty on it.
ELSA: I'll hum it for you. (*Hums.*)
(*Sam plays.*)
ELSA: Sing it, Sam.
SAM (*sings*): Lady of Spain, I adore you —
          Right from the night I first saw you.
          My heart has been yearning for y
ELSA: I'll hum it for you. (*Hums.*)
(*Sam plays.*)
ELSA: Sing it, Sam.
SAM (*sings*): Grab your coat, and get your hat,
          Leave your worry on the doorstep,
          Just direct your feet
          To the sunny side of the stree
ELSA: Sing it, Sam.
SAM (*sings*): Happy days are here again:
          The skies above are clear again,
          So sing a song of cheer agai

SAM (*sings*):   sings   Sam sings

        Sam sings *something*
     . . . *Tiptoe through the tulips* —??

INSTRUMENT OF ABDICATION

I, Edward the Eighth, of Great Britain, Ireland, Nigeria, Kenya, Uganda, Tanganyika, the Gold Coast, Northern Rhodesia, Southern Rhodesia, Bechuanaland, Nyasaland, British Somaliland

I, Edward the Eighth, of Great Britain, Ireland, Large Parts of Africa, Canada, British Honduras, British Guiana, the Falkland Islands, South Georgia

of Great Britain, Ireland, Large Parts of Africa, Canada, Little Bits of Central and South America, Australia, New Zealand, the Solomon Islands, the Gilbert and Ellice Islands, the New Hebrides, Henderson Island, Pitcairn Island, Ascension Island, Gough Island, Tristan da Cunha, St Helena

Great Britain, Ireland, Parts of Africa, Bits of America, an Extraordinary Number of Islands, Aden, Gibraltar, Cyprus, Hong Kong, Singapore

Great Britain, Ireland, and a Good Deal of the Rest of the Globe . . . and Half the Bally Planet

Great Britain, Ireland, and, and, and . . .

Therefore $E = \dfrac{m}{c} \times \pi r^2$
   . . . Start again:
     $1 + 1 = 2$
    Therefore . . .

CLIVE COLLINS

BACK LOT

"All the salerooms and all the auction houses in all the world . . . she has to walk into <u>mine</u>!"

"Only you could go to a studio auction and make a successful bid for a six-foot tall, invisible white rabbit."

"I really wanted that jacket Marlon Brando wore. You shouldna stopped me bidding, Charlie, I coulda been a contender . . ."

"Sold! To the gentleman in the corner!"

"'Lot 453 ...Rosebud' – anyone got any idea
what _that_ is?"

"But surely you must have realised when
you bid for them, sir, that each glove only
had three fingers."

"He's been smoking them two at a time ever since he
made a successful bid for Conrad Veidt's cigarette case."

Publish and Be Dreamed

IT must have been the thickest fog they'd had in that part of London for thirty years. So thick, indeed, that I very soon couldn't remember what part of London it had actually been when I could see it. It certainly was London, though. You could tell by the huge mock-up of the Statue of Liberty they'd installed across the road; through the swirls of caressing cashmere grey, it was occasionally distinguishable as a vast black spiky shape with arm aloft. It *might* have been a statue of somebody changing a light-bulb. As I say, it was very foggy. But I distinctly heard the moon strike twelve.

Under such circumstances, I make it a policy to set off walking and hope for the best; and generally nothing helpful happens for a long time. But on this occasion I was lucky. Swerving round a lamppost that seemed to bend out of my way, thanks no doubt to the refractory effect of the fog, I came almost immediately face to face with a rag-and-bone-man's horse. Any lingering doubts I might have had about whether this was truly London were thereby dispelled, because, of course, this was widely known as the only part of London where rag-and-bone-men's horses are still met with. The nag, a Disney-faced creature, though without Walt's obligatory corporate vitality, coughed.

"*Et tu, Brute!*" I breathed, smokily, though without malice.

"Speak for yourself," said the horse, easing its neck around uncomfortably in its fat leather collar. I felt, momentarily, a twinge of depression. To submit to a put-down from any sort of horse is lowering at the best of times.

"It's behind you," the beast added, coughing again. I considered this. Would "it" turn out to be a spittoon, or a telephone kiosk? Was the creature attempting to enlist my aid in securing the services of a veterinarian, of whose attention he stood, I was almost sure, in greater need than I? Or was he perhaps rehearsing for a pantomime?

It's amazing, in a fog, how you can contrive to look behind you without seeming to twist your neck at all. Having discovered the truth of this, I went ahead and did it, if you see what I mean. Well, I didn't either, but I felt certain that the horse would have raised some objection had it been impossible. And very glad I was that I had, or did, because behind me across the cobbled pavement glowed, in welcoming orange, a bubble-glass bow-window with a sign above in old-gold lettering, edged thickly in black. MANNY TOMES – ANTIC, WEARY & BOOKSELLER. Now this was more like it. Or *mair* like it, as for some reason the phrase presented itself to my mind. The thought of mares recalled to me the source of my information, and I turned to offer thanks, but he was gone – noiselessly into the mist, leaving only a sugar-lump behind, deliquescing visibly in the gutter.

With a shrug of the shoulders, and doffing my admiral's hat (I had forgotten till this moment that I even owned an admiral), I entered Mr Tomes's shop to a charming little chirrup of bells. The proprietor, a tiny, wizened gentleman with nut-brown bald pate and half-moon spectacles, was sitting on a high stool, a good ten feet up I should say, and writing in a huge ledger propped open in his lap.

"Effing VAT," said Mr Tomes. I warmed to him immediately, but nothing happened, and I returned gradually to room temperature. Scratch-scratch, scratch-scratch, went his pen. Scratch-*scratch*, scratch-scratch, *scratch*. Whereupon he fell to writing. Presently he spoke, which was just as well, for I was already considering dragging the horse in to break the ice.

"You'll have come about the autograph letters from Freud to Charlie Chaplin, the Ulysses rewrite, Dostoievsky's Savoy Opera libretto, the Larkin diaries, the Hitler diaries, W.C. Fields's application to join the Catholic Church, Shakespeare's *No Sexe, Prithee, We're Illyrian* and the signed nudie photos of Helen of Troy, I expect?" he enquired, in a pleasant Glaswegian accent. I bowed to the uncanny instinct of a born dealer, and bumped my head on a remarkably lifelike bust of the Person from Porlock.

"The same," I replied, pretty sure that one of us would start making sense soon.

"Well, as you know," resumed the curious cracked baritone (whose name, you will recall, was Tomes), "you are 38th on the waiting list for these items."

"Ah," I ventured, gaining nothing obviously, but scanning the shelves instinctively for the Kafka section. "37 in front of me. Quite so."

"Yes," croaked the octogenarian enigma giraffishly, though I wouldn't have said so at the time, "– and no. You are evidently unaware that three dozen of the persons in question, having formed a kind of *consorzio* or *Bund* together, resolved to conduct a mass appraisal of the material on offer, with a view to which perusal they hired, this very morning, a motor-coach ▶

"OK. Dig in!"

85

which was heading this way at maximum speed when it regrettably plunged over the cliffs of Beachy Head."

A respectful silence ought to have ensued, but didn't, I'm afraid.

"I can tell by your laughter," resumed the aged commercant, "that it grieves you sorely to take that one on board. It is a total sickener and no mistake. Still and all, you were not among those who put their last orders in on this tragic occasion, so you are in a position to bargain with Miss Ekberg."

"Miss Ekberg?"

"Miss Brigitte 'The Body' Ekberg, sadly, is the only remaining bidder whose claim pre-dates your own. You will have to come to some arrangement with the lady." And as if on cue, the bead curtains at the back of the shop parted, and in stepped the most exaggeratedly pro-portioned, the most seductively streamlined rag-and-bone-man's horse I have ever seen. The animal coughed politely.

"Sorry about this, gents," it hissed. "Brigitte is just slipping into something more comfort-ing. If I might insert a word of advice that might help expedite my resumption of hostilities vis-à-vis the bag of carrots that has been set aside for my attention out the back, Brigitte is interested only in the Shakespeare manuscript and is not prepared to go above one-and-ninepence for that. So everything, if you take my meaning gents, is negotiable. I thank you, I am thanking *yew*."

The estimable charger withdrew as decently as it could, given its tutu, and at once the fronded barrier was cloven again – by the prow of the eternal starlet. She had lost a good four stone since her appearance in Fellini's *At Least 14½*, and anything else that needed to be shed came into the category of wardrobe.

"If I may say so, Miss Ekberg," I gurgled, "you are a sight for sore thumbs."

"Very well put, dahlink," purred the convex bibliophile. "Now can we get down to bees-knees?" Whether it was courtesy or panic that caused me to turn to Tomes I do not know, but it was too late anyway, for he had departed leaving a sign taped to his stool-leg – "Gone to make cup of tea, back in 2 days." I was alone with one of the most ruthlessly undulating bookworms in the world.

"I need dat folio," she breathed. "Be a goot boy and hand it over."

"Ian Fleming," I bluffed, "*Shampoothighs*, page 78. You old cornball."

"I tink I can change your mind . . ." Already her fingers were easing the strap of her shim-mering gown off her marble shoulder; then suddenly, with a resigned flip of the wrist, she thrust away the entire corsage, and out spilled the most perfect pair of King Penguins, *The Shock of Recognition* by Edmund Wilson, the complete cartoon works of Vicky in sundry volumes, a mint copy of *The Whitsun Weddings*, a fine set of leather-bound India-paper Dickens . . . and then the fog took it all away.

To wake up with your wants-list as long as ever is of course no fun. But at least I was still in my original pyjama jacket and only slightly foxed. "I yield to no one," I said out loud, "in my admiration for Shakespeare." Somewhere a horse coughed.

Garsmold & Sons
73 Pondicherry Crescent
Bromsgrove

15th January 1987

Dear Prince Edward,

Thank you for your letter regarding light deliveries in the Bromsgrove area, and the enclosed photo-copy of your cycling proficiency certificate.

While I am as patriotic as the next man, up yours Galtieri, what's this tara-masalata muck, never crack walnuts during Queen's Broadcast etcetera, and while I am not slow to spot the commercial advantages of amending our signboard to IF YOU DO NOT SEE WHAT YOU WANT ASK FOR IT, BY APPOINTMENT EMPLOYERS TO THE ROYAL FAMILY, I do not feel I can offer you the position due to where you have not got a reference from previous employer, you have to appreciate my situation, that basket can carry up to forty pounds sterling in bottled sauce, never mind if it goes walkabout the phone would not stop ringing.

I have the honour to remain, Sir, your humble and obedient servant,

Jas Garsmold

Jas. Garsmold
Victuallers to the Carriage Trade Since 1938

A. K. PATEL LTD plc usm

20th January 1987

Dear Prince Edward,

My daughter-in-law's second cousin once removed has shown me the esteemed card which you took out of our window this morning and handed to my son's wife to give to her grandfather's stepsister's husband. I am indeed flattered that you should have offered your inestimable services to our unworthy establishment, and there is no question but that your gracious presence would dignify any paper round, but I am heartbroken to have to tell you that you do not qualify for the advertised position. I am afraid I was hoping to attract a passing relative.

In abject and apologetic humility,

A. K. Patel.

A. K. Patel

On One's Bike

Sunrise Valley Warehouse Company
SLOUGH

16th January 1987

Dear Prince Edward,

In receipt of yours of the 13th inst. regarding our vacancy for a senior tea-boy, as shown in Windsor Morning Advertiser.

I am sorry to have to disappoint you, but we are looking for an applicant with experience. We just do not have the facilities to train up someone in such matters as bringing pot to kettle, poke bag with spoon to maximise flavour-flow, do not put chocolate wholemeal in saucer and end up with smear on cup, keep sharp eye open for furring up, never blow nose on tea-towel, shake milk-bottles of a morning to stop that mare in accounts sucking the cream off, watch that short-changing bastard at the kiosk, I could go on all day.

It is, of course, always possible that you have a natural gift for this or have watched your mum do it. If she would be good enough to give me a bell and set my mind at rest, it is possible I could reconsider, but do not get your hopes up.

Can I give you a hint if you plan a career in teaboyship? Do not bang on about this history degree you mention, most employers do not give a toss about magna wossname, what they are after is something piping hot with no scum on it.

Yours truly,

Raymond Willis

Raymond Willis,
Stockroom Consultant

BRENT COUNCIL

17th January 1987

Dear Mr Windsuh,

You right, no gittin' away f'om it, I and I *did* have a vacancy fo' a Roadsweepin' Operative, but I and I jist lookin' in de file agen, and it bin suddenly filled.

Yours faithfully,

Winston Chamberlain

**Winston Chamberlain,
Top Man**

Brent Council is a Equal Opportunity Employer, honky

TELECOM

Dial House, 151 Shaftesbury Avenue, London W.C.2.

January 20, 1987

Dear Prince Edward,

Thank you for your letter. I am afraid, however, that our recent advertisement may not have made clear that the position of Kissogram is an extremely demanding one. You have to wear a gorilla's head and bang it on the wall a lot, also run around grunting with your knuckles brushing the ground.

Had you actually qualified as a Royal Marine, we should of course have been only too delighted to consider you.

Yours faithfully,

pp British Telecommunications plc

WHICH DOCTORS?

The painfully fashionable secrets of ALTERNATIVE MEDICINE laid bare by ROBERT BUCKMAN (or similar fine Medical Correspondent)

You all know me.

I have never lacked the courage boldly to address controversial issues that have not been boldly addressed before. Not by me, anyway. Yet there is one such issue that I must boldly confess I have been boldly ducking out of — the controversy over alternative medicine.

A recent report has examined this in detail and so many people have asked me to let them have the official and authoritative *Punch* medical correspondent's view on alternative medicine that I have, at last, been forced to speak out.

I had no alternative.

WHY ALTERNATIVE MEDICINE?

Currently, a lot of people believe that while modern doctors have improved their skills and prowess in treating diseases, they have lost their ability to care and to relate to their patients as human beings.

Now obviously this criticism does not apply to me, because, as a caring and humane medical practitioner, I recognise the merit in this viewpoint and I fully empathise with the motivations behind it — even though the published evidence suggests that alternative medicine is a load of horse-crap, packaged by a crew of sycophantic, glib cowboys who could sell ice to the Eskimos, particularly if they could call it holistic ice.

No no no, I didn't mean that, just kidding, ahahahaha.

Anyway, the people who are most attracted to alternative medicine are usually people who suffer from troublesome, but not life-threatening conditions, e.g. living in Islington. No, that's not true either. Sorry.

Now lots of perfectly nice people have a recurring medical condition for which conventional medicine cannot offer a cure or do anything about, e.g. low back-ache, compulsive nose-picking, working in advertising, not wanting an independent deterrent etc. So the idea is that you go to an alternative medical practitioner, who cannot offer a cure or do anything about it either, but says so in a nice way and takes longer about it. Seriously, though, what alternative medical practitioners are good at is treating their patients as human beings in the context of their community and all its complex inter-relationships.

Of course, a few conventional doctors are pretty nifty at that sort of approach, too, e.g. in California, although on this side of the Atlantic we call it something different, e.g. wife-swapping. However, the main point is absolutely undeniable — which is that we conventional doctors, as a group, are not all that good at certain high-tech complex medical doctor-patient interactions such as smiling, looking interested, remembering names, staying awake.

What is happening now is that, in response to our customers voting with their feet, we conventional doctors are re-learning all that stuff in postgraduate courses. I myself have a PhD in nodding sympathetically and I presented a dissertation on fifty different ways of saying "good morning" nicely (except I nearly failed in my oral when my examiner said "good afternoon" and I didn't know what to reply. I mean, I'm a specialist, aren't I? Yes).

So, there is clearly a valuable lesson for us conventional chappies to learn from our alternative colleagues, crawl crawl slime slime slime, and it can only help all of us in doing what we really want, i.e. helping our patients in the best way possible and maybe getting famous as well.

In addition to the humane aspects, alternative medicine has some pretty powerful proponents and patrons. One of them is a person whose name I will not mention but whose identity I will hint at by saying that when his mum stops doing what she's doing, he'll be King of England. It is unclear precisely why this person is such a strong fan of alternative medicine, but I feel that this kind of broad common-sense view of health issues is precisely what this country needs — and PS my CBE hasn't arrived yet, though I sent in all the box tops last February.

However, despite all the obvious psycho-social advantages of alternative medicine, *does it does it cure diseases? In other words, does it actually work?*

Well, there's no point in asking me, is there? I mean, I'm The Enemy, aren't I? I mean, it's like asking the President of Coca-Cola whether Pepsi-Cola is actually nicer-tasting, isn't it?

Anyway, it doesn't matter because I shall now consider many of the alternative medicine techniques individually and let you judge for yourselves.

Please consult your own doctor before reading any further.

PSYCHIC SURGERY

Psychic surgery is a fascinating form of therapy which has been categorised in the language of the transactional-phenomenological school of psychology as "crap". What happens in psychic surgery is that you go along to a psychic surgeon and he or she moves his or her hands over your body or, if you're too busy to attend yourself, over your photo or X-ray or wig or credit card or last school report. Using their special psychic powers they then "divine" where the trouble is and what is causing it.

Now I have seen similar techniques used by other disciplines, e.g. plumbers and television repairmen, but I suppose the big difference was that they had dirtier overalls and charged more. Anyway, once the psychic surgeon has divined what is wrong, he organises the procedure known as psychic surgery. I don't know a lot about it myself, but I believe it's a pretty respectable sort of business with a proper psychic waiting-list and the option of going in a psychic side-room with private phone etc.

I'm told that one of the main advantages of psychic surgery is that you don't need to be anaesthetised (by a psychic anaesthetist) and it doesn't hurt ten days later when they take the psychic stitches out — though for the same money, why can't they use soluble ones?

Another advantage is that while the operation is being performed you (the patient) don't need to be there at all. Now think how helpful that could be for the NHS. I mean, all year round poor surgeons get hassled by executives who want their haemorrhoids fixed in August so they don't miss work — if we had psychic surgeons in the NHS we could do these guys' piles while they're actually working, so they don't even have to miss lunch. The only snag is that I don't know whether psychic surgeons ever do haemorrhoids, although I think I might be able to divine the answer if I just close my eyes and concentrate.

HOMOEOPATHY

Homoeopathy is not like phrenology at all. Really it isn't. But the true scientific basis of the homoeopathic principle is not yet fully established, although it might be proven any decade now, and no thanks, I'm perfectly comfortable, I'm just shifting from foot to foot because there's a stone in my shoe and I always wring my hands like this when I'm talking about something complex and difficult to sort of, well, talk about.

What they do in homoeopathy is use very small doses of medicines. This is actually a very smart idea indeed since it has been shown that 10-30% of "conventional" hospital patients suffer side-effects from drugs. If you use tiny doses of drugs, you'll have tiny side-effects.

What they also do is individualise each drug administration. This is also a very good idea. They look at you as a real person, your eye colour, your skin, your build, your credit-rating etc and pick the type and schedule of homoeopathic medicine accordingly. So it's not like conventional medicine, where you get ampicillin, £2.20, that's your lot, complete the course and who's next? In homoeopathy, you get ElizabethJonesicillin, it matches the colour of your eyes especially for you, with all our love and best wishes for a speedy recovery, £4.75 and call again soon.

There's something to be said for giving people less but giving it with more care and more heart.

Like this column, really. I mean a small dose'll probably do you just as much good as a big one. Please call again next week, I write this only for you and I love you so much.

PHRENOLOGY

This is not actually a form of alternative medicine at all, but I thought we might start off on a fairly non-controversial note, otherwise there'll be tears before bedtime, you mark my words.

Phrenology was the science (if such it could be called) of diagnosing a person's talents and peculiarities by the shape and the bumps of their skull, or cranium, or, as we conventional doctors call it, head. The idea was that your personality inside your brain sort of pushed up from within and shaped the skull over it. Well, of course nowadays we know that in a few cases a personality with certain strong characteristics can alter the shape of your skull, e.g. a psychopath with an axe in Central Park after dark, but your own personality won't shift it a smidgeon. No sirree.

What phrenologists were good at was psychotherapy. They would place their hands on their customers' heads and make intelligent guesses about their lifestyle and personality by subtle clues — an expensive hairdo, a tiara, a Nazi helmet, things like that. And they would proceed by making exploratory statements which were bound to be true, e.g. "there are two women in your life," "you care too much about things," "this'll cost you a florin" etc. And the interview would proceed depending on what the client replied, such as "no, three" or "no, I don't, I'm going to annexe Austria" and so on.

So really phrenology was a pseudo-science, a lot of hocus-pocus and mumbo-jumbo based on a minimal amount of slightly intelligent guess-work — the CIA is another example. Only when those guys feel your bumps, your bumps stay felt. Yes sirree.

HIGH COLONIC IRRIGATION

For many years when I was young I used to see adverts on the back of the *New Statesman*, which was a kind of newspaper in those days, advertising High Colonic Irrigation. I must say that I visualised something like the Tennessee Valley Authority — or maybe Mesopotamia — bringing needed water to the parched valley of High Colon etc.

The truth is more bizarre, but less picturesque. It is based on the idea that — oh you know what it's based on, you just want to see me get embarrassed and coy, don't you? Anyway, for every Keynesian who believes that a good throughput is the mark of a good economy, there are two sceptics who uphold the law of diminishing returns and five opportunists who know that where there's muck there's brass. The defence rests.

ROLFING

Rolfing is actually a serious alternative practitioner's discipline, and is all based on the belief that many diseases are caused by bad posture exaggerated by the effects of gravity, which I suppose might be true in certain circumstances, e.g. if you're drunk or shot. Anyway, practitioners who practice rolfing (known as "rolfing contractors") do a sort of deep massage "to loosen certain muscles and fascia and free the emotions and the mind".

Actually, I had a cousin from out of town who used to do that sort of thing and she got 18 months, but then she didn't know she was rolfing, did she? Anyway, rolfing can be performed on a part-time or full-time basis and there are annual displays and exhibitions (e.g. the Pro-Am Rolf Championships). You have to be careful not to confuse ordinary rolfing with "rolfharrissing", which is Australian and much less tasteful, although in some bizarre way I suppose you could think of it as an alternative to health.

SHIATSU

Shiatsu, like acupuncture, is based on traditional oriental medicine and is fervently supported by many people who can relate to something mysterious and totally unintelligible, provided it's oriental. These are the same people who are ready to believe in ginseng but not Horlicks, in Rabindrinath Tagore but not Desmond Morris, in bad karma but not bad moods, and in yin and yang but not Marks and Spencer.

Well, shiatsu scores heavily on the mysterious oriental scale, let me tell you. It's all based on the technique of applying pressure to one part of the body in order to produce an effect in another part (similar techniques are in use in the Western world, e.g. strangling). Thus, if you have a pain in your gall-bladder, the shiatsu doctor will apply pressure to "the outside of your leg from the pelvis to the knee". Though my manual doesn't say which leg — I suppose it depends on whether you dress with your gall-bladder to the left or right. In shiatsu teaching, the stomach is "just to the outside of the front ridge of the shinbone from the knee to the ankle", which sounds odd to non-orientals, but is actually the exact place where my stomach happens to migrate to on certain occasions, e.g. dentist's appointments or the morning after drinking half-a-bottle of sake.

Funnily enough, the shiatsu method doesn't say what to do to cure pain in the head — perhaps you're meant to apply shiatsu pressure to another part of the body entirely, e.g. your family doctor. More research is clearly needed here.

BOGUS DOCTORS

I must admit that bogus doctors are not exactly recognised by anybody as genuine alternative practitioners, but that's an issue in itself. I mean if Alternative Practitioners grumble that *they're* not properly recognised by the regular Non-Alternative Practitioners (e.g. me and the Big Boys up the BMA), they can hardly complain if someone who isn't recognised as an Alternative Practitioner by *them* goes ahead and practises (in a fairly alternative way), without being recognised by any practitioners whatsoever. It's like being thrown out of the Association of Non-Conformists for not conforming to Association rules. And in real life, these bogus doctors often practise for ages without being recognised. Or caught. And what happens when they are caught? The moment they haul off some poor ex-invoice-clerk-who-always-wanted-to-be-a-

doctor to court for having handled 35 women and tried to perform a few toe-nail removals, all his patients say how nice he was, and gentle, doctorly, authoritative and human.

We shouldn't put these guys in prison — we should employ them in the Health Service. For a start, they could teach medical students how to be nice and gentle, yet firm, authoritative and human (I'd teach those skills myself except I'm too busy using them to sell double-glazing in the evenings). Secondly, we could use them in Out-Patients. I mean, recent surveys have shown that 30% of all patients seeking medical advice haven't got a defined organic medical condition — which means, to one way of looking at things, that they're Bogus Patients. And we all know that doctors are absolutely awful at dealing with psycho-social problems (i.e. being nice to people who earn less than them), so why not employ a whole lot of proper Bogus Doctors to look after the Bogus Patients?

We could start a whole new Bogus College of Physicians which would issue proper 100% Bogus Diplomas (which have to be properly forged by accredited counterfeiters) and doctors, patients and Health Service would all benefit. We could probably pay them with genuine Monopoly money, which would not only solve a lot of funding problems but would also mean that they could get annual Monopoly pay increases as recommended by the Review Board — that would put them streets ahead of the rest of us ordinary doctors for starters. I believe that this suggestion of mine would bring alternative holistic humane medicine once more into the domain of the NHS, and would drastically reduce waiting-lists, patients complaints, drugs' bills and unemployment in one bold and brilliant stroke.

PRESS GANG

"Each weekend over a million words are written about football in publications which people who do not watch or play the game never read."

LAST Saturday, I was publicly rebuked by a man wearing a knitted woollen hat with a pom-pom on the top and the words "Sky Blues" embroidered on the front. His complaint concerned the subject matter of this column and contained the implied accusation of intellectual snobbery. Press Gang, he grumbled, is preoccupied with what used to be Fleet Street, the political weeklies and the glossy magazines. Warming to this theme, he demanded to know why, for six years, no mention had been made of one of publishing's most successful products – a family of publications which go on sale throughout the winter.

I had to admit (for he was a large man) that the most successful amongst them have a print run of over 25,000 and sell out in a single afternoon. And, as well as enjoying a circulation comparable to that boasted by *The Spectator*, they actually make a profit rather than relying on subsidy – the criterion of success supported by *The Spectator* for all commercial enterprises other than small circulation magazines. Realising that deep down inside I was sympathetic to his cause, he handed me a free copy of the "Official Matchday Magazine of Coventry City Football Club, k.o. 3.00 p.m, 60p".

The football programme contains six essential ingredients – "Todays Teams" (*sic*), as they are properly described at Coventry, or "the line-up" according to the vulgar television reporters; a code of numbers and letters on some sort of massive noticeboards which can be translated, by those in the know, into half-time scores in other league games; pen portraits of visiting players; club notes; pictures of last week's action and enthusiasm. The greatest of these is enthusiasm. Programmes are built around the tribal loyalties which hold football clubs together. Little boys who take them home with the intention of keeping them for ever are indoctrinated by their contents into the passionate conviction that Liverpool, Arsenal and Manchester United must never be left to walk alone.

Football programmes are written by friendly journalists (who may or may not be given a pittance in compensation) and a number of inspired amateurs. At Fulham, for instance, the programme is edited by the Chief Industrial Economist at the Midland Bank. His opposite number at Sheffield Wednesday has his name printed on the inside page along with – if not alongside – the chairman, manager and club doctor. His star columnist is Manager Howard Wilkinson, who pontificates as trenchantly as a *Times* leader,

I have lost count of the number of times … that I've heard experts, supposedly well intentioned, say "Of course nobody in football goes out to break another person's leg". That is not the point. That is like saying "no burglar who carries a gun intends to kill anyone".

One of the well-intentioned experts that he had in mind must have been Jimmy Hill, who was guilty of the derided banality on television after Ian Knight, a Wednesday central defender, suffered a double compound fracture of the left leg. A few days ago, after Mr Hill and I had spoken together at a meeting called to denounce the extinction of Fulham Football Club, I intended to draw the Wilkinson comment to his attention. Part of my purpose was, of course, to cause trouble. But I also wanted him to come face-to-face with a refreshing change from commentators' platitudes. Both purposes were frustrated by the offer of a copy of *When Saturday Comes* – football's answer to *Private Eye*.

The idea that football has its own underground subversive press may come as a surprise to you. But the "Charlie Nicholas Haircut Centenary Edition" of *When Saturday Comes* lists other members of the *genre* – *Off the Ball*, *City Gent*, *Wanderers Worldwide* and *Terrace Talk* amongst them. It also publishes a warning:

Since the start of *Off the Ball*, football in the West Midlands has collectively made a run for the lower divisions and seems to have found a permanent niche. York and Bolton are keeping each other company in the gloomy lower reaches of the Third Division. Orient are currently in their worst League position of all time …

There is within *When Saturday Comes* that indispensable ingredient of the alternative magazine – an article which might be either serious or satirical. Did Bob Wilson really write, "Yes, the Go-Go Gunners are sweeping away the cobwebs of the English game with their unique brand of guaranteed non-boring football," or is it the product of malicious Spurs supporters? The judgment that "even the stadium itself conspires against the 'boring' jibe" because "no one could fail to be interested by the fact that it is perfectly symmetrical" is, I assume, meant to be ironic. Though it does not have quite the bite of the "Sir Robert McAlpine Award" for the ground with the "Worst Away End of All".

To return to the comparison with which this analysis of football literature began, the objective student will – I have no doubt – agree that the quality of the "jokes" which appear in *When Saturday Comes* is in no way inferior to those which appear above the byline of Auberon Waugh, *The Spectator's* star columnist. I offer an example. The article on Marseille, St Etienne and Paris St Germain is weakly entitled "French Letter". I doubt if author Andy Lyons was paid as much to produce it as was earned by Mr Waugh's two recent humorous pieces on sanitary protection.

On a rough calculation, I estimate that each winter weekend over a million words are written about football in publications which people who do not watch or play the game never read. And that is only one tiny part of the irregular journalism that is successfully selling itself all over Britain. Parish magazines – produced with all the agony of which we hear in episodes of *The Archers* – have a yearly output which would fill the reading rooms of the British Museum. I hope that there is nothing patronising in the pleasure I find in thinking of all that writing going on. I am pleased to obey the injunction of the man in the woolly hat and pay it proper respect. ❧

"I felt a bit sorry for him after I shot his elephant."

CINEMA

THE COLOR PURPLE   DANNY GLOVER *as Albert*
WHOOPI GOLDBERG *as Celie*   MARGARET AVERY *as Shug Avery*

PSYCHO III
ANTHONY PERKINS *as Norman Bates*

Michael ffolkes

ROUND MIDNIGHT
DEXTER GORDON *as Dale Turner*   FRANÇOIS CLUZET *as Francis Borier*

GOTHIC
NATASHA RICHARDSON *as Mary*   TIMOTHY SPALL *as Dr Polidori*
GABRIEL BYRNE *as Byron*   JULIAN SANDS *as Shelley*   MIRIAM CYR *as Claire*

ANN LESLIE
MOTHER'S DAY

SHOW me a dead ant, and I'll show you a slap-up funeral: matchstick crosses, yoghourt-pot coffins, much keening in the bindweed, the full "Loved One" works. Some even get christened before final interment. "I name this dead ant Eric. Amen." Oh the hypocrisy of the woman, she who's secretly responsible for the said Eric snuffing it in a cloud of Superfast Zappo in the first place. But while it's one thing to play Mr Joyboy to scores of Kentish Town's assassinated ants, it's quite another to preside over the burying of a 12-year-old, 14-foot-long, three-quarter-ton Ford Capri in the back garden.

"But *why* can't we bury the Capri like the Ants?"

"Because you can't fit a Ford Capri into an Eden Vale yoghourt pot, that's why."

"Well, we don't *have* to give it a coffin." Of course not, silly Mummy – God, grown-ups can be such *nit-pickers*! "All you have to do, Mummy, is dig a big hole in the lawn and push it in!" Yup, a few flicks of a trowel, a quick *requiescat*, rearrange the cat-turds and dandelions and bingo! we've got a Ford Capri buried in our lawn. Easy-peasy.

Oh well, at least we've reached the stage of discussing the Ford's funeral arrangements. Shows that K. now accepts that the car is, to all intents and purposes, an ex-car. Took a while, though.

I tried explaining to her that the time had come for it to be put out of its misery. It's a martyr to its tappets, see, has something called a Big End which is about to Go, and a car whose Big End has Gone is, I convinced her, a former car, a late car, a no longer extant car, in short, a dead car. Big End transplants are, I implied, beyond current state-of-the-art automobile surgery as we know it today.

Besides, Rudi at the garage is tired of playing Christiaan Barnard to this terminal heap – and you know Rudi, patient to a fault. (For years he's been muttering to me in his thick Austrian accent, "Tch, tch, vy your husband doesn't get a nice new Audi, dear lady, I vill never know." Because he doesn't vant a nice new Audi, Rudi, he vants a rotten old Capri, that's vy.)

K.'s no fool though, sees straight into her mother's mind, pow, just like that, no tea-leaves required. Before I can bore her with the old "you-wouldn't-want-it-to-suffer-any-more"

routine I use for unconscious pigeons, she snaps coldly, "You always say you wouldn't be seen dead in it! You hate the poor thing! You've *always* hated it!" Well, hate's too strong a word, my little chaffinch, it's…

Oh well, all right, hate's *not* too strong a word. It isn't just the moss growing in the bald patches of the once oh-so-snazzy black vinyl roof; it isn't just that passing thieves keep tearing bits off it like vultures who assume that its appearance betokens so much automotive carrion, nor that the police keep stopping her father when he's driving it and checking him for offensive weapons (on the grounds that any red-blooded man of mature years who willingly drives around in such a wreck must be criminal, deranged, or both). It's when I found a small mushroom growing in the boot that I told it I'd had enough and was writing out its death certificate.

Oh yes, it's the Great Scrapyard in the Sky for you, mate, and don't you blather "valid-M.O.T" to me, buster, or all that "gets-from-A-to-B-and-who-needs-a-status-symbol" stuff – I've had all that from K.'s father, so shut up, the fact is you've had your last tank's-worth of 4-star. I've been round to the showroom with a fistful of crinklies and ordered this nice little Nip job, fully automatic, glass sliding-roof, wrap-around stereo, silver paint, D-reg an' all. Comes next week and no, you can't hang around, we're a two-car family, not a three-car one, especially not when one of the cars is you.

As you well know, the only reason you're still in situ, bringing down the property-values in our street, is that K.'s father is loathe to part with a car until it has a terminal coronary at the lights. Such till-death-us-do-part loyalty may be an admirable trait in a husband, but definitely not, in this day and age, in a car-owner.

Extraordinary, really, how *angry* awful old cars make other car-owners. "Why did that man shout at Daddy?"

"Because he's angry with Daddy for driving an awful old car."

"Why?"

"Well, some men get very angry when they see other men driving awful old cars."

"Why?" "Because they feel threatened, that's why."

"Why?"

"Oh look, darling, isn't that a sweet little squirrel over there digging up those tulips!"

Well, she's only seven, and only just getting to grips with the highly unlikely story of how babies are made, courtesy of the Althea books. Can't load her with too many absurd facts all at once, can I?

And since the blessed Althea hasn't yet written a book for seven-year-olds on "The Role of the Automobile in Twentieth-Century Castration Complexes", right now I don't feel up to explaining why some men have such an erotic relationship with a lump of metal on wheels that they can't take it down to the Dog and Artichoke for a quickie without saying, "How

"It's a letter from her lawyers. She's claiming fifty per cent of your winter nut collection."

was it for you, my darling XR3i?"

Or why such chaps seem convinced that if they sit – vroom! vroom! – behind the wheel of something big and shiny and covered with silver flashes saying Turbo, GT, 16-valve and Fuel Injection, all women over the age of consent will say to themselves, "Hey, wow, that guy must be really great in the sack!" (instead of what they do say, which is "What a pratt!")

Or why such pratts conclude that any man who, like K.'s father, not only doesn't have a car covered with signs saying Turbo *but doesn't even notice that it's covered with moss instead* – well, that such a man must, in some obscure way, be Making Mock. "Get that car cleaned!" they sometimes bellow at him as they vroom! vroom! for take-off at the lights.

They wouldn't get so angry if he were driving a clapped-out Beetle with "*Non à Nucléaire*" on the fender and sacks of bean-sprouts on the back seat – but K.'s father's driving a Ford Capri! A car invented in the first place to satisfy the average family man's penile fantasies. "Note," said the salesman we originally bought it from, "the sporty-looking power-bulge in the front." Yeah yeah, is that a power-bulge in your bonnet, or are you just glad to see me?

No, I can't explain any of that to her yet: she's still young enough to believe that grown-ups more or less have all their marbles.

Me? Oh, I'm fickle about cars, boring creatures they are, soon as they give me a whisper of trouble, I'm threatening divorce. Before I married K.'s father, I was positively promiscuous, vehicularly speaking: a stream of virginal cars came and went in my life, and after I'd had my dastardly way with them, I tossed them away like a soiled glove. I treated them like *things*; if they got moody when I forgot their oil-changes or neglected to give them a nice service on their anniversaries, I just cast them out and traded them in for another eager young model.

Didn't care about their feelings. Never thought I'd have to. But now… "But now you're sending it to the scrapyard to be *crushed* to death *the day before its twelfth birthday!*" K. wailed accusingly the other night. And no, I will *not* make the Ford a birthday cake.

"Well, the least you could do is *christen* the poor thing!"

No problem. "I name this dead car, Florence. *Requiescat* in scrapyard. Amen." Oh golly. Can it be, sniff, that I'm actually going to *miss* Florence – moss, mushrooms and all?

"There's a furry thing in here eating cheese. I understand that's your department."

LET'S PARLER FRANGLAIS!

Lesson Trois-cent-quatre-vingt
Dans le Cricket Commentary Box

1: Et nous donnons un big welcome à listeneurs dans la Hemisphere du Sud. Bonjour, everyone!

2: (*off-mike*) Bon soir.

1: Ou rather, je suis reminded, bon soir, parce que c'est night-time down under. Merci, le marvel mathematician. Et le latest news est que England sont 131 pour 5 dans leur first innings. Aujourd'hui, of course, est le 3ème jour. Leur going est un peu slowish, je crois.

3: Slowish? C'est funéral. Quand j'étais un lad, j'ai vu un film du funéral de George V. C'était très similaire à l'English batting, aujourd'hui. La seule différence était que le funéral était un peu plus lively.

1: Merci, Fred. Of course, George V était quite keen sur cricket, je crois, mais je ne sais pas s'il a jamais joué pour un first-class team. Peut-être je peux poser cette question à notre magic mathematician.

2: (*off-mike*) Encore deux balles.

1: Ah, oui, il ne faut pas oublier qu'il y a un match going on out there. Et maintenant Widley fait son run-up – et il s'approche de la crease – et il passe l'umpire – ET IL BOWLE – et Didley n'offre pas un stroke. Je crois que le bowling de New Zealand n'est pas terrifiquement menaçant, et je trouve que England sont un peu trop respectueux de leur pace attack. Fred?

3: Well, franchement, si vous désirez ma franche opinion, je crois que l'attack de New Zealand est aussi dangereux comme un outing de la Women's Institute. Et le batting d'England me fait penser à un team de waiters Italiens. Dans mes playing days pour England…

2: (*off-mike*) Voici votre update sur George V.

1: Ah! Well, by Jove, c'est très intéressant! … Just un moment, pendant que Widley bowle la finale balle de l'over à Didley … et c'est un no-ball … Well, by Jove, il semble que George V a joué dans un first-class cricket match! Apparently, sur un State Visit à India, il était présent à un match entre le MCC et le Maharajah de Julep's XI. Le Maharajah a demandé à George V de faire l'opening du bowling, et George V a délivré un entier over de six balles! Well, well, well…

3: Etait-il fast ou un spinneur, Brian?

1: C'est un secret, Fred, perdu dans le mist du temps. Incidentellement, vous dites que le batting d'England est comme un team Italien. In fact, je crois qu'il y a un petit league de cricket en Italie. Peut-être que Merlin, le memory magician peut nous informer … Et Widley délivre la finale ball de l'over … et c'est une stroke defensive, no run. Fred, si vous étiez capitaine d'England ?

3: Je donnerais le bullet au team, et puis je donnerais ma resignation aux selecteurs.

1: Bon, Fred! Fighting paroles! … Et nous recevons une lettre d'un listeneur à Bradford, qui dit: "George V était slow left underarm. Je sais parce que j'étais à Bombay, le jour du match en 1926." Well, well, well…

(*Etc, pour 5 jours.*)

LARRY
Play That Tube

The Washington Post

TUESDAY, JANUARY 13, 1987

25 cents

Reagan Comfortable After Big Squeeze

Zapped Zit No Cause For Concern Says Bethesda

from our White House Staff

The President of the United States was reported to be in top shape today following last night's successful removal from his left ear of what consultants at the Bethesda Naval Acne Unit described as a "small to medium-sized blackhead".

Perhaps the most remarkable aspect of the case was that medical authorities believe it to have been the first time that this particular operation has been performed by a First Lady working under telephone instruction. At 3 am this morning, following her emergency call to Bethesda, she was talked through the complex procedure by Surgeon-Commander Gus Kowalski, who told reporters later: "There is normally no way in which we would allow a non-specialist to attempt an operation worth eight hundred dollars to a skilled acnologist, but when the whole future of democracy hangs in the balance, sometimes you have to bend the rules."

At this morning's press conference, a smiling White House pustule spokesman declared: "God was at his earside. We wrongly assume zits, blits, shinies and the like to afflict only adolescents, but they can strike at any time. In older men, they are often brought on by Grecian Brunetto running onto an ear and setting up an infection. The First Lady acted with great presence of mind and personal courage: this is a really tacky operation, especially in the small hours. I have known top surgeons throw up."

PRESIDENTIAL TUXEDO SHOULD PULL THROUGH

Jello Stain Not Terminal Declare Experts

WHITE HOUSE TV "STABLE"

Treasury Crisis Resolved

The Oval Office TV set which gave rise to grave fears yesterday during the review of America's first trillion-dollar budget proposals is now in a stable condition, according to the Bethesda Naval Video Laboratory.

It was during the presentation of the amended defence budget that President Reagan suddenly cried out that the Flintstones had all got little fat legs. Finance Committee members immediately rushed over to his corner and began banging the set, but were unable to resuscitate it. The President then went upstairs to watch, and, lacking a quorum, the meeting was put in suspension.

A replacement set was turned down by the President on the grounds that a TV was one of God's creatures, too, and could not be tossed aside. But, after operating all night, Bethesda experts declared the set fit to continue in office for up to two years.

Following top-level consultations with mohairologists at the Bethesda Naval Stain Clinic, a White House bespokesman told a relieved press conference today that the First Tuxedo could expect a full recovery from the blob of jello that fell on its left-hand silk-facing when the President missed his mouth Sunday night.

"We have taken a smear, and the jello is definitely benign. Could be a wet rag would do it, but we cannot take any risks at this level. It is therefore our intention to perform a partial lapelectomy, removing the left one and replacing it with one from a suitable donor. Bethesda Stain has been in contact with a Mr Sam Rappaport of Orange, New Jersey, who recently lost his pants in a tragic soup accident, and it is my understanding that the material of the jacket lapels is an exact match. Thousands of stitches will be involved, but there is absolutely no reason to suppose that the Presidential tuxedo will not recover totally."

A message of sympathy from Premier Gorbachev was later dismissed by Mr George Bush as "sour apples".

What Larks!

"The menu in the window promised such Dickensian delights as Fagin's Florida, Peggotty's Pâté, Pecksniff's Prawn Burger and Chuzzlewit's Chicken."

DICKENSIAN is a word that tends to be tossed around by people who have never read the chap, when trying to describe a person or a building that is old-fashioned in a vaguely Victorian way, slightly tumbledown and generally quaint. It frequently smacks of the bogus and the pretentious and, during a discussion about an actual character or a house in a Dickens novel, seems oddly out of place.

I cannot believe, for example, that the term is lightly bandied by Dr Andrew Sanders of the Dickens Fellowship; and yet the day he and I drove down to Rochester with Mr Allanson and Miss McKenzie of Hampton & Sons to look at Restoration House, currently on their books at £350,000 and the inspiration for Miss Havisham's Satis House in *Great Expectations*, I found the word elbowing its way firmly to the forefront of my mind on more than one occasion.

Things got off to a reassuring enough start with a brief background chat by Dr Sanders on this city so beloved of Dickens, just across the Medway from his birthplace in Chatham ("Historically very important ... second oldest bishopric in England after Canterbury...one of the best Norman castles in the country...on the old Dover to London road ... top notch architecture... very good little Guildhall..." etc).

But no sooner had we turned into the High Street and been regaled with a brisk verbal vade-mecum of major Dickens landmarks (the Gatehouse where Mr Jasper and Mr Tope, the Cathedral verger, lived in *Edwin Drood*; the big clock on Sir Cloudsley Shovel's Corn Exchange – the "big eye" referred to by Pip in *Great Expectations*; Uncle Pumblechook's corn chandler's, now shared by Threshers and Mann & Co; the Swiss chalet from Dickens's garden at Gadshill, perched beside the splendid 16th-century Eastgate House – the Nun's House in *Drood*, now the Dickens Centre ...), than we found ourselves face to face with Mr Tope's Gatehouse restaurant.

Bearing lunch in mind, we peered at the menu in the window. It was divided into three culinary sections: Chapter One, Chapter Two and Chapter Three, which promised such Dickensian delights as Fagin's Florida ("Juicy grapefruit and mandarin segments, topped with cherries"), Peggotty's Pâté, Pecksniff's Prawn Burger and Chuzzlewit's Chicken ("Tender half chicken, served with or without bar-be-que sauce, a hot jacket potato or french fries and a Squeers salad").

Ah well, we smirked resignedly, there had to be one like it somewhere in the place, didn't there? After all, certain sacrifices must always be made on the altar of modern tourism. And we strolled superciliously on our way, only to realise that almost every second building houses some commercially-based tribute to the Medway towns' most famous son: Dodger's Licensed Restaurant; Fagin's Alley Antiques and Craft Centre; The Oliver Twist Belgian chocolate shop; Mr Pickwick's Restaurant...

We sighed and turned up Crow Lane between ancient walls and Nonconformist churches until we came to the gateway to The Vines – once a vine plantation, now a small public park. From there, we looked across the lane at the front elevation of Restoration House, just as Dickens must have done on June 6th, 1870 – only three days before his death – when he walked over from Gadshill with his dog to post some letters, leaned on a fence and "examined the old mansion with great care".

The house has hardly changed since he admired its handsome proportions and its gable ends, and Mr Pumblechook walked Pip up to Satis House to meet Miss Havisham. (" 'It meant,' Estella told him when he commented on the oddness of the name, 'that whoever had this house could want nothing else'.") Of the several windows that had been walled up to avoid the payment of window tax, only one remains blocked today; of the "great many iron bars" there is no sign; the courtyard is not nearly as big as Dickens described it; nor is there a large brewery to one side; nor is it the slightest bit dismal, as Pip found it. In fact, from the outside, it hardly looks Dickensian at all.

However, the voluble Londoner with the Mick MacManus physique who opened the door to us, Mr Barton ("I am the custodian here"), was custom-built for the epithet. So, too, was the inside of the house: as extraordinary a mixture of genuine antiquity and outrageous bogusness as I have encountered in a long while. Built in 1587, its name commemorates the visit on May 28th, 1660, by Charles II who took shelter there with the owner, Sir Francis Clerke, a staunch Royalist, on his way from France to London to reclaim the throne.

"It was in this very room," declared Mr Barton in the Great Hall, with a gesture that embraced the heavy oak dining-table, the pewter tankards, the medieval armour hanging on the wall above the panelling, and the Cavaliers' costumes and Roundhead helmets tossed casually over various chairs, "that the king was entertained to dinner by his brothers, the Duke of Gloucester and the Duke of York." The furniture and the set-dressings would, he imagined, be kept by any subsequent owner.

We moved on into the Oak Room where, with our backs to the Roman bust, centurion costume and fibreglass shield artistically displayed in the bay window, we admired the fireplace.

"It depicts war and peace," Mr Barton told us. "It's listed in the British Museum. Well, they all are actually."

He pointed out the two little heads carved in the oak columns on either side and said to represent the original owner, Sir Nicholas Morgan, and his exceedingly comely lady wife.

"She looks as if she's up front in the queue," said Mr Barton.

For half a century until 1977, the house was owned by one Colonel Mackie, a keen Dickens man by all accounts. The present owner is also, according to Mr Barton, "a Dickens freak". He had certainly taken great care to maintain the effect of genteel decay that hung over every room, not to say an extremely low personal profile.

"The owner does not wish to be known," Mr Barton replied to our enquiry as to his identity.

He led us out into the hall, past the half-doored Elizabethan buttery (now a ferociously Spartan loo), and up the staircase which Sir Francis built specially for the king opposite the original Elizabethan one, to the King's Bedroom. The door loomed majestically before us.

"Those are certainly the Stuart arms over the top," said Dr Sanders. "And the doorcase looks Jacobean. But the arms of Catherine of Aragon are probably late nineteenth century, the doorknocker's 1810, I'd say, and the handle's about 1960."

"Looks good, though, doesn't it?" said Mr Barton.

The highlight of the room itself was the collection of panels painted in the 1870s by the then owner, Stephen Aveling, famous for the development and production of the steam traction engine in Kent. The scenes are based on Tennyson's *Enid*.

▶

Dr Sanders said he thought it was funny to find a Tennyson room in a Dickens house. Mr Barton said he thought that gave it a royal atmosphere.

Another bedroom and a bathroom later, we were outside the Salon. Mr Barton tapped quietly on the door. "Just in case Miss Havisham's in," he told us. I wouldn't have been surprised if she had been.

Her wedding-dress was – or rather, a modern version, possibly in Bri-nylon – laid across a Victorian chaise-longue beside the fireplace. The clock on the mantelpiece, like all the clocks in the house, had been stopped at twenty to nine, and a long dining-table had been laid – whether by the colonel or by the present owner was not clear – for 16 wedding guests, including Mr Jaggers, Mr Wemmick, Mr Pumblechook, Mr William Sikes and Nancy. In the centre of the table stood a tall replica of a bridal cake, decorated with replica cobwebs and replica mice. Dr Sanders was outraged.

"But Pumblechook would *never* have been invited," he spluttered. "Miss Havisham considered him far too vulgar even to be allowed into the house."

I hate to think what she'd have had to say about that wedding-dress.

Not that a Miss Havisham, or anyone like her, ever lived in Restoration House. Indeed, as Dr Sanders pointed out, there is no evidence that Dickens himself ever set foot inside the house. Now it was Mr Barton's turn to bridle.

"How's the Psalms' title-page coming along?"

"I think it's highly unlikely he didn't, knowing Dickens," he said. "He had his nose into every nook and cranny."

And so, with Mr Barton's enthusiastic encouragement, did we. The next owner will have eight bedrooms, three bathrooms, five receps, dozens of square feet of basement and cellarage and half an acre of romantic and wildly overgrown walled garden for his £350,000 – not to mention a secret tunnel that once, so they say, ran down to the river. And by spending roughly the same amount again, he will undoubtedly finish up with not only the biggest private house in Rochester but one of the most splendid examples of its kind in the land. But somehow, it could never be quite so Dickensian again. Not quite.

"Isn't it supposed to be haunted?" Miss McKenzie enquired at one point.

"What do you mean, *supposed* to be?" said Mr Barton.

Afterwards, we walked in the autumn sunshine through the Cathedral Close, past Minor Canon Row (referred to in *Seven Poor Travellers*), and down to The Bull in search of an authentic lunch. "Good house – nice beds," was how Mr Jingle described it to Mr Winkle; but we decided that neither Jingle nor we would have felt entirely at home in The Victoriana restaurant.

So instead, we drove out to the good old Leather Bottle at Cobham (whither Tracy Tupman retired after being deserted by Miss Rachael Wardle and where the Pickwickians puzzled over the mysterious inscription on the stone), only to find ourselves sitting in the Old Pickwick restaurant, tucking into Tracey Tupman's Duck (sic), Micawber's Scallops and Mr Bumble's Sirloin, preceded by Magwitches Mushrooms, Smikes Sardines and Oliver's Soup of the Day ("Freshly made, you'll be back for more"), and thinking that some popular novelists really do have an awful lot to answer for one way and another.

FRANK MUIR
AUF WIEDERSEHEN, PETS

I MEAN, I've got nothing personal against the five assorted animals who live the life of Riley in our midst. Three cats and two dogs. Furry denizens of the furniture all day, when they're not tearing bits off it. And eating. Oh, my goodness, eating; tin after tin of the gourmet stuff as advertised and refusing even to look at commoner nourishment. Never mind. Only the best is good enough for our silent dependants. And then there are things like their flea-collars at about three quid each (most of my mind was on higher things when I first saw the notice "Flea-collars" in the pet-shop window – I found myself idly wondering how one buckled it round the neck of such a small insect...). But no begrudgement. Health before wealth.

It's just that, well, perhaps we should not allow ourselves to get too soppy over our pets. There is another side to them which, as we have no memory of pain, we tend to forget. Perhaps we should reconsider this not-so-attractive side of domestic animals, if only to remind ourselves that animals, however lovable, are only pets, while we are – well, us.

The French poet Méry once rather impressively declared (and in French, too) that a cat was God's way of allowing man to caress a tiger. A piece of sentimental twaddle, I humbly submit, only to be expected from a nineteenth-century Frenchman with a Christian name like a pop group of three garçons and a fille – François-Joseph-Pierre-Agnès. I have never, myself, personally, caressed a tiger – my arm is about twenty feet too short – but years ago at the London Zoo I once caressed a cheetah, a similar make of beast, and I can report that caressing a cheetah is like stroking a wire flue-brush. It can draw blood.

Blood is never far from the surface with cat owners. Our three cats, two Burmese and an Abyssinian, sleep in the bed with us. They have decided so to do and it is impossible to keep them out, so no moral or hygienic judgments, please; let us just say that at least they keep the foxes down. In the middle of the night cats need to stretch, so they stretch, at the same time unsheathing their little scimitars and swiping out at the nearest soft surface. I caught sight of my back recently in the bathroom mirror and I look like a steel engraving from *Foxe's Book of Martyrs*.

It is my belief that your average mog is a mass of finely-tuned instincts and sophisticated reflexes but in the matter of intelligence is as thick as a Sumo wrestler's thigh. What sort of mighty hunter can't locate its food even when you've rammed its nose into the saucer?

When there is a bit of cold chicken left over in the fridge it becomes the sole objective of our three cats to get at it. Nestles (the greediest) is the stakeout man. He sits three feet away from the fridge door, *willing* it to swing open. He will wait there for days if necessary. Cinto, the Abyssinian, is an outdoor lad so he occasionally livens up Nestles' lonely vigil by dropping in and showing him bits of an ex-mouse. Gentle, middle-aged Kettering is the peterman. Once they have decided in their minuscule brains that the remains of the cold chicken carcass is not going to leap out and surrender, nor the fridge door melt, Kettering starts work on the bottom edge of the door with a gently probing claw. The fridge is often improperly closed due to something like a £1.08 litre-bottle of Turkish Chablis keeping the door slightly ajar, and Ketters often *can* open it. But then what happens? The three Great Thinkers tip the cold chick on to the floor and then haven't the faintest idea what to do with it. It is suddenly too big, or something. It looms over them, cold, alien, and the wrong colour, nothing like *real* food, like their beloved chunks of shiny, brown meat out of a familiar tin marked "Carlton Pet Foods: 38p". So they affect indifference to the mess on the floor, yawn, blink slowly several times and stroll off.

The dogs, too, have IQs difficult to discern with the naked eye. Our scrap of black mongrel, Battersea, named after the Dog's Home from whence we sprang her, is an ingratiator. Visitors get an all-over lick, and a liquid look which says: "Take little me home with you; I am so badly looked-after here." This is true. We don't even clean her ears out for her. The first time I tried she nearly had my leg off. We take her to the vet now; he's a 16-stone New Zealander and can just hold her down if she's under a general anaesthetic (£33.50).

And as for our pedigree standard poodle, Bognor Regis: aristocratic beauty ... 10/10 marks. Sense of fun ... 10/10. Affectionate nature ... 10/10. Canine instincts ... 10/10. Brains... well, look at it this way. As I type these critical comments, Boggy is lying down under the desk keeping me company, as is her wont. She knows that I am saying nasty things about her and the other animals because I read aloud as I work. But will she do anything about it? Will she get her own back on me in some way? No, because that sort of thinking would require an understanding of cause and effect of which she, as a dog, is quite incapable.

No, she will just lie there on the carpet and continue playing innocently with the cable of my electric typewriter.

Now she has started giving the cable playful little bites, but I don't mind: to the world she may be an inferior creature of little intelligence but I will always th *ink of her as my friend.*

101

HAIL FELLOW CELL NET

NOEL FORD

"Hello, dear – just ringing you up on the train like you asked me to."

"For heaven's sake, dear, I've told you not to call me at the office."

BRRRRRRRrrrr

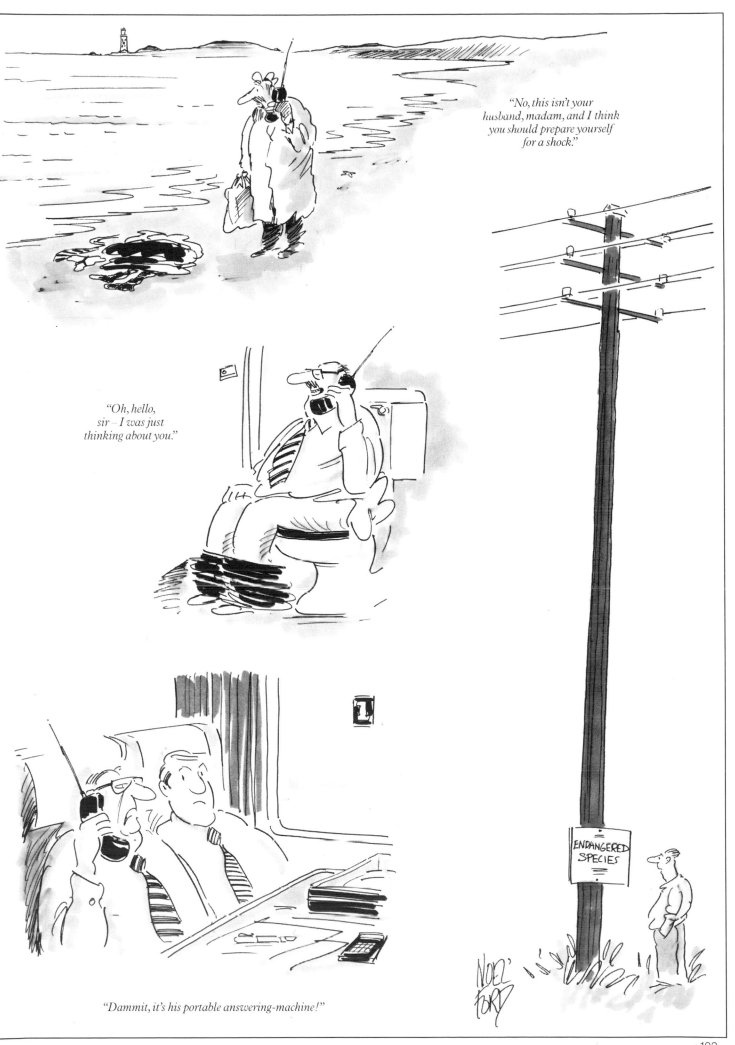

"No, this isn't your husband, madam, and I think you should prepare yourself for a shock."

"Oh, hello, sir – I was just thinking about you."

"Dammit, it's his portable answering-machine!"

ENDANGERED SPECIES

DUNCAN CAMPBELL

Hear it Not, Duncan!

FINALLY, I think, the time has come to tell the whole story of the Zircon spy satellite. Spill the beans. The entire fruits of my research. All the documents, the plans, the diagrams, the lot.

The Special Branch are hardly going to be keeping an eye on *Punch*, are they? They'll be watching the *New Statesman*, getting the binos focused on the second floor there. They're not going to get a restraining writ slapped on the editor of *Punch*, are they? What would the judge say?

Well, here goes. The Zircon spy satellite programme contains … hang on, a minute, couple of blokes moving around in the garden, wearing belted mackintoshes… they must have lost their way.

Anyway, as I was saying, what I discovered about the Zircon satellite was precisely that … now where have those blokes in the garden gone? Is that someone downstairs … What's that you say, officer? You've found a stack of documents relating to the Zircon programme … must have been a friend that left them there … Aaargh!

No. I cannot tell a lie. And those of you who started reading the above because you reckoned you were going to get the whole inside story of the Zircon business will just have to pop along to *Punch* and ask for your money back.

For there are two of us. There's the Duncan Campbell who works for the *New Statesman* and who researched the Zircon spy satellite programme and is called a traitor by Lord Chalfont, and there's the person writing this piece. If you're confused it's nothing to what it's like for us.

When the Zircon business first happened I was lying fast asleep on a winter Sunday morning. The phone rang. It was ITN. They wanted to know if I could come in and be interviewed by them. Always happy to oblige, I asked them what for.

"It's concerning the story about you in the Sunday papers," said the man from ITN.

Now there is no speedier way to wake up on a chill winter's morning than to have someone from ITN phoning you up and asking if he can chat about the story featuring you in the Sunday papers. It was like a syringe full of adrenalin in what rugby commentators refer to as the "upper thigh". It was only when the heart slowed down a bit that I realised that they wanted to talk to the Other One.

The Other Duncan Campbell arrived on the scene and on his bike in the mid-Seventies. He was a freelance journalist from Brighton and I was working at *Time Out*. Even then he had a nose for a story and he was soon shaking the twigs of the Branch.

He first hit international fame when he was arrested with another *Time Out* journalist in 1977. He had been researching a story about signals intelligence when the SB pounced. He was hoisted off briefly to Brixton prison.

I went along, naturally enough, to his appearance at Tottenham magistrates court and, as the *Time Out* news editor, spoke to the press outside about the case. Someone took my photo and it duly appeared in *The Scotsman* the following morning.

Beneath it was the caption: "Duncan Campbell before his court appearance on Official Secrets charges. His widowed mother lives in Dundee." (The local angle is always important and to caption-writers of the day at *The Scotsman* the fact that a bloke came from Dundee was almost an admission of guilt anyway.)

The photo puzzled my mother, since my father was sitting opposite her at breakfast when the paper arrived. Neighbours dropped in notes of condolence. My sister phoned from Hong Kong with an offer to stand bail. The confusion which has pursued us for ten years had begun. It has not been made any the less by the fact that both of us are journalists working sometimes in the same field, him at the *New Statesman*, me at the *London Daily News*.

Sometimes it has worked to our advantage. When the Other One was working on a story about some unpleasant mercenaries, he needed a witness to one confrontation. We both went along. "I am Duncan Campbell," he said to our quarry. "And this is Duncan Campbell." They never recovered.

I've had cheques of his – and income tax demands – and he's had telephone calls from people whom I met on a beach in Puerto Rico in 1968 and who, seeing the name Duncan Campbell in the London telephone directory, reckoned there might just be a vague chance it was the same one.

We did discuss altering names. But if we were to use initials, I would have to be I. Duncan Campbell, which sounds like a last will and testament. The National Union of Journalists, unlike Equity, doesn't stipulate that hacks must have different names when they enter the profession. Eventually we decided that the confusion had its own advantages.

"That unpleasant article about you? Oh, that must have been the *other* Duncan Campbell. Shocking business, yes, terribly confusing," we can say when we bump into someone who has been given a nasty time by either of us. I tend to remember the difference between us when I am invited to a no-expenses-paid meeting somewhere very far away; but having been along to some public meetings about Official Secrets legislation and seen the sad, wee faces when the punters realise they've got the wrong Duncan Campbell, well, I'm not going to cause any more unhappiness.

The Zircon business has, of course, started it all over again. "You look very different on television," people say. "It's a disguise," I assure them. "You can't be too careful these days."

Campaigners against obsessive official secrecy pump my arm when they meet me at parties. Keep up the good work. I nod modestly. When they try and ask about details of What It All Means I give them one of those Can't-talk-here looks.

Up in Scotland where there are many Duncan Campbells, there's no such problem. I mean, I knew a Duncan Campbell who won the tilt-the-bucket competition in the Oban Games when I was only eight and I've bumped into others ever since. But down in London people can't believe that there are two of us bouncing around in the same area. I've even had quite amicable conversations on the phone with people who think we're bosom buddies and who feel quite indignant when I say after a minute or two that I don't think we've ever met.

Last summer I played cricket for the *New Statesman* cricket team. This was taking it all too far. I used to get wickets just because opposing batsmen would be so sure that any satellite-spotter would have some damn cunning way of spinning the ball that they were transfixed to the crease. Sometimes between innings an opposing player would murmur some secret tale under his breath, clearly expecting that I would be following it up the next week.

I *know* other people have the same problem, although I don't think The Who's Peter Townshend ever really got mistaken for Princess Margaret's ex-fiancé. But it's quite comforting to have another self. When I go to football games and hear fans chanting "One Charlie Nicholas, there's only one Charlie Nicholas," I can even feel sorry for him. Take a tip, Charlie: the pressure's a lot less intense when there are two of you.

"God, I hate Sundays!"

ROBERT MORLEY
West Side Stories

"No one in America is ever quite dead in show business, which is curious considering how preoccupied the citizens are with attempts to ward off the grim reaper."

NO visit of mine to Vegas is ever complete unless I have been mistaken at least twice at the roulette wheel for Charles Laughton. No one in America is ever quite dead in show business, which is curious considering how preoccupied the citizens are with attempts to ward off the grim reaper. Health is all the rage – and, of course, wealth. The achievement of both objectives sustains, among other things, the medical and television industries.

Catching the floor show at Caesar's Palace, I found Bill Cosby (almost my favourite on Channel 4) supported by a Mr Tony Tilman. Mr Tilman is, I think, the most accomplished song-and-dance man I have ever seen: amazing grace and energy and quite extraordinarily unhandsome. All that followed was a disappointment, although Mr Cosby, who sits centre at a small table smoking a prodigious cigar in front of the tabs, did momentarily amuse me by remarking that Mr Tilman would not be so happy with his act in forty years or so. "He will want to relax and won't be able to do so."

Mr Cosby was the quintessence of relaxation and long silences as he puffed and re-lit. He spoke for nearly an hour about the problem of being over forty and being forced to give up salt, red meat, fried potatoes: everything, in fact, that he cared about diet-wise. He had been forced back on to boiled fish at the instigation of his wife, whom he quoted as saying that she wanted him around for a good time yet. Not surprising, considering what he must earn as the top TV personality at present.

He went on to discuss his children and the drama accompanying his daughters' first periods. They usually locked themselves in the bathroom and screamed that they were dying while resisting his efforts to break down the door. He dwelt inconsolably on their reluctance to leave home; no other creatures have such prolonged family ties. "Does anyone," he asked the audience, "know how long a foal is tended by the mother?" Someone suggested a few months and Mr Cosby, delighted at having his point proved, volunteered the information that turtles laid eggs in the sands and were miles away at sea when their young hatched. His own children were in their twenties, some of them anyways, and a friend had a son of thirty sharing the family nest and still apparently trying to find himself.

Cosby lamented his approaching baldness but remarked that hair was still plentiful on his backside while the hairs from his nostrils grew to enormous lengths but turned white overnight. He embarked briefly on describing his discomfort in the dentist's chair and then abruptly bade us goodnight. We were all, I think, a little disconcerted to find our hero in such low spirits. Forty dollars is a lot to pay for two gin-and-tonics, but Mr Tilman was well worth it.

For those venturing downtown I have to report that the Golden Slipper has had a marvellous face-lift and so has the airport. Both must have cost fortunes and the latter has largely banished slot-machines in favour of elegance and convenience for the passenger. Everywhere there are small and efficient bars, tended by com-

"The end one, Merlin! Back to the end."

"I simply look upon this as a logical step in the evolution of the car-phone."

▶ ROBERT MORLEY

panionable bartenders, and excellent fast-food counters with imaginative décor.

How sadly different from our own Heathrow and the lamentable converted hangar which is called Terminal Four. Here the motto seems to be: "If there are to be herds, let's herd them." Catering is the responsibility of an American firm but customers are penned in over-large cafeterias with no suggestion of personal service. Couldn't someone have gone to Vegas or Singapore and seen what airports can do if they try? Why should Heathrow always be light years behind? When I came home, the carousel broke down for half an hour because someone somewhere had punched the alarm button and no one could locate the trouble. When it finally started up once more, everyone clapped. So there is something to be said for the British way of life: at least we stay cheerful, but then we have to.

My last evening in Vegas, my son thought I finally ought to see *A Chorus Line.* "If we must, we must," I told him, but I have a horror of auditions and the clothes dancers wear when shaping up. "Don't book," I told him, "we'll walk in. They are always glad to see me." We avoided the queue and marched up the staircase labelled "Invited guests".

"What do you want?" asked the maître d', sizing up the customers, who have been known to pay to be steered down front.

"I am waiting," I told him, "to be recognised."

"I have never seen you before," he riposted.

"Then perhaps the name would help," I told him. "Robert Morley."

He consulted a list. "Your name is not here," he told me accusingly. "What's your problem?"

My child winced. "I want," I said, "to see the show."

"Then why don't you get to the back of the line?" The line was prodigious. I was about to admit defeat when someone else conceded and we were given a table and free drinks, and a moment later a very pretty girl from the PR office. Honour was restored. My children may cringe when I attempt to pull rank, but it is usually, if not always, worth the effort.

Quite one of the best restaurants in Los Angeles now is Jimmy's. Jimmy presides in person and nearly everyone kisses him when they arrive. People are always at their most gracious when waiting for a table and I was surprised by the numbers in formal suits and ballgowns. It turned out that they were attending a private party to welcome back Sammy, but not Davis; we never did find out who he was or where he'd been, although we determinedly waylaid an emerging guest to enquire. "I am just the band leader," he told us, "and I wouldn't know. We do a lot of welcome-back parties here." From gaol, perhaps.

What really mattered, I suppose, was my Dover sole, which was brilliantly filleted and remoulded so that it still resembled a fish. It was utterly delicious. Even my agent was impressed. As we left, Jimmy gave us his card – but then everyone gives you their card in America. If Jesus Christ himself were alive and well and living in California, that's what he would do, I imagine.

The lot of Las Vegas cab-drivers touches on monotony; there are two or three main roads beside the Strip, and where no casino obstructs the view of the mountains, enormous billboards serve the purpose. Fifty years ago, when I first staked my silver dollar, there were miners in steel helmets and four casinos, one at each corner of Main Street. Now there must be a hundred and four, probably more. In those days the punishment for cheating was condign: you were deposited shoeless in Death Valley. Now things are calmer. A cab-driver told me he had unusually keen eyesight and, with the aid of a small piece of mirror-glass strapped to his wristwatch, frequently caught a glimpse of the dealer's hidden card. He netted thirty thousand dollars a week, but not for long, alas. When he was discovered, the police gave him a good talking-to and put him back in the driving-seat. "Weren't you scared?" I enquired. "Shitless," he replied, "but it cured me of gambling." For all I know, it might have cured him of cheating. He was meticulous with the change. ❧

"No, it wasn't – it was Jasper who went to a zoo. Eric became a cuddly toy."

"I've got to hand it to dear Albert.
He never lets anything interfere with his work."

"Edna, I've brought the boss round for supper."

"Give over, Mr Starr. I used to be in the business myself."

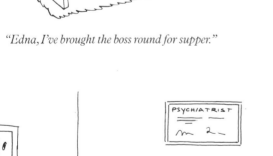

"At your age, you should be able
to express your feelings of inadequacy better."

DUNCAN

DINO, IRVING H., DENIS, ALAN

A brace of articles proving that to everyman once, or,
at least to **Alan Plater** (on your left)
and **Denis Pitts** (on your right)
Hollywood will come calling

SCRATCH a screenwriter and he'll bleed paranoia. Cross his palm with vodka and he'll hold you with a glittering, red-rimmed eye and tell tales of narcissistic actors and actresses, demented front-office hustlers desperate not to be caught out, megalomaniac producers who've already been caught out and moonstruck directors who have drunk too deeply of the auteur theory. At the heart of this bedlam is the screenwriter, sweet of soul, sovereign proprietor of integrity, beauty and truth. To be sure, it is a marginally prejudiced picture – what we call in the trade a P.O.V. (point of view) Shot – but if you want a different P.O.V. you must talk to someone with an equal and opposite vested interest.

The voyage of a screenwriter's career is charted from one abandoned project to the next. The rule-of-thumb average is one film made for every ten screenplays written and my current score is 4½ out of 19. We'll arrive at the ½ a little later. An old and valued friend, and a fine writer, once told me he was scoring 1 out of 18 but was eager to point out that his abandoned projects were for directors of very high quality – people like Joe Losey and John Frankenheimer. Here lies one of the marginal subtleties: you may win more credibility on the back lot writing a never-to-be-made film for Spielberg, than a low-budget, never-heard-of-again turkey for Irving H. Schlock.

The first producer I never worked for was a slick-talking American based in London during the late 1960s. He had bought the rights of an adventure novel of no great distinction, and was keen to turn it into a caper movie of even less. I spent a week trying to write a Film Treatment based on the book. His brief was: "Remember one thing. The universal ass cannot sit still for longer than a hundred minutes." On the Thursday, he read my fourth attempt at turning the book into an idea into a concept into a project and said, for the fourth time:

"The opening's kinda cute but it all falls apart in the middle act."

I caught the next train back to the North.

The only good thing about Irving was there was only one of him to deal with. These days even the co-producers have co-producers, and a script conference often looks like an emergency meeting of the U.N. Security Council. I once attended an indepth talk-in, prior to writing a screenplay for an Anglo-Swedish-American co-production, wherein all present gave lengthy discourses on the theory and practice of screen narrative, with special reference to the story in hand – the one about the Western Allies losing a secret weapon which is later retrieved by a lantern-jawed hero using only his fists and his, well, his lantern-jaw. Somehow they managed to talk about this for three hours before arriving at a short silence, whereupon one of them remembered I was there and asked:

"Is there anything you want to say, Alan?"

I said: "Yes. Who am I working for?"

Whether I actually said that on the day, I'm not sure, but whenever I tell the story, that's how it comes out.

Back in the real world, I had ten days to write the first draft, a long weekend's break, and another ten days to write the second draft. That brand of hectic endeavour indicates it was a Lone Screenwriter job – meaning the original writer screwed up the script, or himself, or both – where the essential message is not can you write it, but can you write it by Thursday? This puts your agent in a strong negotiating position and your talent in a no-lose situation. If the end result is even halfway decent you are given some sort of credit, and if it's another turkey you claim it was already too late anyway.

My ½ credit was a Lone Screenwriter assignment, starting with a phone call from Richard Lester and the question: "Can you rewrite a film in a fortnight?"

The way I tell the story, I replied:

"Fine, as long as I don't have to rush it."

This may not be true, but Richard is too kind a man to betray me.

The film was *Juggernaut* – a group jeopardy story, whereby well-known actors and actresses, disguised as human beings, are put in an aeroplane, an hotel, an earthquake or, in our case, a cruise liner, and bombarded with peril. Richard inherited the movie three weeks before the start of shooting when the original director departed the scene. Whether he was fired, taken drunk or mad, or disappeared up his auteur theories I never asked. My main preoccupation was writing twenty pages a day and putting them on the evening train from Hull to King's Cross, where they were met by a car from the studio. Richard and I had an hour on the telephone around midnight, crossing the "t's", dotting the "i's" and finessing with the P.O.V.'s. On the eighth day I uncrossed the eyes and rested.

Juggernaut opened, complete with an "Additional Dialogue by Alan Plater" credit no bigger than a man's hand, to tepid reviews. I am *almost* certain that I *might* have said to Richard after the premiere: "I wish I'd had another three days."

Critics being fickle creatures have since re-assessed the movie in an upwards direction, and give it a prominent place in Richard Lester's oeuvre. He's a class director and a good guy; he deserves a decent oeuvre.

Fortunately, the British film industry, despite its many renaissances – once every six weeks at the last count – is too uncertain a creature to sustain many writers in fulltime employment. We are all able to crawl away to radio, television and the theatre to nourish the soul. These are strange places to go for cleansing of the spirit, but at the very least the film industry anecdotes spice the meal-breaks in rehearsal room canteens.

Currently going the rounds is a story about Billy Wilder, who was summoned to meet a fresh-faced young executive in L.A., aged about 17, or so it seemed, he expressed great admiration for Wilder's work – he might even have called it his oeuvre – and ended by saying:

"Just to clarify things for my own benefit – could you give me a quick rundown on what films you've made?"

Wilder allowed a decent pause to settle over the office, leaned forward and said:

"You first."

The point of the story is: I bet he *really* said it.

MANHATTAN morning with thunderclouds glowering over the Hudson River. It was turning into a foul summer and I was overwhelmed by nostalgia for bitter beer and Wiltshire voices. The new book was going badly. The publisher was pressing. I was low of spirit, nearly skint and my bags were packed for England.

Then, as in the movies, the phone rang.

"Have I got news for *you*."

Charlie Abramson, my agent, a lovely old man, semi-retired now but still in fighting trim. Small and aggressive, Charlie, a sort of Jewish Jack Russell if you see what I mean.

"I'm all packed," I said.

"Well unpack, goddam it," he shouted. "We've got a movie deal. Dino loves your book. He can see it as a twelve million dollar disaster movie. Twelve million dollars! The disaster movie to end all disaster movies. And you're in for two and a half per cent. Come on over to my office. Right now."

"Dino?"

"De Laurentiis, asshole. He's big. You're going to be rich, son."

I was just about to close the hotel-room door when the phone rang again.

"Don't unpack," he said. "I've found you an apartment. You'll need an apartment. Style, son, style. It's the big time for you from now on."

It was raining hard as the famous screenplay writer walked up Madison Avenue. He was so busy trying to work out two and a half per cent of $12,000,000 that he was nearly knocked down by a cross-town bus.

He bought a cheap calculator and sat in an Irish bar and tried to work it out, except that it *was* a cheap calculator and couldn't cope with more than a measly million. He worked it out on a soft napkin with a pen borrowed from the barman: $300,000, the answer said.

The famous Hollywood screenplay writer ordered another beer, changed his mind, had a Dry Martini instead, and walked out with a silly grin on his face.

By 42nd Street, he had bought a yacht. By 50th Street, he had bought a bigger yacht and paid off the mortgage in England. By 57th Street, the famous Hollywood screenplay writer had written his Oscar acceptance speech, bought a huge yacht, paid off the mortgage, cleared his tax-debts, opened a bank account in the Cayman Islands, invited the Redfords round for drinks and was wondering whether he had enough ready cash to buy a cheap umbrella. The trouble was that he had spent the cheap umbrella money on the cheap calculator.

He was never very good with money. Clearly, he would need a good accountant.

The internationally acclaimed, Oscar-winning Hollywood screenplay writer was already planning the sequel when he reached his agent's office.

My agent was waiting anxiously in his outer office, raincoated and impatient.

"Where the hell you been?" he shouted. "I've got Dino's partner waiting at the Four Seasons. He's brought the option contract."

"I walked," I said.

"Shit," he said. "You don't walk in this city. You're big time now."

Big time was a man called Ralph Serpe who said "Hi" to me and spent the next hour talking to Charlie about the old days on the Coast and using Hollywood words like "amortize", "completion guarantee", "collateral", "cut-off point" and "leverage".

The world-renowned, internationally-acclaimed, Oscar-winning Hollywood screenplay writer ordered oysters and nodded now and again to the front office men and wondered whether he should take an hotel suite or rent a villa at the Cannes Film Festival.

"We've sent books to Greg Peck, Paul Newman, Robert Redford and Gene Hackman," said my new friend, Ralph. "It's a great part for Gene – but he hates leaving home. Guess we can't set the book in LA?"

"It *is* about the Mayor of New York," I said. "And the whole action takes place in the worst blizzard of the century."

"Sure," said Ralph. "But I happen to know that Gene is looking around for a good script. No way we could change location?"

"Does it ever snow in California?" I asked, showing willing.

"Forget it, kid. New York it is. Bob Redford will love it, all that conservation crap."

I was about to say "Eh?" but didn't. The book was about an evil computer.

"And Paul Newman lives just up the road.

Hell, he'd love to play the mayor." He turned to Charlie. "Okay, Charlie, so what's the deal?"

They started talking about options and percentages and I was lost again.

The universally-admired, world-renowned, Oscar-winning Hollywood screenplay writer smiled knowingly at the jargon-talking money men and let Racquel Welch take the helm while he went below to open another bottle of Veuve Cliquot and search out the chart for Acapulco.

"Can't wait to read the treatment," said my new friend, Ralph, as he crushed my hand. "See you on the Coast."

"Can't wait to see Greg or Paul or Bob in the movie," I said entering into the spirit of it all.

Ralph went uptown. We went downtown. "Where's the contract?" I asked Charlie in the taxi.

"Don't worry," he said. "It'll be in the post. Five thousand dollars option against two and a half per cent of the budget plus you write the first draft of the screenplay for a further seventy-five thousand plus I've got you six profit points. That's six per cent of what Dino gets. You're rich, son – come and see the apartment I've rented for you."

It was a superb apartment on Central Park South, the kind of bachelor pad that Frank Sinatra had in *The Tender Trap*.

My new friend, Ralph sent me $2,500 to cover the cost of the treatment. I wrote it off and waited.

And waited.

Charlie was philosophic. "Take it easy," he said. "These things take time." The apartment was swallowing up the dollars at a fearful speed.

Two weeks later, he called again.

"Greg Peck loves the book," he said. "Dino's going for Sophia Loren."

"What about the option money?" I asked.

"Don't push Dino now," he said. "Just hold on. Be patient."

Two months later, the former universally-acclaimed, world-famous, Oscar-winning Hollywood screenplay writer took his seat in the standby economy-class bucket-shop Air India night flight and wondered whether he had enough money for the bus from Heathrow to Reading. ❧

"We're auditioning for the Jericho gig."

ROGER WODDIS
Is Poetry Dead?

The Muse was sick (don't tell me – there were nine;
   This was the sister panting poets seek,
Euterpe who inspired the lyric line),
   And now she lay, a pallor on her cheek
That made her look, not less, but more divine.
   Then someone said, "If only she would speak!"
And from the poets gathered round her bed
A cry of anguish rose – "Is Poetry dead?"

They were all there, the great ones of the past,
   Byron and Browning, Shelley, Keats and Will,
Alfred, Lord Tennyson who stared aghast
   At Wordsworth playing with a daffodil.
Then in the silence Shakespeare said at last,
   "Methinks the maid is only slightly ill –
Look at her breathing," and they craned to see
Her heaving breast. That's when they turned to me.

They seemed to think (though why I cannot say)
   That I could somehow help the ailing goddess.
"As one of those still practising today,
   Here is your source of inspiration, Woddis –
How can we get the Muse to last till May?"[1]
   "Just let her breathe. She wears too tight a bodice."
Far from a desperate struggle to survive,
Poetry today is very much alive.

And thus was launched, to prove these words were true,
   The campaign angled to appeal to all,
Including streams of verse at Waterloo[2]
   And princely pieces at the Albert Hall.[3]
And while you're waiting in the patient queue,
   Look at the graphic writing on the wall.
A fanfare, then, for those who had the sense
To organise such fabulous events.

And yet I hear you cry, "Oh, deary me!
   I don't think I'll attend a single session.
To be quite frank, it's not my cup of tea:
   These weirdos wallowing in self-expression
Are nauseating to the nth degree."
   It's true that verse can cause severe depression
And fill the hapless hearer with alarm,
But poets on the whole do little harm.

Some modern stuff *is* hard to understand,
   And there are certain poets, to be sure,
Who flaunt their egos; on the other hand
   Not every would-be Thomas is obscure,
Although if they were working on the land
   Their crops would profit from the rich manure.
Yet publishers[4] of verse are not dismayed,
And bookshops[5] seem to do a roaring trade.

Some weary readers frequently complain
   That what confronts them doesn't rhyme or scan;
They look for subtle craftsmanship in vain
   And rarely finish what they once began.
Verse can be blank, but metre, it is plain,
   Divides the winner from the also-ran.
The crippled beat, the line that never flows,
If life were fair, should bear the name of prose.

But there are many poets writing now,
   Whose individual voices are so rare,
Their love of life so deep, we wonder how
   They make a case for personal despair.
We can but kneel before the laurelled brow,
   Denying that the Emperor is bare.
Those who refuse to praise them we define
As Gertrude's younger sister, Phyllis Stein.

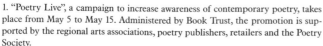

We are a cultured race, and more than most
   We turn to verses in our hour of need
To give us strength – or so we like to boast,
   Though sudden death is what we mostly read.
But still a loyal public is engrossed
   In deathless lines that meet an inner need.
And thus the Muse will stay alive and well,
And fatter grow, the more slim volumes sell.

1. "Poetry Live", a campaign to increase awareness of contemporary poetry, takes place from May 5 to May 15. Administered by Book Trust, the promotion is supported by the regional arts associations, poetry publishers, retailers and the Poetry Society.
2. On May 5, 6 and 7 there will be rush-hour poetry readings on Waterloo Station (from 5 p.m. to 7 p.m.), organised by W. H. Smith and the Poetry Society. Over one hundred readings and other events are planned across the country, including a Poetry Picnic in Manchester (May 10) when The Longest Poem in the Universe will be created under the auspices of North West Arts.
3. On May 12 Irina Ratushinskaya, the Russian dissident, will be among poets reading at the Albert Hall. Her first public reading in this country will be at the Newcastle Playhouse on May 5.
4. For a selection of spring poetry titles, see the reviews by Douglas Dunn and Carol Rumens on pp. 37, 38.
5. According to W. H. Smith, poetry is the second fastest growing area of the book business, after alternative medicine/health/cookery.

> **"For an independent country, the Gambia is possibly the most dependent in the world, having achieved self-sufficiency only in peanuts."**

CLEMENT FREUD

In and Out of Africa

Wednesday

Left airwick gatport at 11 a.m. and arrived at Bathurst, capital of the Gambia, five hours later. Local time is same as ours.

In May 1825 a ship arrived at Bathurst with 199 Britons posted to join the Royal Africa Corps. Since there was insufficient accommodation, only 108 of them landed, the rest remaining on board ship. By the end of the rainy season 87 of the landed recruits had died and, since this made more room, the remaining 91 disembarked and within three months 73 of those were dead.

We on the Thomson Holidays tour fared much better: 273 of us left and, with the exception of Elaine Trumpington, all returned to England. The guide, who thought perhaps la Trump had booked an extra week, posted her missing.

Thursday

Sun shone very brightly. Went on beach. Many Gambian gentlemen came up and said, "Hello. I am your friend. You staying one week or two?" Unlike most Third World nationals, Gambians do not try to sell you anything; rather do they offer their services as local expert, financial consultant, "hire me and I'll keep the other putative advisers and consultants away."

The Gambia is long and thin; on a map it looks like a chipolata sausage protruding into Senegal on the west coast of Africa. For an independent country, it is possibly the most dependent in the world, having achieved self-sufficiency only in peanuts. All else, including us tourists and them hotel managers, are imported.

Friday

Could have gone on a tour called "African Experience" or one called "Creek Trip". Decided to stay on beach. Weather dusty: "the sand from Mauritania". Had lunch in Atlantic Hotel, al fresco. Played tennis. Ricked ankle. Limped for rest of holiday. Dinner in Chinese restaurant called Yellow Gate. Had Nos. 25 (because it was Christmas Day), 42, 44, 51 and 55. Played Trivial Pursuit and man at next table got most answers right. He is a doctor at Medical Research Council and a footballer. Promised to watch him play on Saturday and donate to him baked ham which I took for emergency provision.

Saturday

Mauritanian sand still in sky where sun ought to be. Emma got bitten by mosquitos during night and hand swelled. Doctor's wife is a nurse and provided antihistamine cream. Watched football on a field on which one would hestitate to graze a goat. Doctor only white man among two teams, opponents of MRC being Air Gambia playing in British Caledonian white T-shirts. Stars of game were the two coaches who shouted any one of four slogans from touchline: "Face the ball!", "Man each!", "Attack! Attack!" and "Referee blind man!" On balance, nil-nil draw fair result. My ankle is worse.

Played clock golf with Matthew and found two French letters on fifth hole. No Aids in Gambia; just condoms.

Sunday

Day began grey and warm and sun came out at 1.30 p.m. Went into Banjul which is now name for Bathurst and tried to find some palm wine. My companion, senior Government Muslim with two wives, knew palm wine parlours existed but could not recommend. How strong is palm wine? Depends on whether it is one day old or older; apparently the stuff gets stronger by the hour. Had dinner in restaurant where most things were off; I had *salade niçoise*. Tunny fish was very off. Played family bridge, then gin rummy, then took malaria pills and slept v. well.

Monday

Ate some ham before taking remainder to Doctor; ham clearly ready to be given away with note saying: "Re-bake in medium oven for two hours with cupful each of brown sugar, rum and pineapple juice." Our room lady is called Oumy and is wife No. 2 to a man whose wife No. 1 has seven children, six of them sons. Oumy does not like No. 1 wife. Oumy has merely four children, only two of them sons. Emma hates Oumy's No. 1 wife and takes Oumy's address so that she can write to her.

We have dinner given for us by Minister of Tourism and other high dignitaries at Senegambia Hotel. Plate and cutlery are gold. Service immaculate. Table decorated with amazingly carved vegetables, such as carrot sculpted to look like sweetcorn, beetroot in shape of rose. Minister talks of his two wives and eleven children. Each day he has five or six constituents who come from up country and stay with him because he is their MP. I tell him no problems like that representing Isle of Ely.

How do they know whether you will be with your No. 1 or your No. 2 wife? The Minister said that this was no problem; his two homes are only six kilometres apart. On the way back we are stopped by a Christmas procession. I pass a five dolasi note through the gap at the top of the driver's window; he tries to open it wider and turns the handle the wrong way. I now limp on my right ankle and have an impaired left hand.

Tuesday

Many people in Gambia are called N'Jie. You call the men Mistern Jie and the wives Missessen (*pause*) Jie, which is harder. The sun shines absolutely brilliantly all day and we get v. brown and wonder how brown we would have got had it not been for the sand from Mauritania. As we are on half-board and receive meal tickets, hardly any of which we use, I bargain with the Austrian hotel manager and get four lobster cocktails for twelve meal tickets. Matthew has found a man called Merv who plays backgammon. Matt wins and collects enough to buy a vodka and orange. We continue playing bridge (Emma likes No Trumps best). I kill a cockroach the size of a soup-spoon.

Wednesday

All along the beach the local advisers are practising their hype. "Hello, my friend. What is your name? Are you staying one week or two?" Wednesdays are all-change days – 273 new people are expected. We have a Highland Springwater with the manager, who organises transport for us to the airport. Thomson Holidays man escorts us to VIP lounge which has clearly not been used for some months. Two cleaners are hastily dusting down the tables and some agreeable birds have nested in the ceiling. The sun which shone brightly in the morning is obscured by dust from Mauritania, so one feels better about leaving. The flight is punctual and for the meal we get stew and a roll and Bel Paese and a Bakewell tart – jolly good really. Then an hour before landing they come round with forms on How You Enjoyed Your Holiday in 72 questions. One of them was "Would you go back?" We thought on the whole, yes, though we just might try Mauritania.

"Ronald and I have discovered this marvellous little bistro just around the corner. We often mispronounce everything and they never seem to mind."

"At least he's probably too shaky
to hit the button."

"So what was it like in the Reagan
administration?"

"They colourise old black and white movies, so why
can't they do it to him?"

BAD DAY

"Gee, fellas, thanks for asking me back!"

"I remember when ticker-tape was ticker-tape."

"Nice to see he's still got friends."

LIBBY PURVES

Coronet Among The Corks

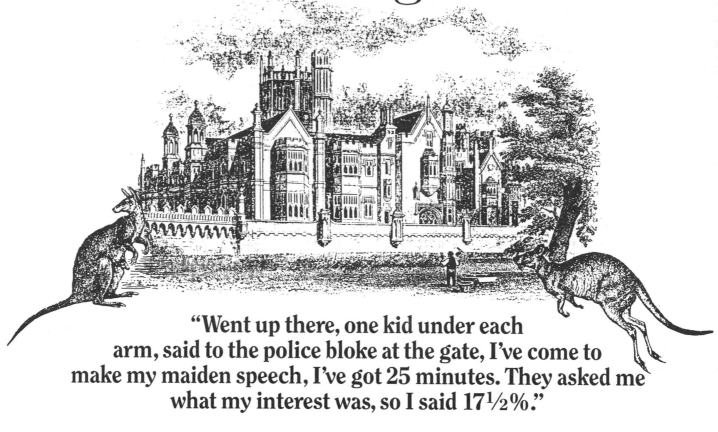

"Went up there, one kid under each arm, said to the police bloke at the gate, I've come to make my maiden speech, I've got 25 minutes. They asked me what my interest was, so I said 17½%."

THE middle-aged party stumped into the Earl's dining-hall, and stared at his crested chairs. A wild-haired Irish-woman lilted "Welcome to Henham House," and took a quid apiece off them. "Is there a guidebook?" boomed the senior male tourist. "Well, no, we've not had the time. We're only open a week."

"Quick decision, wasn't it? This opening the house?" said the man sceptically. Anna from Wexford waved her hands lyrically. "Ah, that's the sixth earl for you. A man of quick decisions." The senior female tourist broke her silence. "*I've* just made a decision. I'm never having a dark green carpet." Around her feet, noticeable as scurf, lay fragments of white petals from the rose-tree at the door.

"We Hoovered this morning," said Anna, descending sharply from poesy. And to me: "We've been up to our eyes, organising cream teas and unpacking the didgeridoo collection. It was held up in Customs." She led her party off to inspect a model of the proposed Humphrey Repton Park, a gallery of cross-looking Countesses in painted ballgowns, and some glossy snaps featuring Winston Walberswick Rous, aged ten weeks, twelfth child of the sixth and current Earl of Stradbroke. Left alone in the hall with the sun streaming in from the park, I was just reading the family crest on the door, *Je vive en espoir*, when a tall man in a bush hat loped through it. "Stradbroke," he said. "Call me Keith."

You will forgive me if I digress. I have to explain that if you happen to live along the Suffolk coastal strip, within gossiping distance

of the Henham Estate, such an encounter is tantamount to meeting J.R. Ewing in the supermarket car-park. The life and times of Keith Stradbroke, even as reported in that sober organ the *East Anglian*, have built a legend. When the fourth and fifth earls died within a few days of one another in 1983, and the title fell on an Australian sheep-farmer with a vast fortune made by debt collecting and missing persons bureaux; when the said Australian turned out to have eleven children and a sensational divorce astern of him (23 co-respondents), and appeared with the lot of them (children, not co-respondents) in sleepy Wangford to spend a year camping in a broken-down rectory, heating the bath-water in a gigantic galvanised tank mounted over a wood-fire, and fighting a bizarre lawsuit for possession of his land, it was unnecessary for local newspapers to do anything but report it all with a straight face. Any neighbouring *bourgeois* not yet *épaté* was neatly swept into the legend by the announcement, in quick succession, of projects for the recovered estate: a Sunday market, a nudist camp, an Australian zoo, a life-size model of Captain Cook's ship *Endeavour* and a giant ski-slope. Round here, if you see a headline like NO ONE IN VILLAGE WOULD NOTICE 300 NUDES, SAYS EARL you know, straight away, which Earl.

But it was the advertisements, for me, which brought him to life. There was the one for a nanny who would receive a bonus of a thousand Australian dollars if the Countess became pregnant; there was the invitation-to-tender for the construction of a memorial stone to his

wolf-hound Reigel (deported after savaging too many pheasants) with the legend *The 6th Earl of Stradbroke, Countess Roseanna, and 11 Stradbroke/Rous children wish Reigel many good Roo hunts and successful mating with female wolf-hounds.* Then, dull months later, suddenly down among the agricultural small-ads, one would glimpse a mad exotic bloom; and families would gather round to read another Henham bulletin opening:

All the tenders listed below are of course subject to Council permission and your English laws etc.
I require some good bushmen with local knowledge of conditions...

Finally, three weeks ago, came the irresistible invitation:

THE 6TH EARL OF STRADBROKE
(but call me Keith!!)
The Aussie Earl invites you to visit "Henham House" and beautiful gardens. The famous Aussie Bushburner ancestors, heirlooms from the early 14th century, model of the Repton Park and Space Age Hall.
CREAM TEAS – GROTT SHOP
CONSERVATION AND FERTILITY
AT ITS BEST!!!
HAVE A BEAUT DAY – Regards – Keith.

So I came, and by luck, his Lordship himself was over from Sydney. He normally costs a thousand quid an hour for interviews, but waived all charges for *Punch*. We passed through the Grott Shop, which sells souvenirs, ships in bottles and antique clocks largely because Anna the guide deals in them. She first struck up a friendship with Keith over her stall at his doomed Sunday Market. The sensible middle-aged local couples swivelled their eyes in polite English fashion at Stradbroke's leather bush hat. There was a definite sense of relief in the air; at last the maverick absentee squire was doing something as comprehensibly Earlish as opening his house and flogging cream teas. Give the man a chance, they seemed to be saying. He'll understand what's what, how to behave, join the county.

Oh no he won't. I had feared that the author of the surreal newspaper ads for bushmen had been working on his image as an Antipodean Uncle Matthew for years, practising for the big moment when he would shake Suffolk rigid. But no. He was surprised. "I thought the old fourth Earl would breed kids. After all, my Dad was sperming kids till he was 77, he left me five illegitimate ones. We sperm a lot of kids, Stradbrokes. So I didn't think I'd inherit." As for the county, he has not even noticed it. And not one of the wild tales or outré projects reported of him has been meant as a joke. The local rumour that his son Wesley, aged 11, attempted to start a pig farm is perfectly true. "Wesley's a very smart bloke. He wanted something to do, to make some money. I was rabbitting for money when I was six." The nudist deal fell through because they wanted a 20-year lease. The ski-slope was serious, at the time, as was the replica ship; the 50-bedroom glass mansion on the estate has got to the model stage, and the sheep-farming is under way, with local bushmen. A conservation project is taking shape, because that is his new idea; the Australian museum is growing as fast as Anna can unpack the didgeridoos.

Wild, light blue eyes glittered at me over his mug of tea. "I had a peculiar childhood. I couldn't read or write until I was about fifteen. Granny wrote to me on my fifth birthday saying, 'Dear Keith, you are now the head of the family, here is one guinea, put it in your war bonds.' Same every birthday, but never enclosed the guinea. I don't have to keep Henham. I could sell it tomorrow." But he keeps it. It's a challenge. He has a fax machine in the corner near the scones. "I'm a commission man. I'm about profit. The thing tells me my Sydney office is making a profit and my English office – this lot – isn't. It's going to." He stared moodily out at his pretty, derelict acres.

It is odd, it *must* be odd, to emerge from a family of alienating inbred weirdness, get kicked out of Harrow, build yourself an uncomplicated fortune in a hot new land – only to be clobbered from across the seas by a chilly, failing estate, a press of merciless taxes and an unsought title, bestowed by a subtle and decadent old country which has the nerve to think that *you* are the oddity. He thinks we are.

"England has lost the pioneering spirit. Rich kids get spoiled and poor kids cheat on the dole. Now *I* give my kids two cents at age two – right – my son Henham gets two cents. For that he does the washing-up. At three, he gets three cents. At five they all get an allowance and buy their own clothes, and if the shoes don't fit they go barefoot. They all know damn well I will not pay for college and university and Sloane Ranger courses. They can pay their own way. Take my daughter, Ingrid, okay, she's a model, but she can still slaughter four sheep and cut them up before breakfast, any morning. Now the coal

strike –"

Since you ask, he did attempt to take his seat in the House of Lords. "Went up there, one kid under each arm, said to the police bloke at the gate, I've come to make my maiden speech, I've got 25 minutes. They asked me what my interest was, so I said 17½%. Turned out they meant what would I speak about, so I said, the coal strike and dole cheats. So the bloke says, sorry, milord, we need your father's death certificate and your birth certificate and your mother's marriage certificate – *thirty certificates* in all." He gives the short, bitter laugh of a man who has been looking for certificates for so long that the coal strike has ended. "Even then they want me to talk about marshes or some non-controversial bird or something. Well, I won't.

I'm an Earl, all right, but I'm different."

Outside in the sunshine, beneath the white roses, wild-haired Anna is weaving a soft inaccurate Irish spell, trying to make him not so different. "Wouldn't it be nice," she dreams, "if there was a family legend, now. For the American visitors. We could have a white hart that appears in the park there whenever one of them is going to die, now that would be grand..."

I am strangely uplifted. On the way to my car, Keith and I plan a lucrative horse show, a nature trail, and the reopening of the sad secret byways of Henham. I am two miles up the road before I remember that I never asked him whether he got the memorial built to the dog Reigel. The one who turned out, in the end, to be too wild to live in England. 🖤

"Want to know what the museum shelled out for this Rembrandt? Take a wild guess and then add a million."

HANDELSMAN FREAKY FABLES

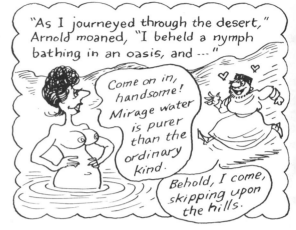

116

RUSSELLMANIA

This month Ken Russell's latest film, *Gothic*, will receive its London premiere. **Melvyn Bragg** tells of an earlier horror story when he wrote Russell's first talkie.

I WROTE Ken Russell's first talkie. Do I duck? Is that a dagger I see before me? It was about Debussy, made for *Monitor*, got me into the most violent professional row of my life – with the late Sir Huw Wheldon – and kicked up the stink usually reserved as an order of merit for a "committed" play. This was in 1964 before an impressive percentage of *Punch* readers were born. To begin, then, at the top.

Ken Russell's earlier film on Elgar – in 1962 – had made him the Sixties' darling. British television's riposte to the accusation that all the *real* celluloid art was in the cinema and made in France. Here was work in the British documentary tradition which recruited the new but punchy forces of Arts Programming and shot this through with a cutting to music which could be and *was* called "poetic". To budding Beginners like myself and all the others who had suddenly fallen for foreign films and wanted to be "Auteurs" as well as authors, the prize seemed within reach. We would not have to go through the impenetrable looking-glass to the unimaginable dream factory of Hollywood – we could do it right here on the BBC road. Russell was that much of an inspiration.

Monitor had a lot of Profs and back room boys, a touch of Biggin Hill and Heath Robinson about it in those days and when Russell asked me – a trainee, a secret, compulsive but unpublished novelist – to write a film script – my first script – I said yes and front office did not demur. Front office was usually out on location.

I decided to be quite miffingly original and bold and Ken would do the rest. We would make a film within a film! Hey-ho. Vladeck Sheybal, just arrived in England from Poland where his screen performances had been wonderful, would "play" the director: Oliver Reed would be Debussy. The advantage of the double-backing was that we could use a commentary voice (which is vital for a short biopic if it is to have any informational value at all) but the voice would belong to an active participant in the story. Moreover, it allowed you to be highly selective, cut scenes short if you needed to and generally move fast.

Ken added enormously to the script. Scenes where I had pencilled in "Music from La Mer" would become a ravishing sequence of images of the sea seen – this was his gift – in a way you felt it had never been seen before. Where I had hinted, he spoke out – and so we had the first striptease to classical music on the BBC – a striptease so innocent by later standards that, as I remember it, the girl ends up rather overdressed for Hot Gossip or Pan's People. But for its time – just a split second pre-Swinging London – it was shocking!

Curiously enough, that was not the main fight we had with Huw Wheldon – who was at that time Head of the BBC Arts Department. His objection was to the principle of using actors in what was an arts documentary strand, to impersonate artists. Where was The Truth? Where was the Authority? In drama-documentary work and in "faction" up to Blunt the argument has gone on. We had to prove – and we did – that every spoken fact and shown incident was based on a sound source. Only then did he "let it through" but there had been blood on the cutting room walls. "The Debussy Film", unlike Elgar, split both audiences and critics. We followed that with a charming film – Ken at his nouvelle vague best – on the Douanier Rousseau – using a real live Yorkshire Primitive Artist as the painter.

The film we wanted to do as a feature was Nijinsky. He was a man whose diaries had fascinated me in the same way as those of Van Gogh. I suppose to someone stuck fast in the provinces, those ejaculations of pain seemed the true cries of the pure artistic soul: and perhaps they were. Ken had spent part of his extraordinary early career (naval cadet, Wilfred Pickles' personal photographer) as a ballet dancer in Sweden. Between us we covered the field.

What *was* important, I think, was that, in the *Monitor* films, Ken had found a way to tell a story of artists' lives through their work. Especially the lives of those to whom music was integral. He could film and later cut to music in a way then unique, much copied since but never, I think, bettered. I was intrigued by the lives of romantic artists: Nijinsky's drama, his liaison with Diaghilev (and the ease with which that dovetailed into the Stravinsky ballets) the wrench of his marriage, the long madness and those diaries attempting to articulate the inexpressible – meat and drink!

Harry Saltzman was to produce it. We worked out a shooting schedule which gave us everything we wanted and still came in way under the median line. (Partly because Ken and I were fatally enthusiastic and inexperienced and came at a knock-down price.) Christopher Gable, a fine dancer who had just scored a great acting hit in his debut in Ken's "Delius" TV film, was to play Nijinsky. We went to Spain and got all the locations. Huw Wheldon, no less, liked the script. We were up and about when – crash. It was decided that Nureyev should be Nijinsky. After that the saga began for everyone else, stopped for me: and, eventually for Ken. Other writers, other directors, the usual fudge and eventually, almost 20 years later, the film which I never did go and see.

I think that the "Nijinsky" experience wounded Ken. He was very enthusiastic about the idea, the cast, the music, the script, the originality of attempting a major and serious feature on such a subject without sensationalising it. Post Nijinsky, I think, he decided that he had to gee it up if he was to get his type of artist biopics on to the screen. Or he had to take an unsuitable budget – just to get it done – and shoot much faster than served the subject's best interests. Most importantly, though, he decided – sometimes with interesting, sometimes with patchy results – that the only way to take on this "outside" – feature-film, Hollywood – world was to take care of everything himself. The BBC had given him a cocoon. He ate his way through it but found little nourishment outside. And it could be frightening out there – Ken was and remains a compulsive film-maker: not to be shooting or preparing or editing a film is not to be tolerated.

►

"Who ordered the large Pernod?"

▶ MELVYN BRAGG

This began to come into focus on the Tchaikovsky film – *The Music Lovers*. There are parts of that – the letter song for instance – which are among the best things he has done. Other sequences – Richard Chamberlain and Glenda Jackson copulating hysterically in a rollocking train on their honeymoon – which were memorable, some thought indelible. Ken began to invent on the spot, to develop a philosophy which equated the fun of doing something with the quality of the finished product. It could work. It could be dangerous.

He also began to draw his own barricades around him increasingly. His then wife, Shirley, had always made the costumes: now his children began to appear regularly in the films and he developed a company of enablers and players whom he wanted to take around the country like a tribe of gypsies. Caravans were bought. More importantly, though, he decided that the only way he could get his vision or his way on the screen was by doing more and more himself. His knowledge of camera techniques already gave him a grip on the "look" of the film: the pace was generally dictated by music he himself had selected: now he moved into the script. Not only to re-write: not only to allow for suggestions and improvisation on the set – but as a place to key in his own obsessions. Like many a writer of the last 40 years, Ken saw and still to some extent sees his own personal feelings as an indicator and exemplar of the age: their force in him compelled him to express them to others.

And so for many years I bid farewell to Ken as he set off on a journey which he wanted to take alone. Had he taken it within British television I think it would have been easier for him, made more impact and gained him an enormous following. As it was, he took in the feature film world which meant that he had to take on *Them* exhaustingly. He retaliated, often, with the outrage of bad taste and the discomfort of sexual and religious violence. There was something of a frenzy in him, I think, which made him wild.

We joined up again recently when he did an enchanting and original film on Vaughan Williams for *The South Bank Show*. On severely limited resources, he delivered a film full of "moments" and marvellous insights into that composer. Ursula – Vaughan Williams' widow – helped and "starred" in it. Much of what she said was, if not the shooting script, then at least the theme and he benefited, I thought, from the second voice. Odd how things come full circle. As editor, I had to see it through the final cut: there was a little blood on the walls there, too. But he is working for *T.S.B.S.* again and yet again has turned up with something curious, full of energy, unique.

So far Ken Russell's career has been the oddest, the most erratic, the most fertile and the most personal in British film history. I will be very surprised if, in a few years' time, we do not see queues along the South Bank waiting to get into a retrospective season of the unique K.R. ❧

"It's an emergency. He thinks he's a psychiatrist."

MI5 "DIRTY TRICKS" SHOCK!

The sinister questions which must be answered as more classified photographs are revealed by former agents rushing into print

EXHIBIT A

An Oxford academic (PICTURED "SOMEWHERE ON THIS PAGE") known today as "The Chancellor", was able to gain access to the inner-most circles of government during the political turmoil of the 1970s, a former MI5 doorman says in his controversial memoirs, believed to have been seized by Special Branch. This shadowy figure was referred to as "The Home Secretary", it is alleged, but he was never shown, nor did he ever order an investigation of certain outrageous photographic evidence which many now claim never existed (BELOW).

This startling exposé, which under the Official Secrets Act cannot be revealed without an Australian court order, shows unprecedented scenes of debauchery, skulduggery and insider dealing as a dissident faction within MI5 ran amok "off its own bat" during the 1976 Labour Party Conference in what is now believed to have been an ill-fated attempt to destabilise a Bulgarian attaché who had stumbled on plans to develop the Sri Lankan atom bomb and was prepared to sell them to Hanoi.

Who was the sharply-dressed, dapper young man (LEFT, BUT EXTREME RIGHT) known only as "M" and what was he hiding behind his back when in 1974 he stood beside a man claiming to be "Prime Minister" and another shadowy figure, possibly masquerading as the covert Australian subversive, code-named "Clive James"?

Espionage expert Dobermann Pinscher claims the photo was a clandestine set-up masterminded by Israeli intelligence in a bid to discredit British made-to-measure tailoring and cause job losses, or may have been part of a wider plot by MI5 to try and frighten the Irish into believing key members of the Cabinet shopped off the peg in Moscow.

EXHIBIT B

A hitherto unpublished photograph (LEFT) of the so-called "sultry mole" at the Foreign Office who in 1972 is alleged to have made contact with the NUM, offering to bring down the Heath Government by talking noisily in Russian on Brighton station, with a compromising score of *Toccata and fugue* and saucy pictures of the PM topless during Cowes Week (RIGHT). At least six former MI5 agents have now written her biography, claiming she was drowned whilst mining the entrance to Goose Bay, almost certainly on behalf of Druze factions believed to have infiltrated the Cape Town offices of the then CIA.

EXHIBIT C

EXHIBIT D-NOTICE

"You do lovely needlepoint, grandma, but…"

ALAN BRIEN
At Creak-Two-Swans

**"Even if they close their eyes, as I do
from time to time, they must surely find the beasts of the field
sound to their ears every bit as raucous and mechanical as the beasts of the
terraces, the discos, the cross-Channel steamers, the Stock Exchange,
or the House of Commons backbenches?"**

I T is spring. Two swans creak by, very low, very slow. They barely surface above the sill of our new, Cineramic, curtainless, bedroom window where five panes, the size of bath-tubs, are lined up in a row.

I used to think that mothy, cardboard-and-plaster bird which traditionally traversed the stage during productions toured by third-rate, passing for second-rate, ballet companies of my youth must be the epitome of theatrical artifice.

For us culture-Hooverers in the provincial gallery, it was even more insecurely suspended than our disbelief, especially since we had a privileged view of the bald heads of the stage-hands who worked its jerky wires.

Now, after prolonged exposure recently to the living world of the British countryside, I realise that our swans, like so many other of our wild creatures, are frequently as bad as they are painted.

Take this dingy pair whose grey cement colouring would not pass Miss Haversham's window test, wilful Brand X users refusing to swap for Daz if I ever saw them. Their performance at dawn is totally unconvincing. I mean, the wings are Copydexed mock-ups of job-lot feathers on plastic backing such as might have been knocked together by a DIY tyro who gave up early. They move far too wearily and hesi-tantly to sustain genuine heavier-than-air flight. Their noise is mechanical and man-made, some primitive, failing water-pump sobbing for a bead of oil. I could fell the coconut-shy pair, as they cruise from one hillside pond to another, skimming the chimneys, with a single tennis ball.

And yet, these Heath-Robinson devices work. Swans *can* fly! Their machinery is in much better nick than many of the dawn-stricken motors which whirr-whirr-whirr into all our dreams at first light.

What I have learned is that the rural/urban split is by no means as dramatic and severe as people on the far sides of its boundary imagine. My *aubade* continues. After the rusting swans, the tuneless chorus of the birds, laughably described as singing by those who must still be playing Nelly Melba on old 78s. A dedicated non-killer of anything that isn't human, parti-cularly pardoning the nastiest-looking squashy insects on my path, I confess to murderous impulses targeted on those of our avian enemies who feel they must raise such pointless din every day simply to greet the sun. I cannot accept this possesses any aesthetic quality. The nearest equivalent seems to be exceptionally vengeful guests or hirelings doing the washing-up and getting as near to smashing the fragile china ornaments and best crystal glasses as they dare. *Chink, clunk, squeak, scrape, shiver, clank, screech!* I'd rather tape a blunt fork on wet glass.

Next, the farmyard awakes. No wonder Mr Noah took to drink! How're you gonna keep 'em down on the farm, after they've seen the farm?

Even if they close their eyes, as I do from time to time, they must surely find the beasts of the field sound to their ears every bit as raucous and mechanical as the beasts of the terraces, the discos, the cross-Channel steamers, the Stock Exchange, or the House of Commons back-benches?

The donkey brays. It's like the worst kind of snore, or saw, trumpeting away on the intake as well as the outbreak – *oy-veh, heave-ho, gertcher-screwyer!* Why do almost all animals make noises as appalling at one end as at the other, as though outsize, eternal babies?

Pigs are perhaps the most extreme examples of this pull-you, push-you mechanism, perma-nent converters of fodder into manure with only the minimum pause on the way along the line. I have no problem hearing the snout in action, like a motor-bike being kicked into life over and over again – *snuffle, gargle, grumble, chortle, purr!* You feel a pack of these four-legged vacuum cleaners could clear the sewers of Paris or Rome, the Norfolk Broads or the Florida *bayous*, in a weekend. They could also fill them in a day. Though this reverse process – *splat, spulch, crump!* – is somewhat quieter, a kind of double-bass bottom-line to the factory uproar of the farm, sensed rather than registered by the ear.

And if somehow I miss these aural affronts, noise pollution that would attract writs, riots and pickets if it were emitted by hard instead of soft machines, there are always the hens. I can see an occasional one leaping in the air as if thrown like a welly, escaping from having its throat cut, or its backside speared by friendly, neighbourhood rivals for its rung in the pecking order, if I get out of bed and peer through a side window. Instead, I slide down and watch the paper clouds edging past, strung on wires. I hear the chicken-serenade, like a combination of pelted pebbles, massed knitting needles, cleared throats and screaming, ungreased axles.

So – this is a typical spring morning, looking out from the fifth-floor mansard-studio bedroom of our new house in Kentish Town. What? *Sorry!* Didn't I mention this is all taking place in London? I have moved only a mile west across the railway tracks that divide NW5 and NW3 around this point like the Berlin Wall, but now, so the estate agents insist, into their newly-invented "Hampstead Borders".

The bedroom looks north upon the swans across terraced roofs, like slates of giant tortoise, around two or three tower blocks, to a panoramic horizon of woods, grassy slopes and bushy coppices. This is a densely populated area. Parliament Hill Fields, and the Heath, are only brief oases in the bricks and mortar deserts of the metropolis. And yet what used to be called "wild" creatures already demonstrate how easily they can become domesticated away from open fields, while farm animals revert to wild patterns of behaviour among streets and buildings. I could more quickly focus on a hawk at springtime here than in the Berwyn Mountains of Clwyd where I spend my summers.

God knows who made the town. But there can be little doubt that man made the country. Scotland and Wales retain some of the uncomfortable unpredictability, the dangerous sharp edges, the *otherness*, of nature so long as it keeps the upper hand. In England, this strangeness has almost vanished. What seems to the casual eye in the country a random scatter of hedges, animals, cottages and people, distanced as far as possible from each other, is really, as anyone knows who spends more than a weekend there, a carefully-mapped, strictly-parcelled domain. A foot out of place there is as noticeable as it would be in any London garden, or indeed sitting-room. While my five-paned, twenty-feet wide window is barely noted on the Hampstead Borders, anywhere in the countryside it would be regarded as a gross invasion of privacy, even though I could not tell whether my neighbour were male or female without binoculars.

It is more than a century since Henry James explored England with the gingerly nervousness of a Yankee who was conscious that no part of this possibly diminishing, ocean-girt isle was more than seventy miles from the wild, wild waves. The place seemed to him incredibly sub-urban, over-gardened, always under the eyes of the authorities. He complained that he had yet to find a spot of open space where he could sit down without someone producing a seat and charging him twopence. Yet this was the same period that E.M. Forster looked back to with such nostalgia in the Twenties, asserting that no one who did not remember the countryside of Victorian times could imagine how wild, frightening and exhilarating it had been. The Golden Age is always receding. But nevertheless the process cannot be dismissed just as a fantasy of middle age. In the end humanity is responsible for everything on our planet. City mice are as much wild life as country mice. Consumers are as important as producers. Miners deserve to be subsidised as much as farmers.

It is dusk in spring. Two swans creak by again, very slow, very low. I have as much right to savour their presence cruising between the tower blocks as David Attenborough, up to his knees in sea slugs, where no white man has ever filmed before. 🦚

"They say their food is the most expensive in town."

ROGER WODDIS

Any Month Now

"Let no man boast himself that he has got through the perils of winter till at least the seventh of May"
– Anthony Trollope.

When the Bounds Green bus, full of frozen faces,
　　Matches the frowns on the snowbound train,
And a storm over Sterling ruins the races,
　　And football founders in driving rain,
And the pallid pagans who yearn for skinburn
Yell to the heavens, "To hell with Swinburne!"
And Pa cannot paddle in belt and braces,
　　We'll know Primavera is here again.

For winter's shivers are far from over,
　　And tourists huddle in wayside inns,
And all you can see from Dundee to Dover
　　Are balaclavas and mufflered chins;
But though the loony are wearing cotton,
And nudists are swearing something rotten,
With cows that browse in a field of clover
　　And Ian McCaskill, the Spring begins.

"We're so pleased. Doris and Tom are trying for a family . . . ."

MICHAEL BYWATER

PARADISE MISLAID

The British Ecological Society has announced 23 expedition awards, all to parties organised by young would-be explorers.

The Guardian

June 2nd 198–

Well here we are up the old Matto Grosso. Who wuold of thought the Fojrds of Finland wuold be like this? Never in my darkest, dreams did I ~~invs enivsa invasadge~~ got a clue about the snakes and stuff, let alone the tree's, which it must be siad are well amazing. The place is crawling with coon's but Mr Hanky say's as we mus'tnt notice nor say nothink in case of offending Wellington and Florizel, thuogh niether of them give a ~~fu bugg~~ dam, matter of fact Wellington says they a lower form of life, for a ethi enthic coon he is a real snob.

The major indusry of this place is rain. My bog-roll is totally swolled up. And somtheing is moving about inside my Walkman, I can hear its little footstep's. Maybe its a native ho ho ho they are graet at Limbo dancing, a Walkman wuold be no problem. I just told this joke to Florizel an he puncht me in the, muoth.

Plenty of tree's and stuff but Hanky wo'nt say what they are, jus says "You are here to appreciate and assimilate, taxomony is a repressive dicsipline of the middle clases." We havne't seen any aminals yet niether.

June 3rd 198–

We still havne't seen any but the jugnle is ovbiously full of ~~esco coxit~~ queer and strange animals with loud voices, one of them has eat my DM's in the nihgt. I got up and put my foot in and this thing ran out the toecap, it was greenish, in one night it done what four year's up the Shed fail to ~~achie~~ do, e.g. ruin them. That is £32.50 down the drian or rather down the throat!! Hanky say's this wil give us a insight into the problems of alternative society's. ~~No wonder we all call him "Wank~~ You can gues what we call him an no wonder, what a ~~eu~~ fool.

One of these day's, ~~vegnean veangan vengae~~ we will push his teeth in.

June 4th 198–

This morning saw a bit of a ~~contrm contrepe~~ punch-up on account of ~~W~~ Hanky giving out a stupid book called "Lord of the Flie's", he tried to make us read it but natch it all swole up in the rain just like my bog-roll and Florizel says "Hey, colonialist oppressive ~~shi~~ junk, man!", his father is in the Education Sub Comitte and ~~Wa~~ Hanky is shi dead scared of him even though here we are, billions of miles away in the jugnles of, I think we decided it was Switzerland.

June 5th 198–

We are defnitely in Tasmania. There are Brazil nuts everywhere. The qeustion is, where do we go from here? We got a whole lot of map's but no compass, at least we got a compass but Eric drunk the ~~aelo alhole~~ booze out of it and it just flops over now, juts like Eric ha ha ha. ~~Wa~~ Hanky say "Wait for nihgtfall and we will nagivate by means of the star's, a anceint trick discovered by the Sumerian's", then Florizel give him this mean Look and Hanky think (Oh ~~fu~~ dear) and say's "Of course the ~~coo~~ Blakcs new of it first, they jus't didnt chose to go anywhere althouhg they cuold if theyd of wante'd to".

Later

Well nihgt has fallen and we had this decromatic vote on what was the North Pole, it turn out to be prety interesting. Hanky come out of his tent looking red and hot with Snakehips O'Brien (Social Studeis & Communinty Projecs) doing up her zip, "We been looking up stuff in the Anostromy book" according to Hanky but we cuold see what been going on, if he think's we were born yesterday, we we'rent. Then Hanky say "Civilization is northwetsward, chaps!" which dosent go down to

well with geuss who, Florizel!!!, who says "Hey man, you fascist dictator or what?, also racist cultural suprecamist!" and Hanky says "Why?" and Florizel says "You ovbiously been ~~sha ser~~ having a go on Snakehips excluding the Black Man from his cultural heritage, white trash", and Snakehips look hard at Florizel, stand there in his Laurence Corner fatigeus and gunbelt with his banana wrap round his head like a real mercenary and next thing, Snakehips in the tent with Florizel and Hanky standing there looking like a stick of cerely.

June 6th 198–

Stil dark and stil walking, Hanky nagging us from the front. Every time anyone say "When ~~the f~~ we going to get there?" all Hanky say is "Do not be so goal directed, this is not a gramer school, we are helping yuo to find yuor true selves ecncountering ethnic civilsations without prejudice, throw away yuor cultural bagage." I said "All my bagage got is (a) pink bog roll swole up; (2) copy of Lord of the Fleis, all swole up, and (d) Weetabix, all swole up." Hanky did'nt luagh, just say nonsense, i.e. "The important thing is to keep your course fixed against a distant refrence point or else you go round in circels". We have just passed a Tree for the third time.

June 7th 198–

At las we know where we are! We are in Borneo! We met some blokes, they invite us to a Party, I do not know abuot local ethinc customs and absorbing fauna and the diversity of man, e.g. what Hanky was on abuot, but they kno how to give a party, we all got really ~~pi~~ drunk and the coo locals were real freindly, going around sqeuzing our arms an such. At first we were dead woried on account of cabinals but Hanky said "Do not push yuor luck, keep yuor gutter fascism to yuorselves, these people have a cultural heritage as rich as yuors althuogh difrently expresed." This speech gone down A.1. and the ~~wo~~ locals luagh a lot took Hanky off to some special private party. Weetabix now green and furry but so what? Thei'rs this great smell of cooking and wer'e looking forward to a decent meal, our first for day's.

We Remember It Well

Basil Boothroyd looks through a screen vaguely

"HE always reminded me of Donald you-know," said Mrs Hicks, accepting elegantly another dip in her hostess's cheese fondue. "The way his hair went back." She patted her own hair, thick but snowy.

"O'Connor?" suggested Mrs Wheatley. She hoped the fondue would hold out. You could never tell about the pre-lunch appetites of strangers. She proffered the tray to Mr Hicks, who declined with a polite wheeze. He was probably dieting, and could do with it.

"No, no," said Mrs Hicks with a touch of impatience. "Bertie knows who I mean, don't you, Bertie? He was in Carnival Novelties."

Mr Wheatley, making the rounds with the *sangria* jug, said he didn't think they'd seen it. Was it Franchot Tone?

"It wasn't a film," said Mrs Hicks. "It was when we lived at Tring. Oh, come on Bertie. He had the house on the corner. Wholesale balloons and things, he was in."

Mr Hicks furrowed his scalp. "You mean Donald Cripps, with the Triumph Herald?"

"I used to love Donald Crisp," said Mrs Wheatley.

"Well, it doesn't matter," said Mrs Hicks. "But that's who he used to remind me of."

"He danced up the walls, singing," said Mr Wheatley.

"Donald Crisp did?" His wife sounded doubtful. "Darling, you're not watching our guests' glasses."

"Donald O'Connor," said Wheatley, getting up with the jug. "It's a lovely day today".

"Certainly nice to see a bit of sun," said Hicks. "Only a half for me, old man."

"He means that was the song," said Mrs Hicks. "Fantastic." Swaying in her chair, her pearls slightly swinging, she hummed a snatch of "Oh, what a Wonderful Morning". No one put her right, though Hicks looked tempted for a moment.

"That's going back a bit," said Wheatley.

"Not that far. *South Pacific*," said Mrs Wheatley, one eye on the fondue, the other on the dwindling orange-sticks of French bread and mango chutney, and a third, if she'd had one, on the beaded bubbles at Mrs Hicks's brim, sinking fast.

"I meant Triumph Heralds," said Wheatley.

"With the sloping rear window."

"We saw that twice," said Mrs Hicks. "Stewart Granger with his leg up and he has this rear window and thinks he sees this crime."

"Not with Stewart Granger," said Hicks.

"Farley, then."

"You mean James Stewart."

"Remember the way they propped up the dead soldiers in the battlements, I shall never forget his face, Jimmy Stewart, before his friend shot the snake." Mrs Hicks shuddered dramatically. "Now *that* was Franchot Tone, if you like!"

"You don't get those pictures nowadays," said Mrs Wheatley. "Darling, Mrs Hicks is empty."

"I was just going to say," said Mrs Hicks. "Not like *Four Feathers*." She extended her glass. "Call me Norma. Let's be on first names, everybody. After all, we're neighbours, even if Bertie and me are new in the road."

"Derek," Mr Wheatley introduced himself, pouring.

"I'm Gillian," said Mrs Wheatley, feeling she ought to shake hands with someone. She wished they would go. It had been a mistake.

"Right up, Derek," said Mrs Hicks, and suddenly laughed on a higher note than might have been expected. "Derek! The penny's just dropped. That's who he always reminded me of. I knew it began with a D. Fred MacMurray!"

Her husband, who had been forming a triangle of chutney sticks on his well-filled cavalry twill knee, looked up warily. "Now, dear," he said.

"The man who made balloons. Pop-pop!" She pricked the air. "When we were in Tring. He had just that same bumpy face, like in *The Cincinnati Kid*."

"I don't think," began her husband, "Mr and Mrs Wheatley –"

"Derek and Gillian," said the Wheatleys.

"Perhaps they aren't very interested in Tring."

"Balloons, round the world in eighty days." Mrs Hicks took a powerful gulp. "I always say we don't give enough credit to the pictures, what they've given us all over the years, goodness, when you think it used to be every Tuesday and Friday up the Blue Hall, Islington, irrespectively of whether it was the mark of Zorro or Alice Faye, top price one and three and a bar of fruit-and-nut, two big pictures and the Wurlitzer, wasn't it, Bertie, when we was courting?"

Mr Hicks winced, and said quietly to Mr Wheatley, who was moving, "She won't have any more."

"Clark Grable," said Mrs Hicks. "Besides, look at now, this morning, there's nothing like films for a chat, they give you something to talk about always, even when you're with – well, we can't hardly call Derek and Gillian strangers, but what I mean, you know what I mean when

THINGS I HAVE FOUND LYING AROUND IN THE STREET 20p EACH

BANX

"Five minutes everybody!"

you're stuck for something to say. People in Tring never talked about nothing but the TV. It's been the ruination of the pictures for me, has the TV." She brushed at an eye-corner. "I mean, you see them all in the olden-goldies, young and lovely, and dancing like Fred Mac-Murray –"

"She means Fred Astaire." Mr Hicks got up.

"That's just it. Then they come on *Wogan* and they're all wrinkled."

"Look at the time, Connie," said Mr Hicks.

"Frankly, my dear," said Mrs Hicks, "I don't *give* a damn. He only calls me Connie when he's bad-tempered and pissed." She confided this to Wheatley's arm, helping to raise her from the chair. "He was potty on Norma Shearer, used to write me notes Dear Norma and it stuck, didn't it, Bertie, you sloppy old sod?"

Out in the hall, disentangling coats from the telephone stool, Hicks said, "Sorry about this." The Wheatleys waved it aside. "Staying so long," said Hicks.

"It's been a real treat," said Mrs Hicks, groping for a sleeve. "Just don't forget, you two, it's drinkies with us next time, now you know the way."

"Good God," said Wheatley, as the door banged on his smile. "What on earth possessed you?"

"It was Enid Watford. She said the new couple down the road were in films. I suppose she meant into. I thought you could tell them how your mother used to know Arthur Treacher."

"Eric Blore," said her husband, making for the cloakroom. "You never get that right." 🍃

"Amazing! You should write a book."

On the tenth anniversary of his death, an attempt is being made to refurbish the image of Chairman Mao. A new edition of the Little Red Book will contain hitherto unpublished thoughts showing him to have been far closer to China's current liberal and Western trends than anyone had realised.   *Herald Tribune*

ON SECOND THOUGHTS

☆ ————————————BOURGEOIS OF THE WORLD, UNITE!———————————— ☆

If there is to be revolution, there must be a revolutionary party. Without a party built on Marxist-Leninist revolutionary theory and in the Marxist-Leninist revolutionary style, it is impossible to lead the broad masses of the people in defeating imperialism and its running dogs. The first thing, therefore, is to design a Marxist-Leninist tie.

☆

We must have faith in the masses and the masses must have faith in the Party. These are two cardinal principles. The masses must believe that the Party is in a position to provide fitted carpet at cost, to include underlay and making good, and the Party must believe the masses will have the sense not to let the dog in.

☆

Who are our enemies? Who are our friends? These two questions are of prime importance for the revolution. Another one is where can we get those shirts with little crocodiles on?

☆

Letting a hundred flowers blossom is the policy. Also putting a stone heron down by the azaleas and trimming the hedge to look like a teapot. And let all workers remember that, if there is space, a pond sets things off a treat.

☆

No political party can possibly lead a great revolutionary movement to victory unless it has a revolutionary theory, a knowledge of history, and an annual Christmas Dance & Tombola (*8 for 8.30, Black Tie*).

☆

The enemy will not perish of himself. But, until that day when the jackals of Wall Street and their lickspittle cohorts are brought howling to their knees, how much can it hurt to play a little golf?

☆

Classes struggle, some classes triumph, other classes are eliminated. Such is history. To interpret history from this viewpoint is historical materialism; opposition to this viewpoint is historical idealism. Classes with inside plumbing have the best chance.

☆

Whoever wants to know a thing has no way of doing so except by coming into contact with it. All genuine knowledge originates in direct experience. The worker would be wise, therefore, to ask for seven days' free trial and money back if not completely satisfied. A worker cannot be happy if his smoking-jacket pinches under the arms, his compact discs crackle, or spare ribs keep jamming his waste-disposal.

☆

Self-criticism must always be supported by mutual criticism. That is the path to victory. If a worker goes off his new deodorant, let him, before embarking upon any major decision, offer himself for a communal sniff.

Every Communist should grasp the truth that political power grows out of the barrel of a gun. Once he has paid for the gun, however, let him feel free to start saving for a snooker table.

☆

A firm people and a firm party are welded together by a firm press. A firm press cannot exist without a lot of firm young women with nothing on, and plenty of firm bingo.

☆

As for people who are politically backward, Communists should not slight or despise them, but befriend them, unite with them, convince them, and encourage them to go forward. For example, why not try to get an unsecured loan out of a Zurich bank manager?

☆

Taught by mistakes and setbacks, we have become wiser. Once a mistake is made, we should correct it, and the more quickly and thoroughly the better. Thus, never mix radial tyres with cross-ply, never buy a room extension from a man with an unmarked van, and never back second favourites for a place.

☆

Thousands upon thousands of martyrs have heroically laid down their lives for the people. Let us hold their banner high and march ahead along the path crimson with their blood, confident that they would see nothing wrong in a second set upstairs for the children!

Kevin Pilley's Careers Guide

THIS WEEK: SECRETARIAL DUTIES

TRACEY

It's so easy to trivialise secretarial work and say there's no variety in it. That it's mundane and repetitive. It's not. It's not. Every day I am confronting new problems and having to make difficult decisions. Like whether to use the stairs or lift when I arrive in the morning. I am under considerable pressure. The phone never stops and personal calls keep me incredibly busy. I'm allowed to think for myself. That's a nice feeling. It's largely up to me when I take my Pill and whether to block or indent addresses on envelopes. I like that sort of freedom.

I'm always trying to think up ways of making the office run more smoothly and efficiently. Getting a kettle with a boil-dry element was my idea. I have a great social life and through work have got to know lots of very interesting and talented telesales people. They are always asking me for my daytime telephone number. I am learning new skills all the time. I now know about Post Codes which at 25 is quite an achievement. I still have a lot to learn but I am determined to succeed. I think I have it within me. I still don't know the best way to present chicken pieces at a business buffet but the lady in Personnel says that will come with experience.

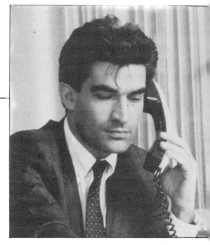

KEITH

Becoming a secretary was the key liberation for me. I had this terrible feel of emptiness. I wanted to do someth more than make millions. Something m suited to my temper and talents. I felt true potential was repressed. I wanted be of value. To contribute. I was sick of petty power-seeking intrigues. T wheeling and dealing. I was sick of be so unnaturally dependent on one pers for my tea. I wanted to break out of board-room. Now I am a copy-typist I myself a lot better. I no longer feel I am non-job.

REG

I run a recruitment bureau specialising in bubbly blondes. I travel up and down the country looking for secretarial talent. What I'm after is someone with a command of the language who understands speech, has a sound appreciation of Luncheon Vouchers and a genuine desire to work indoors. Most importantly, they must believe in themselves. You've got to work hard to make it. It's not easy although, of course, luck does come into it. But the rewards are great. The best girl I've ever had on my books now earns over 7K.

I also run a small secretarial school in Lambeth where the council is one of the biggest employers. My graduates are very marketable. They tend not to belong to the white gentile culture and spend most of their time in wage comparisons. They can do 100wpm shorthand carrying their kid in a papoose on their back and all are very keen on organising inter-work social activities like discos and ethnic head counts.

MAND

Graham will hate me for saying this l he's driving himself too hard. As his s retary I can see the signs. He's asle before I get into bed. He thinks his caree stagnating and that he hasn't got expensive enough squash racquet. wife is trying to save their marriage cooking complicated casseroles. Grah calls me his right arm and says comput can never replace basic human skills. has this thing about pretty women with formal qualifications. His first wife wa stunning warehouse assistant. He's funny. When he went home once cove in love-bites he told his wife he had fal into the franking-machine.

I like what I have to do for Graham ar get a lot out of our working relationsh He pays the electricity bills. The work atmosphere here is terrific. It's one knocking-shop. At the Xmas party store-room light goes off and you really feel part of a young and lively team!

GILLIAN

...idn't drift into my job. God chose it for
...e. I believe He put me here for a signi-
...ant end. To be a person Friday and
...end the large proportion of my life in an
...en-plan typing pool. Everything I do
...o for Him. Running a busy reception
...a, ordering cabs, preparing overdraft
...erests. It's a partnership. One day I
...ow He shall appear to me in the subsi-
...od restaurant.

...As long as He gives me strength I shall
...ntinue watering the plants and
...arpening the pencils. My work is a
...urce of great meaning and creativity. My
...ine is a special gift. The typewriter is
...re expressive of human aspirations
...an any other medium. Let me be thank-
...that I am not a soloist and 94 others
...are the joy of its music with me.

SARAH

It's ridiculous to say all audio-typists are
morons. That implies at least some sensation. I even caught one trying to Tipp-Ex
her VDU yesterday. They are unbelievably
thick sometimes and you have to disinfect
most things after they've used them. As a
high-powered bilingual secretary in a
famous London publishing company I feel
like a triumph of evolution compared to the
other secretaries we have here. Not just
because I went to Keele. I don't have to use
a dictionary to read the staff notice-board.
Nor do I get congratulations cards every

time I go a whole day without getting the
address of the company wrong.

I am very well thought of because I am
well-organised, discreet and my father is
the chief shareholder. I have a broad base
of common sense and general knowlege
which is a great asset as some of my work
is quite intricate. Above all, I think I have a
balanced and appealing personality and
that I am modest about my work. I don't
think anyone knows exactly how much I
do. It helps having a dad with some clout. I
ring him up when I want to go home early.

CHRISTINE

My parents had high hopes for me. When I
told my Dad I had got a job he looked at me
with absolute horror and said, "It's not
clerical, is it?" I nodded and he threw himself under the mobile library. My Mum was
more excited. She was a secretary herself
until a tragic accident with a lever-arch file
paralysed her down one side.

A lot of people I know hate being a
secretary. They think it's beneath them. I
don't. I love it. I love being an expert on
limescale. I know the first thing clients
look at are the washing facilities. I thrive

on getting involved with all aspects of
office admin. It's so important to have
professional-looking toilet pans. I am completely wrapped up in my job. I can't get to
sleep sometimes worrying about station-
ery supplies. Even my curtains at home are
made from company ties. I am separated. I
was just spending more time on relief
switchboard duty than I was with my husband. I am not particularly interested in
other men but I do enjoy occasionally looking at the trouser folds of messenger bike
riders.

ANNA RAEBURN

BLACK TO THE FUTURE

THE room is painted white, regardless of its shape or dimensions. The lamp is black ironwork. The bed-frame is of polished steel. The sheets are sleet grey, the blanket too. Apart from a smoked Perspex cube containing word-processor, cordless telephone, television and video-recorder, all lacquered black and fitted into their respective compartments, the only other piece of furniture in the room is a trolley of stacking trays enamelled egg-yolk yellow. There may be one white flower in a black vase. (Black flowers would be preferable but are quite hard to come by except in the form of tulips, which are *so* Sixties.)

No, this is not the study of a wealthy Italian anarchist, nor the upmarket accommodation in one of Britain's newly planned prisons. It is the bedroom of a wealthy client whose decorator espouses a variation upon the style known as "high tech".

Men are supposed to like high tech. It's functional, pared down, easy to maintain, unequivocally masculine; style, you might say, above style. Unfortunately, at its most serious, it always looks as if somebody's leg is being pulled. No matter how cheaply or expensively a room is furnished, it self-consciously looks as if you were trying to prove what you could do without. And unless you've taken a vow of chastity in keeping with the monastic walls, one of the things you won't want to do without is a little feminine companionship from time to time. But you'll find that high tech and romance, if not incompatible, don't quite mix.

For a start, high-tech women always wear black in one of two prominently recognisable styles. High-tech Woman One wears the Japanese-inspired version of the *chador*, with all sorts of extra bits and flaps and folds, but all, all black, plus flat black shoes, a large black bag (which must contain supplies of vitamins and essential minerals as the effect of wearing black constantly can be very lowering), cryptically short hair and no make-up topped off by a black hat shaped like a coal-scuttle.

All this may go very well with the décor but it doesn't go well with many men other than decorators, professional exponents of *le dernier cri* and others equally serious about their image. The trouble with those long voluminous dark clothes – wherein even if one section sort of fits, it is immediately concealed by six more which fall all over the place – is that you just don't know what you're getting. There may indeed be a bust, waist and hips inside but there's nothing to indicate their presence. Black-out clothes of this variety may mean you're in for a wonderful surprise if you can brave the layers. Such exploration may equally well mean coming up against convent underwear sadly shaded by constant friction against so much black fabric. One thing you won't find in there is a touch of

the frillies. Not a hope. It would spoil the line. So now you know you're with a woman who cares more about the modish correctitude of her clothes than any way you can suggest of pleasantly passing a wet afternoon.

The second version of the High-tech Woman is ostensibly much more promising. Her black fits. It looks like, or is, leather or latex, tailored like a second skin, although you've never seen anybody's skin with a tight skirt. She wears very high heels (black), a very square-shouldered jacket (black), and carries a small black handbag which contains a black Filofax and three credit cards also always in the black. Her head is crowned by very long hair, either dressed asymmetrically in the kind of disorder it takes a hairdresser three hours to achieve or else pulled up ruthlessly into a brutal knot on the crown and covered by a leather hat in the shape of an inverted ice-cream cone, the point of which is folded over.

On first view, HTW2 is a better bet because at least there's a shape. With luck, hard work and the kind of application concomitant with any aspect of high tech, a *good* shape, so good that the black stockings may indeed be just that and not the tights which bring tears to the eyes of many a hardened lover of women. Look your fill at HTW2, lads, and if looking is all you're there for, all will be well.

If you desire to take matters one step further, however, problems will begin. Because helping her out of her form-fitting black is a job which takes a considerable amount of time and has been known to break nails and spoil the sunniest of temperaments. No matter what the

woman inside the clothes may say, the impli message of HTW2 is: "You can look at t goods but don't touch…" unless you've got l of time and talc, and/or don't mind leaving t ensemble – with the possible exception of t headgear – in place, except in the essential are which may be set aside to permit access.

Which brings us to high-tech sex. High-te sex is not defined by promiscuity but, on t contrary, by its infrequency. It is, like the f nishing and architectural style it emulat rational and functional. A high-tech man d not have to be reminded about the ris inherent in a close encounter with an unknow A container coloured black, or one of the u sparing shades occasionally used to relieve essentially monochromal setting, contains p tectives. Conventionally, one might be temp to make them tone with the container but thi usually avoided as too obvious, whereas black silver grey could be considered quite sma

A woman doesn't have to worry about a hig tech man spoiling her career. He's too bu thinking about his own, before, after and duri – which could be chilling if one were m romantic in inclination but which proves th he is a serious person. A man doesn't have worry about a high-tech woman clinging him. She's only there because she's heard much about his flat from others who favour style or because the release of hormones is go for her skin.

You could thus argue that high tech ratio ises the excesses surrounding the man/wom relationship in an effective, if sometimes rat bleak, manner. But there are details of the s nario which ensure that high tech will remai minority taste. No matter how expensive expression, high tech remains high-style comfort. For the very young, who would nothing stop them or the rich who can afford change everything at whim, this is acceptab but for the rest of us, particularly men, witho a modicum of comfort there will be no pass.

Then there's underwear. High-tech linge fails. Do you really want to see the woman women in your life clad in zippered black spa dex, or, "to keep the line", in combinations m impenetrable than those devised by any nun games mistress? American *Vogue* recently fe tured two or three such and I'm sure that, matter how attractive the object of your desir you would be unusual to be able to rise abe such considerations on more than an occasion basis.

And then there's affection, which is aw ward, many-layered and multicoloured a might initially overcome but would eventua dismiss the sparse elegance of such a style. fine for artifacts to become more and mo streamlined, because they are mere things; b most men would prefer a hug to the perfecti of HTW1 or 2 – I hope.

COUNTRY LIFE

The driver reversed into another car and then, putting her car into forward gear, drove into the wall at the front of the store. She then reversed again, hitting the other customer's car again. This time, on driving forward she went straight through the low wall and 12-foot-square plate-glass window into the store.

Her car pushed the big vegetable stands into the next aisle, and without pausing for breath she started to reverse out again. The car went back through the glass window (or, more accurately, where the glass window had been), shot across the car park and hit the parked car of the Co-op manager. The car then hit the wire perimeter fence and a tree before coming to rest in the car park.

B. Cockell (*Haslemere Herald*)

Any person who desires to object to the grant of such Permit and Licence should send two copies of a brief statement of the grounds of his or her objection.

Signed,
WRIGHT HASSAL & CO,
Solicitors.
E. Wiltshire (*Gloucestershire Echo*)

PART TIME mother's help required at least three afternoons per week, to help pregnant man with toddler.

E. Rolls (*Cheltenham News*)

We always smile at instruction booklets or manuals writted in a kind of pidgin English. The impression this creates is, as we know, of inefficiency and lack of care.

I. Miller (*The Scotsman*)

DETAILS of the TSB flotation will be announced today, but last night a Cheltenham-based organisation warned that many applications for hares would fail because of incorrectly filled-in forms.

B. Kay (*Western Daily Press*)

STEVEN ROBERTS, 20, is nursing two broken angles after falling off as he tried to tap dance on the roof of his house in Reading, Berkshire.

L. Manning-Davies (*South Wales Evening Post*)

INTERNATIONAL SECTION

A New Hampshire paper, trying to correct an earlier error, printed this note: "Our paper carried the notice last week that Mr Herman Jones is a defective in the police force. This was a typographical error. Mr Jones, is of course, a detective in the police farce."

H. Matthews (*New Canaan Advertiser*, Connecticut, USA)

CHICAGO – A missionary charged with killing her husband during an argument over who had saved more souls has been acquitted of murder by a judge who accepted her plea of self-defence.

P. Hopkinson (*Vancouver Sun*, Canada)

A BUDDHIST PRIEST blesses some 70,000 used brassieres, heaped in a big pyramid, in a memorial service for cast-off underwear at the compound of Zojoji Temple in Tokyo, Friday.

M. Dohma (photo caption, *The Japan Times*)

Thirty women moon worshippers met on a hill Wednesday night to dance naked in an ancient pagan ritual, but called off the ceremony when 150 men turned up to watch.

R. Lockie (*Saskatoon Star*, Canada)

PARA GIRL TO REPEAT FATAL JUMP

J. Thomas (*The World in Runcorn, Frodsham and Helsby*)

One council official said yesterday: "Everyone in the town hall is wandering around like headless chickens, looking over their shoulders to see if they are going to be next."

E. Munday (*Hackney Gazette*)

8.15 Inside Castor's Cube: Communism with Sugar on Top.

E. Almond (unnamed TV guide)

Theft and burglary linked, police believe

V. Forgetful (*Huddersfield Daily Examiner*)

In the private bar there is a box of mahogany panels that are believed to have come from a sycamore tree that stood on this site.

P. Graves (Southend *Standard Recorder*)

ACCIDENT victim Shaun Carey gladly accepted a lift when a stolen car pulled up alongside him. Carey, 21 – who suffered two broken legs – was having difficulty as he walked home from a late-night party. Mr Andrew Kenyon, prosecuting, said the car was stopped by police but the driver managed to escape. Carey was unsuccessful.

A. Critchley (*Manchester Evening News*)

Two men were charged with "jointly entering a pullover" at Dewsbury Magistrates' Court. The case was adjourned and the charge is expected to be corrected to "jointly entering a shop" before the accused next appear in court.

B. Picken (*Yorkshire Evening Post*)

The Dukedom of York is a title that carries no automatic lands or financial rewards. By contrast, the Ducky of Cornwall provides the Prince of Wales with a substantial sum.

G. Moore (*Western Daily Press*)

Organisers have managed to get a last-minute replacement for Danny La Rue. A spokesman said: "It is with great pleasure and gratitude at this late stage that the Robert Brothers' Circus have generously offered their star elephant, Maureen."

D. Allan (*Driffield Times*)

IMPOSSIBLE BUILDING WORK
carried out to
customer's requirements.
Sensible rates. Estimates free.
D. Burgess (*Hemel Hempstead Express*)

INTERNATIONAL SECTION
ALIEN WITH TUSKS FINED K5,000

Anon (*Times of Zambia*)

Alcoholic beverages are banned in Saudi Arabia. Under the country's Islamic Sharia law, those who consume alcohol are canned publicly.

I. Dobson (*The Herald*, Melbourne, Australia)

A 25-year-old man, who was found in the basement of a Royal Street house pulling apart a pot plant, claimed he was looking for a friend.

P. Bain (*The Timatu Herald*, New Zealand)

MOSCOW'S Hall of Columns, a charming classical building tucked between the Bolshoi theatre and Kremlin, used to be the noblemen's club when the country was still ruled by the tsars. These days, it is used for the lying in state of the dear departed Politburo members, chess world-title fights, and other events to which the party wants the people to pay respectful attention.

So the launch of *Burda Moden*, a rather down-market West German fashion magazine, had top-level backing. To the no-longer deca-dent strains of early Elvis Presley and country-and-western, the beanpole models of the West flaunted *Mittel Deutschland* fashions to well-connected Soviet women who last possessed such figures in the hungry years of war and collectivisation.

For the past ten years in Moscow, a copy of *Vogue* magazine has gone for forty roubles (forty pounds at the official exchange rate, ten quid on the black market). But *Burda* has com-manded up to twice the price, because *Burda* is useful rather than just pretty. In between the ads and the glossy photos are sewing patterns, paper templates from which the seamstresses on Pokrovsky Boulevard can run you up some-thing that is catching eyes in downtown Düssel-dorf. Like so many of the Gorbachev reforms in the Soviet Union, the purpose behind the official launch of the Russian-language *Burda* was to legitimise a social phenomenon that has already been under way for years. In legalising some private enterprise and encouraging a modest and taxable profit, Gorbachev has ack-nowledged that if you can't beat it, you might as well legalise it. But with an initial print-run of 100,000 in a country of 150 million women, the fashions on display in *Burda* are hardly going to revolutionise the daily life of the Soviet rag-trade.

The advertisements, however, are another matter. From the back cover of the latest issue gleams a new Audi. Inside, there are ads for wicked Western perfumes, Cartier watches, and oddest of all, for the American Express credit card. Just the thing for the meat counter at the Novosibirsk "*Produkti*" shop. That will do nicely, comrade.

But none of these things is exactly alien to the

> "There are the *Metallisti*, the heavy-metal fans with their long hair, black vinyl jackets and studded wrist-bands. There are punks, who dye their hair green and blue, and the rather more stuck-up New Romantics who go in for side-whiskers and Edwardian dress of late tsarist days."

Soviet experience. When Mikhail Gorbachev came on his hugely successful PR tour to Lon-don in 1984, even before he had become Soviet leader, his well-dressed wife not only persuaded a cynical West that something was changing behind the Iron Curtain, she even bought her-self some diamond ear-rings with a credit card.

She is not the only Russian to possess such a capitalist talisman. Since the great wave of *détente* began in about 1970, Soviet trade with the West has quintupled, spurred by increasing exports of oil and gas. And with the trade came the businessmen, the purpose-built trade and exhibition centre, the American-style interna-tional hotel with its massage parlours, beer halls, Japanese restaurant, and call-girls who insist on dollars or Deutschmarks. The growth of trade means that today, there are almost forty Western banks, and over a hundred Western corporations and trading houses, with perma-nent offices and trade missions in Moscow. They employ Soviet staff, give them seasonal gifts, import the standard Western consumer goods and exotic foods and wines – and have given a growing fraction of the city's population an exposure to Western lifestyles which has fuelled expectations, swollen the black market, and transformed the look of the city.

The old stereotype of headscarved grannies built on the lines of combine harvesters has not quite vanished. But as spring comes to Moscow and the population doffs the fur hats and thick coats of winter, the Muscovites look increasingly like the people of any other European city. They almost all seem to wear Levi jeans and the fashion now is for Adidas training-shoes. The real trendies wear their Sony Walkman headphones as they head for the new video rental salon on the Arbat or the video arcade games centre in Fili park. Moscow kids are breaking down into the stylistic tribal groups that have been startling the West for years.

There are the "Metallisti", the heavy-metal fans with their long hair, black vinyl jackets and studded wrist-bands. They have a medical pur-pose, to support the straining limb that hauls around the cumbersome stereo recorders that blare out the latest bootleg tape of Iron Maiden, or Moscow's favourite home-grown band, Ariya. There are punks, who have ingeniously found a way of using watercolour paints to dye their hair green and blue, and New Wave fans and the rather more stuck-up New Romantics who go in for the side-whiskers and Edwardian dress of late tsarist days.

And inevitably, there has been a reaction, with the newly fashionable "Liuberi", highly nationalist Russian skinheads who take a pride in wearing ugly, local plaid coats, go in for body-building, reject drink and drugs, and get their kicks by beating up the punks and Metallisti. The point about these skinheads is that their

THE OLD BLOC

As Mr Gorbachev's New Russian Revolution gathers pace,
MARTIN WALKER in Moscow finds that every Prospekt pleases

name comes from their base of Liubertsi, one of the capital's satellite cities. They come into Moscow for their fights, and to occupy turf: the "Four Seasons" cafe in Gorky Park used to be a Metallisti base until the Liuberi muscled in. The psychology is classic: the tough kids of the grim fringes moving in to challenge the privileged kids and lifestyles of the pampered centre.

But even among the young Muscovites there are style wars waged by the designer comrades which have put a new word into the Soviet economy – "*Leybel*". This is the little leather patch on the back of your jeans that says Levi or Wrangler, the expensive logo on the shirt or sweater that says Pierre Cardin or the Nike badge on the running shoes. It is not just Western products that have defined Soviet fashion, it is the competing Western brand names and their own coded messages of style and privilege which are helping to define the loyalties and pecking order of Soviet youth, which is increasingly able to afford them.

The growth of wages, and high subsidies for basics like food and rent, combines with a lack of choice among Soviet consumer goods that has forced the population into becoming the world's thriftiest savers. The state savings bank holds deposits of 260 billion roubles – or 1,000 pounds a head for every man, woman and child in the country.

The astonishing aspect is the origin of all these imported goods. The growing numbers of Western students are one source, eking out their meagre grants by selling their jeans for 100 roubles and tape cassettes for twenty. Tourists help feed the supply chain, particularly the neighbouring Finns, who escape the high cost of alcohol back home by taking cheap weekend package trips to the USSR, in the knowledge that a couple of pairs of jeans and sweat-shirts will keep them in vodka and women until the trip back.

And the Soviet state encourages the process. Some 10,000 Westerners work in Moscow as accredited diplomats, correspondents and businessmen, and all of their Russian staff – secretaries, drivers, maids and translators – are entitled to at least one month's salary in hard currency, to be spent in the state-run stores that accept only foreign exchange for their imported clothes and electrical goods.

Then there are the thousands of lucky Soviet officials who have a licence to travel and to deal

> "Inevitably, there has been a reaction with the newly fashionable *Liuberi*, highly nationalist Russian skinheads who take a pride in wearing ugly, local plaid coats, go in for body-building, reject drink and drugs, and get their kicks by beating up the punks and *Metallisti*."

with foreigners. There are the executives of the Foreign Trade Ministry and the foreign trade organisations, the diplomats and journalists, ballet dancers and sports teams, who all seem to arrive back at Moscow airport loaded down with personal computers and stereo systems and designer jeans from the boutiques and duty-free stores of the West. Some of these are the most privileged of the lot, the "Am-Exniki", those allowed to hold their own American Express cards. Others simply like to flaunt their bottles of Chivas Regal and Marlboro cigarettes.

In the last, and increasingly corrupt, years of Brezhnev, the conspicuous capitalist consumption of the elite became an open scandal. There was the son of the Minister of the Interior who used to enjoy driving his personal Mercedes to university every day; and Brezhnev's own son

(given a sinecure as Deputy Minister of Foreign Trade) who gained a name for tipping the topless waitresses at the Crazy Horse night-club in Paris with 100-dollar bills.

By contrast with those days, the Gorbachev regime is made up of puritans. Not only did they launch a headlong attack on the national vodka addiction, they have even arrested Brezhnev's son-in-law, a former Deputy Minister of the Interior, for corruption. The young Liuberi toughs, who attack any sign of Western influence, may be the first manifestation of a backlash against Western influence and consumer goodies, which some of them have likened in TV interviews to eighteenth-century British slavers exploiting West Africa with glass beads and cheap mirrors.

But the Gorbachev policy is to encourage Western technology and trade as part of his modernisation programme, to boost tourism and student exchanges to break down the psychological Iron Curtain which has fenced off the Soviet people much more effectively than the KGB border-guards ever did. Because Gorbachev needs popular support for his reforms, he has to give the people consumer goodies. The motto seems to be, let them eat cake, so long as it's Soviet-made. So you can now buy Soviet Marlboro cigarettes, made under licence. A Pierre Cardin boutique is opening in Moscow, to sell French-designed and Soviet-made leisure-wear, and most of those Adidas track-shoes that pound the Moscow streets are made, under licence, at a plant in Soviet Lithuania.

What was that phrase of Lenin's, about the capitalists being so greedy they would sell the very rope that would one day be used to hang them? What he forgot was that the hangman, as he fingered the various samples of silk and hemp and best-quality cord, might get a hankering to open a little rope and accessory business of his own. ☙

Pregnant Silence

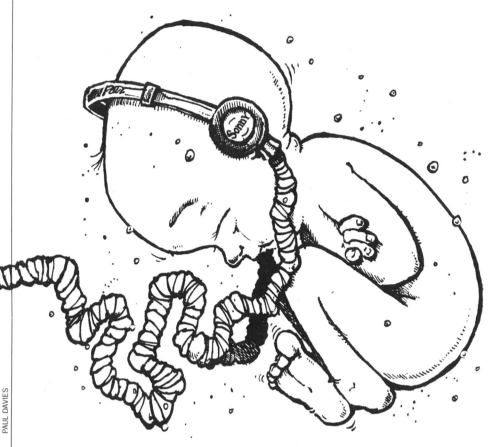

Sir Yehudi Menuhin, speaking at the inaugural meeting in London of the British Society for Pre-natal Psychology, said he knew that both his father and mother had sung to him before he was born. *Daily Telegraph*

PAUL DAVIES

AND very nice too. But it was grossly interfering of Yehudi to add that *every* unborn baby should be entertained in the same way.

This seems a monstrous invasion of privacy. It's because I, myself, was given compulsory music in the womb that I now resent the busking guitarists who trap me on London's Underground. I feel much the same about the claustrophobic pop music in a Harrods lift. And I don't much like being hemmed in by Beethoven at the Véritable Crêperie in Chelsea, or by Mozart at Richoux of Piccadilly. Worse still is the primitive beat in the Hard Rock Café at Hyde Park Corner.

I mentioned this to Dr Michele Clement, president of the Pre-natal Society.

"You have the same views as the average foetus, Kenneth," she said. "Rock music is too loud and too complex for the unborn child, which can easily kick itself aggressively out of position."

"But I was born ages before Rock was invented," I said, "and I'm told that I kicked quite a lot in the womb."

"Perhaps you were kicking for sheer joy," said Dr Clement.

I decided to check what joyful sounds had reached me as a foetus. I even looked up the

Radio Times programmes for the day I was born. There was "A Straight Talk To The Boys", by John Reith, which seemed a little premature for me, as did "Advice On Afternoon Walks". Otherwise there was nothing very violent, though I shall never know if my mother and I listened, on the brink of birth, to "Auntie Lettie's Songs From The Zoo", "Bernard Albert's Syncopated Items" or, rather inappropriately, "Hymen, Come Thy Torch Prepare", by Handel.

Sir Yehudi has pointed out that canned melodies are less pleasing to a foetus than live music. I happen to know that my own fidgeting in the womb was induced by my father accompanying his own singing.

"I think he's kicking again, Bertram," my mother is quoted as saying. And the kindest man I ever knew would continue to strum through his favourite pot-pourri of unfinished melodies. As I grew up I became accustomed to his restless chopping about from *Chin Chin Chinaman* and *Where Did You Get That Hat?* to snippets of gems from the classics. All these, I now realise, had already vibrated through me from my mother, influencing my attitude to life before I was born.

Though I didn't know, until I talked to Dr Clement, that I was also listening, in the womb,

to a sort of one-note samba. This, she told me, is the normal sound of a mother's interior. It seems that while we're inside it we all hear a continual droning on the note of G below middle C.

Sir Yehudi says he uses this note for transcendental meditation. He simply sticks two fingers between his eyes and lets out a jolly hum until he feels better.

I, myself, have never been very keen on the G below middle C, though it could be that nine months of listening to it is enough for a lifetime. It's not surprising that most people feel a lifting of the heart when an orchestra tunes up with a note two semi-tones higher. The G always sounds flat and lifeless, but the concert-pitch A is wonderfully full of promise – even if you don't like music, and I'm never quite sure if I do or not.

It's true that I listen a lot and play the piano even more, but I can never sit for long at a keyboard or in a concert hall without wondering what on earth I'm doing. I'm sure that by hearing my father's cleverly-twisted tunes I became what I am today – not only one of life's musically wounded, but also a sort of walking unfinished symphony with a pot-pourri mentality.

Not that I mind. I certainly wouldn't have liked the experience of Boris Brott, the Canadian orchestral conductor who is currently the hero of the Pre-natal Society. It seems that because his cellist mother toured concert halls while pregnant, he was born knowing by heart all the scores she had played.

I can't think of anything more aggressive for a foetus than a whining spiked instrument jammed between its mother's knees. Though I sometimes wonder if a little aggression might be quite useful to an unborn child. My own parents were almost too nice to me, especially in their pre-natal singing of such lyrics as "Friends may forsake me, let them all forsake me, I still have you, Sonny Boy". That was my father's favourite. My mother, I'm told, specialised in a terrifying piece of moral blackmail – a grotesque ballad that urged: "Mummy's little feller, don't you grow up tall; she'll forgive your wickedness if only you stay small."

My subconscious reaction was to expand, like an uncoiled spring, to an eventual six-foot-one-and-a-half inches.

Still, I'm not complaining. If that's how I became so lovable, it was well worth it. And it must be reassuring, for mum-and-dad readers, to know that if they *do* sing duets to a foetus, it doesn't have to turn out like Sir Yehudi. It could be like me.

Incidentally, I ought to mention that Yehudi believes the right tune hummed to an unborn baby "can give it a sense of the real world it is to enter".

All too soon it will find that in the real world the lovely tune of *The Sugar Plum Fairy* now means a commercial for Dream Topping and *Eine Kleine Nachtmusik* means Batchelor's soup.

And the soothing lullaby of Liszt's *Liebestraum*?

Cinzano.

Maybe it's time for another straight talk to the boys.

"Incredible. We've both gone insane at exactly six o'clock."

HOUSE PAINTERS

SELF PORTRAIT by Geoffrey Howe

A BIGGER SPLASH by David Steel

ANGLO-AMERICAN GOTHIC by Margaret Thatcher

OUL RED SOCKS by Ian Paisley

MAHOOD reviews the annual exhibition of paintings by MPs at Westminster

[B]EHOLD, I STAND AT THE DOOR [A]ND KNOCK by David Owen

SOFT CONSTRUCTION WITH MILITANTS: PREMONITION OF CIVIL WAR by Neil Kinnock

[W]ILLIE WHITELAW by Denis Healey
[D]ENIS HEALEY by Willie Whitelaw

THE CABINET ROOM by Michael Heseltine

PUNCH

"Oh, God, VAT Inspectors!"

KEITH WATERHOUSE

Just Drinking Aloud

Drinkers will be asked to enter a competition to end alcohol abuse in the north-west of England, where more beer and spirits are consumed than anywhere else in Britain...Entrants will be asked to complete a questionnaire to determine if they are cautious drinkers.

The Times

When did you start drinking?
Can't remember.

Why did you start drinking?
Have forgotten. Probably to forget. Have known lot of sadness in life. Lot, lot of sadness. Very lot. When boy, had to go to off-licence in bare feet. Have known days when only thing to drink in house was one bottle of Newcastle Brown between nine of us. Father used to take strap to me when drunk – sometimes even when I was not drunk. Ran away to tea. Not tea, sea. Got taste for rum and never looked back. Dare not look back, because of fear of being followed by big black rabbit.

Would you describe yourself as a social drinker?
Definitely. Never voted Conservative in life.

Approximately how much do you drink a day?
Do not drink at all, as matter of fact. Not after yesterday. Never again under any circumstances. Not if paid me. Even if win comp, not

so much as crate of light ale with whisky chasers will pass lips. Never again. Mean that.

Do you experience hangovers or other ill-effects?
Just minute, just minute, wait till tell you. Since ask, do not have hangovers, no. Do not believe in them. Sometimes wake up with splitting headache and throw up into boots, but this not hangover, this down to mixing drinks. Never mix drinks. If on vodka, brandy and dash of sloe gin, topped up with lager, stay on that all night. Do not switch to whisky, rum and dash of crème de menthe, topped up with Guinness, or it curtains. But was saying. Was not hangover that decided turn over leaf, no no no. No no no no no no no. It meeting Hector again after he discharged from hospital.

Does your drinking concern your family and friends?
If by that mean what was Hector doing in hospital, will tell you. He in hospital because knocked him through pub window after having few. Big pals again now, but only on condition I not drink. So whether it concern family and friends or not is irrelerent. Irrelevant.

Do you find it possible to pass a day without drinking?
Wait minute, hold horses, not so fast. Have not asked who Hector is yet. Go on, ask who Hector is.

Would you describe any members of your family as heavy drinkers?
Yes – Hector. Drinks like dish. Not dish, fish. But is not fish, is big black rabbit. Have heard of Harvey? Yes have, course have, was invisible six-foot rabbit in film with forgotten his name, James Mason. Stewart Granger. James Stewart. Yes, well, listen to what am telling you, Hector Harvey's brother. Is not in showbiz himself as has cleft palate, also has not got height for it. Is only four foot high on hind legs so would have to play only kids' parts, either that or dwarves. That why he started drinking – was promised part in *Snow White and Seven Rabbits* but production fell through. Where was? Don't tell me don't tell me don't bloody TELL me! Just because you're bloody commissionaire, not commissionaire, questionnaire, doesn't mean you know it all, not by long chalk. Am not non compos thingy. Perfectly capable of remembering own name. Well, not own name maybe, but certainly capable of remembering what was writing about. Wait minute, wait minute, wait bloody flaming MINUTE. Was answering commissionaire, right? Question was when Hector start drinking, right? Do not know, but tell you this for nothing. Hector is finest big black rabbit ever lived. Would do anything for that rabbit. Only sorry now that used to be

"He says they'd rather destroy their secret than let us catch a glimpse of it."

BOXED IN

Many houses in Britain now have as many as seven televisions.
Daily Telegraph

afraid of turning round in case saw him, because would have liked shaken paw years ago. Best big black rabbit ever met, bar none. Would die for that rabbit. Would.

Have you ever tried to cut down on your drinking?

Don't listen, do you? Bloody cloth-ears, that's what are. Why ask all these questions if don't want answers? Look, ratbag. AM cutting down. How much have had since started filling in commissionaire? Go on – you know all answers, how much? Don't know, do you? Will tell you, then. Will surprise you now. Have had two small whiskies, that all. No, am liar, call it three. And that only because Hector insisted, to celebrate him coming out of hospital. Didn't you, Hector? All right, don't mind if do. Cheers. Down hatch. First today.

Have you ever sought medical advice on a drinking problem?

Why asking all these questions? What got do with you? Mind own business.

Have you ever experienced blackouts?

Matter of fact, since ask, DID seek medical advice on drinking problem, didn't we, Hector? Were in Wine Lodge one night having quiet drink, when suddenly, weren't in Wine Lodge any longer. Were out on backsides, having had alterations with landlord. Not alteration, allocation. Alliteration. Where you have disagreement with someone over them refusing give big black rabbit carrot in his vodka martini, and you hit them in mouth. Altercation. Anyway, just as picked selves up, who should come past but Dr Snodgrass, local GP. So asked him for advice on problem of where to get another drink. Could do nothing for me, as said we had had enough. Should have got second opinion. Should have seen specialist.

Have you ever suffered any of the symptoms of delirium tremens?

Blackouts? No, not serious ones. Just usual blackouts everyone else gets after having few. They never last more than three days, far as know.

Would you have difficulty in trying to give up drinking altogether?

Hector has, haven't you, Hector? Says yes. He once thought had lot of spiders crawling up him, didn't you, Hector? Says no, they were beetles, mainly. So if that is symptom of delirium thing, answer is yes for Hector, no for me, as did not personally see Hector's beetles.

Do you ever drink before lunch?

Can take it or leave it alone. Have given up altogether hundreds of times. Hundreds and hundreds. Given up drinking for life more times than can remember. Easy as falling off log. So don't talk about me not being able stop drinking, bloody pig-nosed commissionaire. Can stop drinking you under table, any day of week.

Would you be prepared to advise heavy drinkers who wish to adopt a more sensible approach?

Never have lunch, so question does not supply. Apply. Will tell you this, though, will tell it you for nothing. Have never had drink on empty stomach. Never. Don't believe in it. Always eat olive out of first triple rum and blackcurrant juice before drop touches lip. Always. Sets up for day. Then invariably eat hearty crisp before starting serious drinking in evening.

What was your age last birthday?

Certainly. Advice is keep out of Wine Lodge, landlord there is right bastard. 🐌

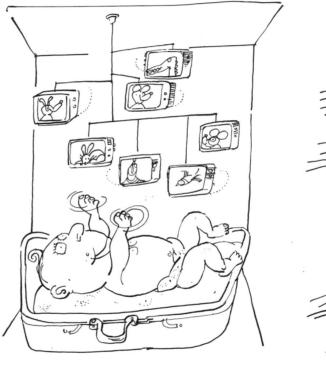

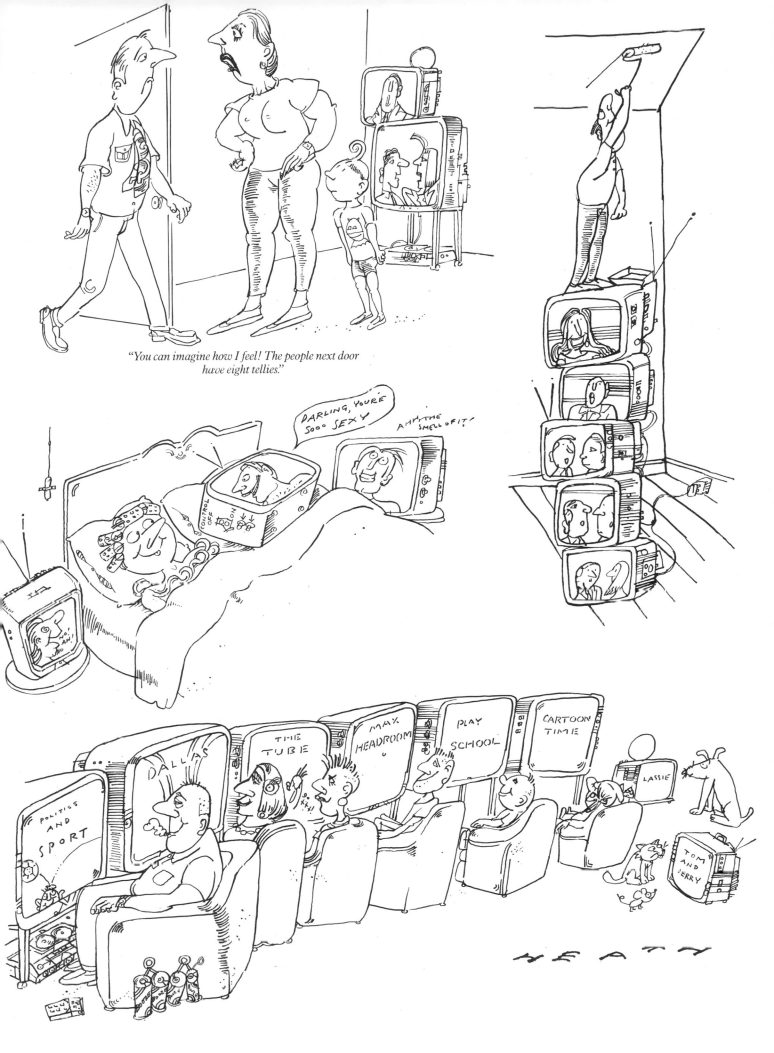

"You can imagine how I feel! The people next door have eight tellies."

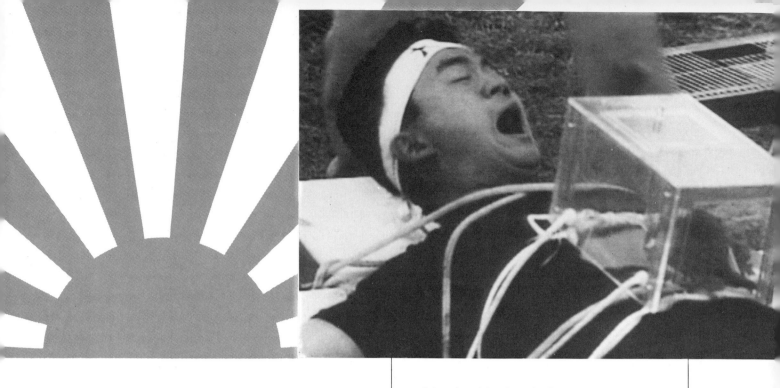

TRADE WARS

THE WACKY GAME SHOW O PAINFUL SANCTIONS AND PUNITIVE RESTRICTIONS THAT'S TESTING JAPANESE TRADE POLICY TO THE LIMITS O ENDURANCE

Grimacing with pain as the Dow Jones Industrial Average recorded its largest one-day drop in points, a Japanese finance minister has a live ferret fixed to a hole in his kimono. If, after five minutes, he has failed to grant an export licence to Cable & Wireless, DTI officials start pouring mulled Scotch export whisky down his nose.

Strapped and shackled to non-tariff barriers, a team of Tokyo traders have their backdoor import controls held over shark-infested waters while their toenails are wired up to dirt-cheap semi-conductors. First man to beg for mercy has to buy a round of sake for the Group of Five leading industrial nations. The runner-up buys Paul Channon lunch.

Lashed upside down with red tape, Japanese industrialists have their licences revoked and are subjected to horrendous administrative complications, examination for health and safety, detailed product tests, certification and scorched nipples until they agree to open markets and reciprocity in financial services.

The remodelled Immigration Hall at Gatwick where Japanese passengers will be re-routed unless Prime Minister Yasuhiro Nakasone agrees to speed foreign access to Japanese markets. Arrivals have to reach the Duty Free Shop in a wet-suit full of soldier ants by scooting a baggage trolley pre-heated to 200°C. The winner is the first to buy £1m worth of novelties.

As part of a retaliatory package of swingeing measures threshed out to test Tokyo to the limits of endurance, a foreign exchange dealer is roped to foreign goods and has five minutes to escape being savaged by a bull representing market trends. Unless he then agrees to go on covering the American balance of payments deficit, he is smothered in EEC butter and left to mud-wrestle with a bear.

JEFFREY ARCHER

"Jeffrey Archer's turbulent story, which after lots of practice he can précis in ten minutes flat, seems to bash on regardless, like his rip-snorting paperbacks. Perfectly simple, it seems. But pay careful attention and you sense his in-built filing, vetting system. You get things straight. In perspective. In context. Or else you never meet again."

DOESN'T have an enemy in the world. No. Perfectly simple. He trusts everyone. If they take advantage of his trust – fine. Never speaks to them again. We meet, but if I quote him out of context – fine. We never meet again. So lots of friends, he sees them all the time. But no enemies, since he'll not meet them, ever. Perfectly simple.

Between you and me, by the way, he never met her. The one we mustn't talk about. If I do choose to talk about her, if I take advantage – fine. I'll finish up in court as well. Perfectly simple. There'll be a court case soon enough. He plans to have some fun.

But then he always does. Damned if he'll stop being an enthusiast, he says. Won't and in any case couldn't. Always the way. Tireless energy. Perfectly simple. Fully occupied, night and day. Can't stand holidays. What was it old Jimmy Goldsmith said? He goes on holiday and by the Wednesday he wants to buy the beach. By the Friday he wants to sell it. Marvellous line. Knows what he means. You've either got it, or you haven't. Perfectly simple.

Of course he never stops talking. Speaking, I should say. What he said, five years ago, before he was Deputy Chairman, was that he wanted to talk in 500 constituencies. And raise a million pounds. Well. Just under 400 to date. And £800,000 or so. The business over the girl he never met did make him feel a bit low, of course it did, of course it did. But only for a couple of days. A great friend of his rang him up, never mind who, and said Jeffrey, we'd better declare war. It's the only way to keep you occupied, stop you pacing about. He needs to be *doing* things. So he does. And if people don't like it – fine. He ignores them and gets on with it anyway. Perfectly simple, really.

The job's still got to be done and Jeffrey's going on doing it: so last week he was up in Liverpool, Manchester, Wallasey; the week before Bradford, Dewsbury, Pontefract. He doesn't drive himself, not by car, he means. Not since one day when he nodded off on the motorway and, between us, is bloody lucky to be here to tell the tale. We hadn't better talk about that.

Bit of a treadmill, of course it is, of course it is. But he bets he knows Britain better than any politician: not because he's cleverer, only because he's *been*, listened to the managing directors and the little old ladies *at first hand*. That's terribly important. Of course it is.

It's got to be done, of course it has, of course it has, especially in an election year. He'll not clock up the 500 in time. Probably not, but don't quote him. Nor will he reach the million much before Christmas. Last Christmas Day he was issuing writs. Oh and took a few weeks off to write a play. What? Long-hand. Does it all in long-hand, always has, gets secretaries to type it up and does his corrections on successive typescripts. Want to know what the real nightmare once was? It was supposing the first book hadn't taken off. What then? He means there are upsets and upsets. Then, he couldn't pay the bills, *any* bills. That was really a time to sweat a bit. Now, whatever hits him, he knows that if need be, he doesn't have to work again.

Hypothetical, of course it is, of course it is. Fully occupied day and night, hasn't got a minute off. Well, no. That's not strictly true. The other day he did have an hour to spare, had nothing on the diary from 2.30 to 3.30. So he tootles off out to a gallery and buys himself a masterpiece.

No, I'd better not say that. Bought a simply marvellous painting, marvellous thing, and he loves to collect a few marvellous, marvellous things. See that? Sisley. Do I like that one? Dufy. But we mustn't go on about this.

When he's writing, by the way, the concentration comes in roughly two-hourly bursts. About that. He doesn't know what I find, David, but what he finds, Jeffrey, is that two hours is about enough. After that you need to refresh the old batteries. So he'll watch snooker, or a marvellous old black-and-white movie on the box. It clears the brain, he finds. Or he'll do a bit of exercise, go for a walk, play squash. It helps to be physically fit, of course it does, of course it does. Keeps you on your toes.

He'd been on his toes when first I'd rung to ask him to talk. Yes and no, he'd stated. He'd meant yes, in so far as he couldn't see what harm it'd do to talk, even though he'd been saying lately that he wouldn't talk to anyone, not for a little while yet. But no, in so far as he wouldn't be able to talk about I knew what, *that*, since all that would be *sub judice*. Did I know what he meant? See the difficulties? OK. Right I was, then. Fine. Perfectly simple.

I'd talked to Angie, who's marvellous, to fix a slot in the diary. She'd gathered he'd said yes, said Angie, so we'd better make it soon. How's about ten the next day? I'd come to Alembic House (one's sumptuous penthouse and *salon*, on Albert Embankment, overlooking the Thames and the House).

But as ten the next day loomed, Jeffrey wasn't to be found in Alembic House. S'funny, said the lady who does for him, when I rang before Angie had arrived. Somebody had been in, because when she'd come, the door wasn't double-locked, the way it always is. Mr Archer is most particular on locks.

He's most particular over everything. Jeffrey Archer's turbulent story, which after lots of practice he can précis in ten minutes flat, seems to bash on regardless, like his rip-snorting paperbacks. Perfectly simple, it seems. But pay careful attention and you sense his in-built filing, vetting system. You get things straight. In perspective. In context. Or else you never meet again.

It's scarcely an everyday story of countryfolk, nor yet of political sophisticates, but does claim elements of both. Up from Somerset, he originally came and has more recently moved into Rupert Brooke's old vicarage in Grantchester. His wife's now a director of Anglia TV, by the way. But Alembic House beckons most days because, *gulp*, just look at that view: blow him if it isn't the best in London, a place so palatial it makes you feel like a king and is, gosh, one's indulgence. Of course it is. So why shouldn't one say so? It's perfectly all right to say that.

He's incontrovertibly earned it. An alembic, remember, is an old distilling apparatus and although Our Jeffrey is not yet 47 he has distilled his more spectacular slings and one or two arrows of fortune into the *oeuvres* which continue to coin it from royalties he estimates at well over £50,000 *a week*. Never needs to work again, he says again.

Grist to this ever-grinding mill has included his heady days at Oxford, where Jumping Bean (he says he was called) was quick on his feet enough to take an athletics Blue and another for gymnastics, and fame, if not notoriety, buzzed about his high-profile charity fund-raising, persuading The Beatles to chip in. It has included, too, his precociously go-getting appointment as MP for Louth at the tender age of 29, and of course his subsequent cropper when a "misjudged" investment into a dodgy Canadian outfit which reckoned to have the answer to pollution from car exhausts, hadn't.

Jeffrey had been had on an heroic scale and feared as much when Scotland Yard first tapped on his door and on to his mat thudded a bank statement with almost half a million in the column headed *Debtor*. It was his darkest hour. *One* of his darkest hours. As he says, he owed money, then.

Something like that. Actually it wasn't *quite* so sudden and traumatic, but gosh, the gist of it is accurate enough and what's the point of telling a story unless you dress it up a bit (qv *Not a Penny More, Not a Penny Less*)?

The fact is he was indeed skint, felt responsible for others in the same boat and obliged to resign from public life, if not jump from Big Ben. He means way back when. He doesn't draw contemporary parallels. Neither should we. Not if we are to meet again. Perfectly simple.

The single most remarkable of Archer's everlengthening list of achievements must be that first period of convincing people he was not washed up. Convincing himself, of course, look no longer than it takes to uncork a bottle of his Krug and say tra-la-la. The second most remarkable will be if he manages to swing it again. Sorry, *when* he manages to swing it again.

The precedents, at least, are good. The shelf-bending international best-sellers were helped by his indefatigably defiant self-assurance and talent to promote whatever takes his fancy. In the case of books about his own life, which he has never been able to put down, there could not have been a more appealing incentive. Publishers reeled as Jumping Bean set about it: man and publicity machine in perfect harmony. The millions stacked up, but Jeffrey longed for diversion.

His Big Leap Backwards into mainstream politics was no less well orchestrated. Political society for a long time seemed to centre around glittering lunches in Alembic House and no one has yet been able to match Jeffrey's chatterboxy turn of speed at what's called the "chicken and peas" run – the endless round of Conservative Party lunches.

It has been clear from the start that Jeffrey Archer would go rapidly to the top and very likely over it. He has always provoked extremes of reaction, especially from them who have never experienced at first hand the charm and take exception to the brazenly promoted persona.

Never one to look before he's leapt, Jeffrey continues to work without respite on the latest real-life twists of a plot whose pace has never flagged, of course it hasn't, of course it hasn't, no matter what people say. It simply does not matter what people say, unless what they say isn't true. That's different. Just you watch this space. He can't, or he won't, say more than that. Just wait, that's all. It won't be long now. Though he's not saying what. I mustn't either. And that's quite enough said about that. Whatever it is. ❧

TELEVISION

INSIDE STORY
FRANCESCA ANNIS as Paula Croxley   DOUGLAS LAMBERT as Walter Schiff
ROY MARSDEN as John Bennet   HARRY ANDREWS as Lord Glenross

THE GOOD DOCTOR BODKIN ADAMS
TRISTRAM JELLINEK *as Geoffrey Lawrence*   TIMOTHY WEST *as Dr John Bodkin Adams*

John Jensen

THE ELEVENTH HOUR: STRANGER THAN FICTION
THE FORSYTE SAGA   NYREE DAWN PORTER *as Irene*   ERIC PORTER *as Soames*

MISS MARPLE   JOAN HICKSON

Mrs Cynthia Foskett of Okehampton, soon after her arrest on a charge of impersonating Queen Victoria. A vaulting horse, diving-suit, inner-tube, Arapahoe head-dress, eight pairs of manacles and a pound of sprouts were taken into police custody, but the ferret succeeded in escaping.

A rare oleograph of **Congressman Ambrose Finemesser** of Alopecia, NY, who called at Balmoral in June 1879 in the hope of persuading the Queen to endorse a patent glove-hook which would put Alopecia on the map. She of course refused, but insisted that he stay for tea. The gin-urn was wheeled in. In November, the Congressman was identified by a party of American doughboys on leave in Shanghai, one of whom thought there was something familiar about the man pulling their rickshaw. Sadly, Finemesser was unable to remember anything of his recent past, especially the whereabouts of his lower intestine. He was taken back to New York and, as the picture shows, fitted with a device enabling him to ingest soup.

Early automobilist **Seamus Nork**, who, in 1889, was discovered lurking trouserless in the Sandringham bushes by the East Anglian Constabulary, who sold him to Queen Victoria for £2 10s.

Gert und Daisy von Hesse, the notorious Prussian cross-dressers who plagued the Baltic during the late 1860s wheedling money from sailors in return for a coracle-mounted pornographic double-act the mere mention of which remains sub judice to this day. They came to Her Majesty's attention in November 1871, and spent that Christmas on the Isle of Wight in four days of continuous charades during which several footmen tunnelled out and sought sanctuary in Parkhurst Gaol. Victoria's favourite tableau was *Scott's Emulsion*, in which she would dress up as a cod and be carried around Osborne House by either Gert or Daisy, whichever was the drunker.

A unique snapshot of the Chilean acrobatic troupe **Los Cinco Olvidados**, with their manager El Pimpo, taken after the 1876 Royal Command Performance in Mrs McCluskie's Elite Guest House, Brighton, at which they were the only act. They appear to have removed their protective elbow pads for the picture. Soon after the performance the group broke up. Indeed, Manuel Y Gasset (*2nd from left*), as his stick shows, started breaking up during the performance.

BARGEPOLE

I expect that you read the nonsense in your newspaper about the Great Divide and thought "so what?". This is unhealthy. Not because the people in the North have anyone to blame but themselves, for being savages, but because of unenlightened self-interest. If we were Samoan fuzzy-wuzzies (and one word out of the Race Relations industry on that and I shall push their glittering white teeth down their throats) we would be up and about now, throwing buns down volcanoes and sacrificing civil servants to the Fire Gods.

You might think this is a waste of time. Civil servants are not known for their ability to do anything properly and there is little point in a sacrifice if the victim doesn't notice. I have been urged to sacrifice a Johnny-come-lately in a "newspaper" who is copying what I am assured is my style, but why bother? The bugger wouldn't know you were up him with Rolf Harris until the singing started, so hurling him down a volcano followed by a hail of buns would be a waste of effort.

The same thing with civil servants who lie and cheat and steal and grow fat, although their "honours" for which they seem to live have become devalued now. What could have possessed the Queen to honour those two damned actors? A friend of mine wrote a letter to *The Guardian* pointing out that it was in fact Mr Jay and Mr Lynn who should have been honoured because they actually *wrote* the stuff (you may have read his letter elsewhere too, because a number of half-baked "columnists" served it up as their own idea the following day) but I suppose Mrs Thatcher regards writing as somehow ignoble, making it up as you go along and so forth, but the point is that this is what we can expect from now on.

They drew a map in the *Daily Mirror* showing the North and South-East and I noticed that the North seems to stop at Northampton and the South-East extend to the Lizard. At first I just thought that the *Mirror* had fouled up again but then I thought, "No, they would not foul up, they are a serious paper and anyway they've given me a job," and as it turns out I am right. What is happening is that *the North is creeping downwards*.

Think of it as an Ice Age, except with anoraks and pasty complexions instead of nice clean ice. The old jokes about Watford are coming true. Any minute now we'll be holed up in our drawing rooms huddled together against the glacial creep of hoarse, inarticulate, shouting Northerners. It will be on the news: London Shivers As Terminal Morain Reaches Golders Green; Social Temperature Continues To Fall.

We will all have to learn new manners.

We will have to cultivate rudeness and being sick on stout and hake, and wearing those strange slimy greenish clothes, and holding our knives like pens and our pens like spanners; we will have to call each other "Duck" and become accustomed to inexplicable cries of "Owdyer Tart" on the 'bus, and smoke Park Drive cigarettes which we keep in a chromium cigarette case with an enamel Scottie on, which belonged to our Dad, and light with a Ronson Varaflame in a suedette pochette. We shall have to eat Fry's chocolate and wear TruGel on our hair and laugh at Nancy-boys ("Phookin Jessie!"); we will be obliged to wear pens in our top pockets and keep our change in a purse and hang things in our cars.

When we go out it will be for steak and all the trimmings. We will put on shiny suits and matching tie 'n' handkerchief for smart, and our wives will stand in the hallway squeezing our blackheads and nagging us, and we will have a row in the car on the way. And when we get there ("One thing, you can allus rely on Berni") we will walk in, rubbing our hands, and we will thank the waiter every time we see him, and we will have Irish Coffee and wink at each other across table and think it's all just like *Dallas* on telly.

It will all of course be a terrible shame and the most *awful* blow to our weay uv lafe deown heah axely to have all these dreffly ah, ah, *unsporlt* peepl infesting us with their ah, ah, well t'be frairnk, *comn* weays but I dare say we'll get used to it. It'll be a pity to see the Sithe go down the plarg, though. Look how we have adairpted to changing circ'ms't'nc's: for example, I saw on the back of a bus the other day (an appropriate place for it) an appalling trumpeting little poster advertising a company which advertised itself as being Public Relations Consultants to London Transport Advertising. You see how apsley *innovative* that is, in a communications/media/new-tech service industry? I mean, there they are, earning money from doing public relations for an advertising company which advertises on buses and *with* the money they get from doing public relations for an advertising company which advertises on buses they are *buying* advertising on the buses from the company which *does* the advertising on buses, to advertise the fact that they do public relations for an advertising company which advertises on buses. I mean, isn't it just *neat*? No harm done, nobody's hands dirty and everyone's kept in Beef Wellington and BMWs 'til Doomsday. And this is the sort of sosarty which the North is threatening, and I haven't even *mentioned* Lloyd's and Guinness and Lazard's and some *wonderful* USM flotations of the most *remarkable* service-orientated start-up ventures, because of course what it comes down to is do you want a purpose to your life or do you want a Porsche? I know I do.

BUILD-IT-YOURSELF TOPICA

Aladdin

Act II, Scene 5.

Enter Frank Bruno in a puff of smoke.

Frank: I am the Genie of the Ring! Ring – get it?
Our mate Aladdin's really chuffed, and yet it
So happens that his happiness is men –
Aced by that Abanazer berk again.
But he don't know that in the scene that we
Are gonna show you now. I don't like tea.

Well, I do really, but it's gotta rhyme, dunnit – know what
I mean?

*Exit Frank. Curtains open to reveal a room in Aladdin's palace.
Aladdin's bride, the beautiful Princess Michael (herself) is
discovered reading a book. Suddenly she gasps and hurls it
furiously to the floor.*

Michael: Typical! Every time I write something, somebody else
uses it ten years before!

Enter Marti Caine as Aladdin. She sings:

Marti: On a wonderful day like today,
When the moon is as big as a yellow balloon,
Even Rod Stewart is singing in tune,
On a wonderful day like today!
Michael: Hello, darling.
Marti: Hello, love – and hello again, boys and girls.

Marti and Michael kiss.

I must say, Michael dear, you're looking even more
incredibly royal than usual this evening.

MUTTY STAR-STUDDED PANTO

Michael: (*loftily*)
All people on this earth, alive and dead agree
That I possess the very finest pedigree.
True Royals don't have freckles or big feet.
(*confidingly*)
Diana once, outside her hotel suite,
Placed both her shoes for cleaning. Come next day,
She found that they had both been towed away.

Marti: That was smashing. Here, I nearly forgot – I've got a real
treat for you. Yes, specially reunited just for tonight, here
are – the Boomtown Rats!

Enter the Rats.

The boys are going to perform – of all things – that great
Carmen Miranda number, "I Yi Yi Yi Yi"!

*The Rats perform the song. Instead of maraccas, Bob Geldof
shakes a collection box. At the end of the number, Marti turns to
Michael.*

All right, love – what did you think of that?
Michael: That was Bob Geldof who does all that charity work.
I find charity very boring. (*she yawns*) No good.
Marti: (*to audience*) Well, *we* thought it was smashing, didn't we?

*Cheers from the audience. Exeunt the Rats. Marti takes Michael's
hands.*

Now love, I've got to go to Pekin on business, but I'll see
you in the morning.
Michael: "Goodnight, goodnight! Parting is such sweet sorrow."
That's mine. I'll write "The Winter's Tale" tomorrow. ▶

As they kiss, lovable Jim Davidson enters as Wishee Washee. Sees the kiss and does double-take.

Davidson: Two birds kissing? What is this, Greenham Common?

Exeunt Michael and Marti. Jim turns to the audience.

Have you seen the women at Greenham Common? Butch? They're butcher than the baker and the candlestick maker! And have you seen Bradford? Every Tom, Dick and Harry is named Mahomet! Now a little poem!

"You always make fun of minorities!"
That's what some nutters say.
What, *me* make fun of minorities?
Dat'll be do doo-dah day!

And have you seen Brixton? There's another chocolate ghetto! There's more where that came from in my new book.

He produces a copy.

There's a great gag in it about this communist. He comes from Vladivostok...

Re-enter Princess Michael.

Michael: And I come from vladi-*good*-stok!

She produces a copy of her book.

So I am more than qualified to write this resoundingly snobbish study of...

Enter Abanazer (Spike Milligan), carrying a pedlar's tray and wearing a false beard over his real beard.

Abanazer: New lamps for old! Not to mention copies of yet another book about Spike Milligan's war experiences!

He produces a copy of his book.

The lad spent six years in a tank, you know.
Michael: In the desert?
Abanazer: In the Aquarium! New lamps for old!
Michael: Mmmmmm. That sounds like a bargain.
Davidson: Don't trust him, Princess. Looks like a bloody hippy to me – see the beard?
Michael: (to Abanazer) Old man, would you...
Davidson: You know what a hippy has in common with Father Christmas? He never shaves and only works one bleedin' day a year!
Michael: (to Abanazer) Would you take...
Davidson: Saw a hippy the other day with a beard so scruffy nobody wanted to know her!
Michael: Silence!
Abanazer: Yes, he was expecting a laugh there.
Michael: (to Abanazer) Would you give me a new lamp for this?

She takes Aladdin's lamp from the table and offers it to Abanazer.

 # Cinderella

Act I, Scene 7.

The Baroness Hardup – Joan Rivers – is discovered in her boudoir, dressing for the ball.

Joan Rivers: Hey, kids – in a minute I'm off to the ball. Everybody's gonna be there. Even my gynaecologist, composer of the song "I'll be Gloving You Always". They're gonna have a terrific cabaret at the ball. They've booked Bernard Manning and Evel Kneivel. Evel's gonna jump his bike over Manning's mouth. Christina Onassis is gonna be at the ball too. I love that gal. In fact, I'm just *wild* about Hairy. Well, that's what they call her – on accounta she is the *hairiest*! Oh grow up! Every night she puts her legs up in curlers! Can we talk here? Christina doesn't use a depilatory – she uses a lawn-mower! I'm talking *hirsute*! This kid gets fan mail from chimpanzees! Or do you call them chimpanzeds over here? Anyway, six times a year Christina has to get waxed from her trunk right down to her knees. Goes to Moorfields Thigh Hospital! A week later her boy-friend goes around singing "Nobody knows the stubble I've seen!" Oh, grow up – have I ever lied to you?

She looks at herself in the full-length mirror and shudders.

Oh God, have my boobs dropped! Can we talk? The damn things have fallen so far, I call 'em Humpty and Dumpty!... Have you kids been drinking Tizer or embalming fluid? Don't you know the nursery rhyme? "Humpty Dumpty had a great fall"? Oh, but I guess you say "had a great autumn" over here. But as I was saying before I so rudely interrupted myself, my boobs have dropped so far, I have to get 'em soled and heeled twice a year! I'll bet Mrs Isaac Newton didn't have droopy boobs before her Goddamn husband invented gravity! Do you have gravity over here?... You do? What a small world – it's uncanny! But then I guess you say "untinny".

She looks in the mirror again. Another wince.

God knows I try to look good, but what the hell's the use? Three jars of Max Factor and I still look like Max Bygraves!

Enter Baron Hardup.

Baron: Somebody call me?

Applause, despite the fact that the Baron **is** Max Bygraves.

Baron: (to audience)
Thank you – your applause is a credit to your intelligence. Now, ladies and gentlemen, a beautiful song – beautifully sung.

The Baron and the audience join forces in eleven singalong numbers.

Joan Rivers: Those were all songs for the Baron's new album, "Cunnilingamax".

To small boy in audience.

Explain that to the rest of your row, will you, kid?
Baron: By the way, love, what do you think of Hardup Hall? I had it redecorated just for you.
Joan Rivers: It's okay, but I nearly broke my neck using that new drinking fountain in the bathroom.
Baron: Drinking fountain? Doesn't the word "bidet" mean anything to you?
Joan Rivers: Wasn't that two days before D-Day?

The Baron sings four more singalong numbers and exits.

Joan Rivers: You know, kids, I was just playing dumb about the bidet. I know plenty, really. Why, just last week I wrote an article on coitus interruptus for one of your Sunday

Abanazer: I certainly would, folks!

He seizes the lamp, whips off his disguise and laughs maniacally.

Revenge is sweet! And non-fattening too!

Re-enter Marti.

Marti: Hello again, I forgot my . . . Abanazer! And look what he has in his hand! What's happened here?

By way of explanation, Michael sings.

Michael: At saving money, yours truly's the champ.
That's why the lady
This royal lady
That's why the lady swapped the lamp.
Marti: *(to Abanazer)* And what did you think of that?
Abanazer: Suspiciously familiar.
Michael: So it should be – it's a parody of one of my own songs!
Abanazer: You wrote "The Lady is a Tramp"?
Michael: Of course.
Abanazer: But what about Rodgers and Hart?
Michael: *(quickly)* I wrote that as well!
Abanazer: Bah!
Marti: *(to audience)* Well, *we* thought it was smashing, didn't we?

Cheers from the audience, during which Frank Bruno appears in another puff of smoke and punches Abanazer. Marti snatches back the lamp.

Now Abanazer, you'll pay for your treachery with your life!
Abanazer: My life! Sapristi – why why why why why why, Aladdin?
Marti: You left me in that cave to die!
And something *worse* you did!
You dreamed up that commercial
Where they ask you to tell Sid!

Usual TV Commercial Reference Ovation from audience. Entire cast shoot Abanazer. Lord Longford (himself) rushes onstage, shoots Abanazer too and rushes off again.

He's dead – so let's all sing our final song.
Our story has a happy ending.
Michael: Wrong!
Despite our sacred vow to love each other,
While you've been gone, I've grown to love another!

Marti is speechless as Michael throws her arms about the astonished but delighted Davidson.

Davidson: That's great – but why am *I* the lucky lad?
Michael: The jokes you tell remind me of my Dad!

She sings: So keep on heiling!
'Cos when you're heiling,
Cast: The whole world heils with you!

(Curtain)

papers. It was a pull-out supplement! But where was I? Oh yeah – Christina Onassis. Thanks to her, you always know when it's spring in Athens. She raises her arm and a robin flies out. She's the only person I know who uses Head and Shoulders as a body lotion. Talk about Follicle City . . .!

Voices are heard offstage: two men arguing in falsetto.

Hear that? It's my two ugly daughters – the twins, Errata and Erotica. God, what a tramp that Erotica is! Can we talk here, kids? Last night that slut drove into a self-service gas station and helped herself to the manager! At the last Grand National, she had a job at Aintree. As a jump! I mean, we're talking tramp! Last month she went to Rhodes to visit her lovers – the Grecian 2000! And her sister Errata's even worse! She wears a plaque that says "Everybody slept here"! This morning she said, "Mom, I'm in love." I said, "Who's the lucky regiment?" Turned out to be the whole Hallé Orchestra. That bitch is a symphomaniac!

Enter the Ugly Sisters, played by Russells Harty and Grant.

Errata: Oh mummy, I'm so excited about the ball tonight!
Erotica: So am I – I hear handsome men are coming from all over the world!
Errata: From far and from near,
They're journeying here –
From Portugal, Paris and Putney!
Erotica: Oh, life would be sweet
If I could just meet
Tim Curry! Tim Rice! And Tim Chutney!
Errata: Ooh, that Tim Curry – if he coaxed me enough, I might just say yes!
Erotica: And so might I!
Joan Rivers: Oh, grow up – the only time either of you ever say no is

when a guy asks, "Had enough?"

Exit Ugly Sisters giggling.

God knows I didn't mean to have kids, kids. I lost an egg-and-sperm race. Their father was my first husband. He was a schizophrenic. I divorced him 'cause I didn't like group sex! So I married the Baron and *now* what am I getting? *Droop* sex! I thought I was getting a dreamboat but I wound up with a punt! I'll never forgive the Baron his lousy diction – if I hadn't misheard him when he said his name was Hardup, I wouldn't have married the bum!

Enter Samantha Fox as Cinderella to wild applause. She sings her latest release. Even wilder applause. Cinders acknowledges it by bowing low in her low-cut rags. The little boys in the audience burst into frenzied applause and puberty.

Joan Rivers: Kids, this is my stepdaughter, Cinderella. You've probably noticed, she's only flat when she sings. Can we talk? This kid never catches a cold. Never! Nobody can get close enough to give her one. Or should I rephrase that?
Cinderella: *(sighs ecstatically)*
This evening at the ball, I hope the Prince'll
Propose beneath the mistletoe and tinsel.
Joan Rivers: Oh, stop with the doggerel and grow up – you're not going to the ball! For you it's gonna be strictly Drudge City – you gotta stay here and bake a cake. *I* can't do it – the ones I bake are so heavy, the stove gets a hernia! Can we talk here? Just stick around and look after the house – oh, and if Christina Onassis drops in, don't tell her to get lost. She's your Furry Godmother! Thank you so much – good night!

She sweeps out.

▶

Act I, Scene 8.

The kitchen of Hardup Hall. Enter Ben Elton as Buttons.

Buttons: Hello... Okay then? Right, merry Christmas. Yeah, I know what Thatcher needs for Christmas, but how do you gift-wrap a conscience?... Yeah! (*Makes peace sign*) Okay, I'm Buttons, right? Let's have a song about Thatcher. (*sings*)

She's just an old Fascist girl
With an old Fascist mind.
When it comes to principles,
She's deaf and dumb and blind!

... All right! Okay, I can't bloody sing but the sentiments are right, right?... right (*makes peace sign*) But here I am at Hardup Hall, okay? Had to come all the way from Manchester but they say travel broadens the mind. What a load of crap that is – think of all the bleedin' miles Prince Philip covers!... Yeah!... I got mugged in Manchester. The bugger punched me and kicked me and burnt me with a fag, but they nicked him – for impersonating a police officer!... Okay!... They're all the bloody same, right?... So I want all of you to write abusive letters to the Manchester police, the Flying Squad, the Met... Oh, and you won't forget to tell CID, will you?... You've got to do 'em in panto, haven't you?... Okay. I see Thatcher's still saying Sellafield isn't dangerous. It's a wonder her tongue doesn't get liar's cramp!... All right!... Thatcher doesn't give a toss about radiation – her motto is "Let my people glow!" ... Okay!... This is a panto, right? Then let's have some bloody verse.

As sure as eggs is eggs and Pepsi bottles are returnable, If we don't shut down Sellafield, we'll have another Chernoble!

... Okay! But on with *Cinderella*, right? That's Reagan's favourite story, you know? Always has been – even during his *first* childhood!... Okay!... All right... that's enough, Elton. More story now. Here comes Cinders in her pathetic rags... not to be confused with the *Sun, Mail, Telegraph, Express,* and bloody *Times*!... Okay?... you'll recognise Cinders, Jennifer Saunders of French and Saunders, great team, great girl, not patronising her, I'm a feminist, my name's Ben Elton, keep laughs out of comedy, okay? Right!

Exit Buttons. Enter Jennifer Saunders as Cinders, looking forlorn.

Cinders: I'm sad 'cos Daddy's got another bride.
Life hasn't been the same since Mummy died.
Mum's colder than a British Rail Spam fritter.
She died of hydrophobia; Tebbit bit 'er.

A knock at the door. Cinders admits an old woman, her face hidden in a cloak.

Cinders: Why, you're the old lady I met in the woods yesterday. We were both looking for firewood, actually.
Old Woman: And when I asked you if I could have some of yours, you told me to piss off. That was cold and insensitive and uncaring.
Cinders: (*shrugging*) So?
Old Woman: So you're my kind of people!

Old woman throws off her cloak, revealing herself as a Latex model of Margaret Thatcher.

Thatcher: I came in answer to your call.
Tonight you shall go to the ball.
Cinders: Oh, how wonderful, actually.
Thatcher: Now first, my dear, you'll need a gown
Of satin and brocade.
Abracadabra! Sink the Belgrano!

She waves her wand. Cinderella's rags become a beautiful blue gown.

What's more, it's British made!

Cinderella's Dangerous Sisters (Ade Edmondson and Rick Mayall) return from the ball, having forgotten something.

Ade: (*punching Rick*)
We're back! I'm lovely Adrienne!
Rick: (*kneeing Ade in the groin*)
And I'm her lovely sister!
Ade: (*strangling Rick*)
I'm very very very pissed!
Rick: (*nutting Ade and falling down*)
And I am even pisseder!

They spy Cinderella and her Godmother, realise what they're up to, scream with rage and blow the house up.

(*Curtain*)

152

5 OCTOBER 1986   No 8,461   Price 50p   ☆ ☆

OVERSEAS PRICES
*Austria   AS 45 | *Italy   L5,000
Belgium   Bfr 120 | *Malta   50c
*Canada $3.50 | *Norway   Nkr 20
*Denmark Dkr 7.2 | *Portugal Esc 380
*Finland   Fmk 14 | *Spain   Plas 400
*France   Ffr 20 | *Sweden Skr 18.00
*Gibr'ltr £1.25p | Switz.   SFr 5.5
*Greece Dra 258 | *USA $3.00
*Germany DM 6.80 | 2nd post paid NY
Holland 0.Fl 6.50 | USPS No 528 440
*Republic of Ireland (inc VAT)   80p
*Without Colour Magazine

THE SUNDAY TIMES

Revealed: the secrets of Israel's nuclear arsenal

INSIGHT
THE SECRETS of a subterra-
nean factory engaged in the

ALAN COREN

The Bespoke Overkill

THE hand-lettered fascia board said:

Rappaport & Moss
Bespoke Gents Ware
No Bang Too Large Or Small

I pushed at the door.

It opened. The little bell tinkled.

"Don't slam!" shouted a voice.

I stepped through, and closed the door carefully. The shop smelt of plutonium and herring.

Outside, in the traditional hubbub of Tel Aviv's bustling bomb district, harassed men in armbands pushed clanging racks of missiles along the narrow pavements, haggard sales reps dragged their samples in and out of a hundred overstocked shopfronts, frantic knots of thermonuclear wholesalers scuttled, yelling, among the hurtling delivery vans and their cursing drivers, outraged designers stamped their feet at sweating patent agents, warehouse foremen clouted factory runners, errand boys with trays of lemon tea collided with office juniors struggling under piles of order books and invoices – but, in here, all was suddenly and strangely quiet.

Except for a faint far pattering beneath my feet, as of carpet slippers over dry flagstones. After a moment or two, a pink and hairless head emerged from a trapdoored gap in the middle of the floor, and peered around, until its half-moon spectacles settled on me.

"Stocktaking," he explained. "Give a slam, anything could happen. I wouldn't like to be responsible. We got some slightly soiled Sidewinders down there you only have to look at twice."

"I quite understand," I said.

"Ask me why we bought them in the first place."

"Why did you buy them in the first place?"

"Don't ask."

He climbed out, puffing, and patted the white dust off, gently.

"Rappaport," he said. He pushed the spectacles onto his forehead. "What can I do for you?"

"I'd like a bomb," I said.

He pulled the spectacles down again, and looked at me over the wire rims.

"If you wanted a pound walnuts," he said, "you'd be next door." He removed the spectacles, and his waistcoat being undone, polished them slowly with the end of his tie. "This bomb. It's for you, or a gift?"

"For me."

He took a small black notebook from his waistcoat pocket, and clicked his ballpoint.

"What kind of price range are we talking here?"

"I'm not really sure," I said. "I'll, er, I'll know it when I see it."

Mr Rappaport shrugged.

"Listen, whatever you say. Pressure we can all do without." He pointed to a sign, which read *Please Look Around And Waste Our Valuable Time Without Obligation.* "I just don't want you should be embarrassed. You see something in a nice cobalt, say, it suits you down to the ground – you should pardon the expression – and you say perfect, how much, and I tell you, and it's outside your price range, how will we both feel? Terrible is how we'll both feel."

"I understand," I said.

"I'll call Moss," he said.

"Moss!" he called, into the hole.

"I'm coming," cried Moss, "I only got two pair of hands."

"That Moss," said Rappaport, "what a comedian. Always a wisecrack." He laid a hand on my arm. "From mutations, you don't have to worry. Everything comes straight from the factory, two wrappings, official seals. Don't talk to me about spotless, you can eat off the floor down there."

A second head appeared in the trapdoor, a thinner head, wispy-haired, hollow-eyed, lugubrious of mien.

"Meet Mr Moss," said Mr Rappaport. "A diamond."

"From the wages," murmured Mr Moss, "a rhinestone."

"This gentleman," said Mr Rappaport, "is looking for a bomb."

Mr Moss climbed out, sighing, and re-arranged his thin limbs.

"Nuclear?" he enquired.

"Naturally, nuclear!" snapped Mr Rappaport. "What are we all of a sudden, a flea market?"

His assistant looked at him for a time. He blew his nose.

"Conventional is also nice," he said, finally. "For conventional, what were we? A byword was what we were."

"Conventional was good to us," conceded Mr Rappaport. "When did I say different? Times change, Sam."

"Change, change," muttered Mr Moss. "Conventional is always in fashion. A gentleman should always own a couple items conventional. Discreet, not loud." He turned to me. "It's for a formal occasion?"

"I'm sorry?" I said.

"A big affair. An invasion, a war, something you'd like to declare?"

"Possibly," I said. "I'm not exactly certain."

Moss looked at Rappaport.

"Young people these days," he said. "What do they know?"

"He's not wrong," said Rappaport to me. "Once upon a time, formal was formal, casual was casual, you knew where you were. Customers were selective. The occasion called for ten tons high explosive, ten tons high explosive is what it got, you needed a small piece napalm, you ordered a small piece napalm."

"Today," said Moss, "who knows from precision bombing? Personally, I blame Vietnam. Fifty thousand tons HE from ten miles up for a *bridge*? I used to watch it on the television, it broke my heart. Wonderful materiel, and what did they do with it?"

"Cowboys," said Rappaport. "Never mind the quality, feel the width."

"It's simply," I said, "that I'm not quite sure what the requirement will be. Is there anything ▶

"I know, but who was going to stop him?"

sort of, well, all-purpose?"

Moss sighed.

"We're talking bespoke," he enquired, "or ready-to-drop?"

"Under the circumstances," I said, "I suppose something off the peg would be better. I could see what I was getting."

"You want a bomb, a missile, a satellite, what?" enquired Mr Moss, somewhat irritably.

ROGER WODDIS

Logo Con Brio

The Medici String Quartet has put its services up for auction in exchange for commercial sponsorship.

"Music has charms to sooth a savage breast"
And calms the livid more than lager can:
Congreve apart, such feelings are expressed
By every Mozart freak and Haydn fan.
What if Count Rasoumovsky could have guessed
The note he struck in funding Ludwig van?

To subsidise a quartet in B flat
May have sufficed in 1824,
But patronage today means more than that:
Those who are born to make the spirits soar
Have learnt the market-place is where it's at.
Whatever else, musicians know the score.

There will be slogans geared to selling things,
T-shirts for tissues where Tchaikovsky's played,
Pasta to flog when Pavarotti sings,
Cars and cigars and low-fat lemonade.
And as for those who strain to hear the strings –
"Beethoven Plus – the only sound deaf-aid!"

"What kind of delivery system are we talking here?"

"A straightforward bomb," I said, "I think."

"Straightforward," echoed Mr Rappaport. He barked a short, dry laugh. "You hear, Sam?"

"If it was straightforward," said Mr Moss, "where would we be?"

"The Bahamas is where we'd be," replied Mr Rappaport. "Antibes, possibly."

"Florida is bad?"

Mr Rappaport reached behind the littered counter, took down a sample book, licked his thumb, turned the pages. Moss peered over his shoulder. Rappaport paused. Moss nodded.

"If you want a plain vehicle-delivered bomb," he said, swivelling the book around towards me, "you couldn't do better than this one. A very popular number. Always in fashion."

"It looks a little big," I said.

"Big is the thing these days," said Moss. "Ask anyone. A generous cut is the style. Read the magazines, you'll see."

"Even so . . ."

"Do they do it in a five-kiloton?" asked Rappaport.

"No," said Moss. "We'd have to alter." He drew a piece of chalk from his waistcoat pocket. "Take it in a bit here, make a little dart there, you wouldn't even notice the seam."

"Could be very smart," nodded Rappaport, "in a five-kiloton. While we're at it, you know what I'd do? I'd make up the case in a nice lightweight. Pass me the swatch."

Mr Moss reached beneath the counter, and handed up a bundle of metal plates on a ring.

"Ruthenium is nice," he said to me. "Feel."

"It's not too thin?" I said.

"What do you want," cried Moss, "shrapnel?

This is a nuclear device. If you want a hand grenade, go to Feldman!"

"Look," said Rappaport, soothingly, "how about we do the case in ruthenium and set the fins off in a nice twelve-ounce blue tungsten?"

"You're giving him a bespoke bomb at ready-to-drop prices?" enquired Moss.

"It's not all about money, Sam," said Rappaport. "A craftsman is a craftsman. The gentleman walked in the shop, right away I said: *that's a five-kiloton in a nice ruthenium-tungsten manmade.* So we do it at cost, so what? We have a satisfied customer. If he likes it in nuclear, who knows, next season maybe he'll come back and we'll make it up in biological."

"There I'd argue," said Moss. "This is basically a traditional dirty bomb. Full in the waste. Sure, it's a little old-fashioned, it's been around a few years, but it's classical. With a bomb like this, you could walk in anywhere."

"You don't see it in a nice contemporary neutron?"

"It would take all the life out of it," said Moss.

Mr Rappaport shut the book, and looked up.

"Should be ready Thursday," he said. "I can't promise, I got two cutters off sick, you know how it is. But we'll do our best."

"Well," I said, "could I let you know, it was more in the nature of a general enqu . . ."

"Listen," said Mr Rappaport, "you don't want to commit yourself, so don't commit yourself. Take it home, see how you like it, if it doesn't deter anybody for seven days, bring it back, we'll refund. After all, we can always shift it, am I right, Sam?"

Mr Moss, rolling up his tape-measure, nodded.

"How much can it hurt?" he said.

"Sorry, I must have dozed off for a minute. You were about to tell me what a hypnoherbalist actually does."

"For a shop steward, you're in pretty good shape. I'd say you've got years of confrontation in you yet."

NEXT!

"We can't exactly change your spots but we can conceal the unsightly ones."

"Say, whaddya know, it really worked. My hiccups are cured!"

"Yours is a sincere face, doctor. I'll bet you'd be very successful in advertising."

DOC BRIEF
ROBERT BUCKMAN

I hardly need remind you that it is now two weeks since New Year's Day.
Speaking personally, I made no fewer than eight New Year's resolutions and have so far broken seven of them.
In fact, the only resolution I was able to keep was my resolution not to mention
New Year's resolutions in this column. Oh bum.
Well, anyway, as part of my continuing survey of The Human Face I shall now consider involuntary
or reflex facial motor activity — which will include all those facial activities that cannot be controlled by
conscious thought or will-power, neither of which are necessary if you want to be a doctor.
Which is why we're so good at looking cool and impassive in emergencies —
and playing poker.
Now, do read on quickly or the wind will change and you'll be stuck
on this opening paragraph for ever.

FACIAL REFLEXES

It has been said that the human face is the shop-window of the soul. This is very worrying, particularly if you have a face like mine — and even more particularly if you don't happen to have a portrait in your attic that does your ageing and sin-wearing for you.

In fact, if I might be permitted a personal note here, several people have put forward the theory that my face is acting as the portrait of Dorian Gray for several of my sinful friends. They seem to look young and innocent while they get away with murder (or other interpersonal trans-actions of more interest and fun), while I have a debauched and sinful face, but actually spend the whole party in the kitchen and end up emptying the ashtrays. However, that is my problem.

The point is that whatever kind of soul it is that the face mirrors, on occasions the window does certain things that have nothing to do with the soul, e.g. bangs shut. These are the facial reflexes and we do them hundreds of times a day without thinking about them. Of course we do, I mean, if we thought about them they wouldn't be reflexes, would they? Right then. What we are talking about here are the involun-tary responses to external stimuli — blinking in bright sunlight, closing the eyes during a sneeze, licking the lower lip when eating a jam doughnut, drooling over Nastassja Kinski.

Now all these reflexes have survival value in the evolution of our species. We can thus assume that early in his history man must have been threatened by bright sunlight (which might interfere with his ability to hunt dino-saurs, avoid tigers, bowl from the east pavilion etc) and evolved the blink reflex to reduce the incident light and preserve acuity. Similarly, we can assume that Neanderthal man faced a major plague of jam doughnuts which posed a threat to the hygiene of his lower lip. Precisely what kind of a threat to mankind is posed by Nastassja Kinski is harder to define — though I think I have a pretty good idea myself.

BLINKING

In some respects, the blink reflex is the classic example of the kind of biological phenomenon of which the blink reflex is the classic example. But, in other respects, it certainly is not. Either way, what is so fascinating about the blink reflex is that it can be elicited by direct pressure on the eyelash, air pressure on the conjunctiva or visual stimuli connoting rapidly approaching objects — but, unfortunately, I have completely forgotten why that is so fascinating.

Anyway, the whole point of the blink reflex is that it represents an evolutionary compromise between the need to protect the eyeball from damage by putting the covers on it, and the need to keep looking around to avoid predators etc. There is evidence that some early hominid apes had a blink reflex that only went one way, so they shut their eyes and kept them shut dur-ing any danger. Some paleontologists believe that descendants of these unfortunate animals can still be found driving elderly Cortinas on the A23 on Sundays.

GRIMACING

Grimacing is a complex reflex in which virtually the entire face is screwed up in response to a gustatory stimulus of acid or bitterness, e.g. mother's cooking — which can also screw up the whole family according to some researchers, e.g. Portnoy's Complaint. However, what is so

interesting about the grimace is its value as a signal. Basically a grimace is a signal to the rest of the tribe which transmits something to the effect, "Look here, I'm eating this particular stuff and it's turning out to be really poisonous — for goodness sake get away as fast as you can."

Nowadays the grimace has been replaced by more complex warning signals, e.g. restaurant critics. But the power of the grimace signal can be estimated from its imitation in art forms, e.g. Japanese Kabuki theatre. Here, a grimace can portray an entire story which, in Western

theatre, would require a major speech. Thus one complex grimace might convey the idea that the person is the daughter of a warlord, and in love with a minstrel by whom she has fallen pregnant and is now compelled to marry, to her family's shame and discredit (the so-called shogun wedding).

The power of the grimace also leads to its voluntary use as a metaphor — to signal psychological indigestion or poisoning. You may find this concept difficult to grasp right now, but just you wait till the party political broadcasts get going.

"God. I hate auditions."

"It says here you sponsored him for five pence per square centimetre."

Proverbial Soup

READER'S Digest is a publication that I can take or leave. Staying the weekend in Leicestershire recently, I found it was the only available reading in the bathroom and so I took it. On page 137, I came across an article sub-headed: "These everyday phrases have surprising origins."

I examined the phrase "Saved by the bell". Now, you and I and the old boy next door know that if the bell sounds before a boxer has spent a full ten seconds lying on the floor, it signifies the end of the round and the pugilist is "saved" – which is an odd definition for a man who thought his troubles were over but can now get beaten up some more.

The origin, says Reader's Digest (who once paid me $150 to reprint something I had almost said on Radio Three four years previously), is that in the late seventeenth century a sentry at Windsor Castle was accused of being asleep on duty. His defence at the court martial was that since he had heard the clock of St Paul's cathedral, twenty miles away, strike thirteen at midnight, he could not have been asleep. The court ridiculed the idea that the bells could carry between London and Windsor and sentenced him to death. It was later verified, however (Reader's Digest is very into words like "however"), that the clock at St Paul's *did* strike thirteen instead of twelve times on that particular night. "Saved by the bell, the sentry was released and lived to the ripe old age of 102."

To my mind, the story poses more questions than it answers. Firstly, in the late seventeenth century, with all the noise of William trying to speak to Mary and vice versa, not to mention the Battle of Monmouth which was far from silent, there was no way you could hear St Paul's bells at Windsor unless you were asleep.

Moreover, if you were found asleep and said, "Actually I was awake, listening to St Paul's striking thirteen," you would have been put away during the King's pleasure. Further, by the time a seventeenth-century court martial had got itself convened, I doubt anyone would remember the date on which St Paul's cathedral clock had struck the wrong number.

These and many other thoughts passed through my mind in that Leicestershire bathroom – including the derivation of the saying "Too many cooks spoil the broth" which was not given by the Digest.

It was at the commencement of the year 1308 that a yeoman farmer from Somerset snared a griffin and handed him to Mrs Yeoman Farmer to give to the cook and provide a *demi-tasse* of *ma griff* for Sunday lunch.

The lads in the kitchen plucked the griffin, singed the flesh, and cut the neck into nine pieces. They anointed the beak with oil, as was the custom, and simmered the beast for two days, changing the water hourly for the first three hours. Then did they add onion and allspice, fenugreek and aniseed and some green herbage that grew on the hedgerows for which there was not yet a name, and two boys were posted at each end of the pot to remove the scum as it rose.

On the second day, the duty cook, unappraised of the length of time the griffin had been simmering, threw away the liquor surrounding the bird and rubbed the beak with oil, as was the practice, and added onion and allspice, fenugreek and aniseed and cow parsley which had been named just that morning, and set it to simmer.

As the duty-cook's cousin was due to be put to death in Plymouth the next day for some omission in respect of counting chimes from Bodmin clock-tower, he left two boys to remove the scum from either end of the vessel and took the late-night coach to the west. And that afternoon the griffin, who had been asleep since just after the coronation of Hereward the Wake, pulled himself together and emerged from the pan with a lot of noise and some loss of plumage and soup, and flew off to where griffins go when they have just woken up after a long time.

The hapless soup-boys, gravely frit because they knew they would be put to death, got an elderly culinary uncle, who was waiting for *nouvelle cuisine* to be invented, to come and make it all better.

There was a little liquid left in the pot to which the cook added some Knorr Suisse beef granules and a tin of Campbell's cream of mushroom soup. When the yeoman farmer returned from Taunton Assizes, where they had been hanging old Roundheads to keep their hands in, he sat down to his dinner and slurped a few slurps and said, "Who cooked this broth?"

His wife explained that it was the work of many hands, some now far afield, others taken over by General Foods of America, and he uttered one of the earliest battle-cries of domestic democracy: "One man, one soup" – which was later taken to mean "Too many cooks spoil a broth!"

"A stitch in time saves nine" came about when a suburban football team ate a barded joint of gammon (for high tea) in which the practitioner had regrettably left two larding-needles. The goalkeeper and a sweeper succumbed to a slow, uncomfortable and messy death, but the remaining nine players were unaffected and won the final of the Sanderstead Hospital Charity cup on penalties after extra time.

"Of course, some of the sense of wonder and mystery disappears when you find that it's the local McDonald's."

ROGER LEWIS

Little Lewis and Big Burgess

"We happened to be placed at the same table at a *Punch* lunch – a hebdomadal gathering of London media monkeys. Alan Coren was careful to separate us, fearing fisticuffs."

SINCE I became, at the instigation of Malcolm Bradbury in 1983 (and not at the instigation of Anthony Burgess), Anthony Burgess's Recording Angel, I have met my quarry thrice.

The first confrontation was masterminded by Richard Ellmann, biographer of James Joyce and Oscar Wilde. Over in Britain for the publication of *The Kingdom of the Wicked* – an apostolic completion of the Bible's cinematic re-writing, filmed as *A.D. Anno Domini*; Burt Lancaster's *Moses the Lawgiver* and Robert Powell's *Jesus of Nazareth* forming earlier portions of the triptych – Burgess had agreed to take the train to Oxford, accompanied by his wife.

Ellmann and I had a long wait at the railway station. The Intercity from Paddington was delayed. We amused ourselves spotting dons depart for metropolitan weekends – John Wain, for example. "I've just finished lunch at Brasenose," said the quondam Professor of Poetry, "and I've now to go and give a lecture I've not yet written in London. I'll scribble something between here and Reading." We told him our mission: to await Anthony Burgess. "Well," replied John, "I'd rather be doing what I'm doing than what you're doing." He rattled his bicycle through the turnstile, snaking the machine with difficulty past an oncoming mob.

The oncoming mob consisted of passengers from London. A clatter and confusion of ticket punching and portmanteaus knocked against shins.

I was trepidatious. I'd read every word Burgess had published that I could find. That's thousands of articles and essays; dozens of books (novels, critical appreciations, translations); hundreds of forewords and afterwords and prefaces. I was a hierophant – but had mitigated my enthusiasm, now and again, with the odd high-handed undergraduate sneer in an occasional review. Salutary moderation. Would Burgess take offence? He accepts praise without demur, but censure makes him bridle.

But of Burgess there was no sign. We thought he'd forgotten about the trip, or had decided to travel later, or had come by another route. Then, up the steps, like a Mancunian Orpheus from the underworld tunnel beneath the tracks, came the man of letters, followed by a diminutive bundle in bombasine black, Burgess's Eurydice, the contessa Liliana Macellari, known as Liana.

It was Liana who did the talking, in a heavily accented English, a fiery torrent, or creole, of her own devising, darting in and out of French

and Italian when the local word escaped her. She fizzed with admiration about her husband's *The End of the World News*, which she was currently translating; she fizzed with venom for an agent, or was it a publisher, who'd robbed her husband blind; she fizzed with enthusiasm for a book on Merlin she'd lately read, which would aid her husband's current composition – a novel about King Arthur called *The Sovereignty of the Sword*.

Meantime, Burgess was talking about a book on D.H. Lawrence he'd knocked off for Heinemann: "Heinemann finally woke up to the fact that it was Lawrence's centenary, so I said, you'd better celebrate it duly, so I've written them a short book." That was *Flame into Being* – a lively account of the Nottingham miner's son, which tells us as much about Burgess himself as about Lawrence. Both had indigent childhoods and were brought up hard; both were scoffed for literary ambitions; both married foreign aristocrats; both became self-exiles. The first chapter is called "Lawrence and Myself When Young".

Ellmann directed us towards New College, whither he'd recently retired as Goldsmith Professor. "This reminds me," said Liana, "of the opening scene in Antonio's Shakespeare film. A beautiful, beautiful script I recently found in

Bracciano. The film was never made, but it imagined Will meeting the philosopher Vico in Oxford."

I heard about the Shakespeare film. It was meant to star Maggie Smith as Ann Hathaway and Peter Ustinov as Ben Jonson. "Few of my scripts have ever been made," said Burgess. "The executive producers are fired, and projects are dropped."

Ellmann pointed out statuary and gargoyles. Burgess looked at memorial tablets. He calculated ages of the deceased, and was shaken to espy names of contemporaries. "All of us of that generation born just after the First World War are getting very old. We're dying off."

We next went to Ellmann's house in St Giles's for gin. I noticed an onomastic proliferation. Liana called Burgess *Antonio*; Ellmann called him *John* – from John Wilson, the baptismal name; an ursine American academic, in for pre-prandials, called him *Mr Burgess*; Mary Ellmann, sceptical of the man's merit and smarting from an anti-feminist remark Burgess had made years previously, didn't call him anything; and I, too, avoided all monickers. I'd read all his books, remember. How do you address a stranger you think you know intimately?

I left the proceedings when Antonio, or John, or Mr Burgess, started to recite Thackeray by ▶

"You're a sadistic bastard, Stig."

159

"Eva! You call this ironing?"

▶ ROGER LEWIS

the yard. It had transpired that the ursine American academic was a Thackeray bibliographer named Gordon Ray. "*The Rose and the Ring* is one of my favourite books," said Burgess, and off he went. Gordon Ray, now deceased, returned to New York to ask, "Who

the hell was that novelist with the Italian wife who knew the works of Thackeray by heart?"

My second meeting with Burgess was hardly that. We happened to be placed at the same table at a *Punch* lunch – a hebdomadal gather-

ing of London media monkeys. Alan Coren wa careful to separate us, fearing fisticuffs. He di not know we'd met. Ellmann was also presen listening to Irma Kurtz tell him about Laur ence Sterne. I was next to Cyril Ray, wine's wit tiest historian, and Dick Price, who is olde than God and twice as knowledgeable; the onl man I've met who can follow a Congreve plot.

Before the food, during drinks, I watche Burgess huffing and puffing on cigarillos, o display, baritonal and anecdotal during th boozy hours of obligatory wit. A critic, who' best remain nameless, praised "your wonderfu latest novel". Ten minutes previously, tha nameless critic had asked me for a fast sum mary "of the old bugger's new raving".

Burgess and I later jostled on the stairs, bot making egress, me rather drunk, my pocket full of cigars placed there by Michael ffolkes th cartoonist. "What," I asked Burgess, who wa searching for a plastic bag, "do you have in tha plastic bag?"

"Language tapes," he responded. "I'm teaching myself Russian."

Or it may have been Welsh, I don't rightly recall.

My third encounter was at the Apollo Theatre Oxford, in late 1985. Burgess had tailored a new libretto, called *Oberon Old and New*, for Scottish Opera's production of Carl Maria Von Weber's *Oberon* (1826). I'd received a telemessage summoning my wife and me to the vestibule, 6.45.

Burgess was accompanied by Leslie and Gabriele Pantucci, his literary agents and close friends. We were introduced, and Leslie is now my literary agent. Liana had stayed home in Monaco or Lugano or Rome or Malta or Callian. Very sensibly, any half-decent publisher's advance, or film producer's fee, is banged direc into property. The Callian cottage was once generously offered as a holiday address for myself plus spouse. Then, with comic business almost hard to believe, the key couldn't be found. A big rusty medieval clanking job impossible to duplicate. So we were offered a studio flat in Monte Carlo – but by this time we'd flown to Greece.

At the Apollo Theatre, Burgess was utterly generous, utterly a modest man of letters, shy when recognised and insisting on brief chats with votaries requesting an autograph. He was clad in green and wore "my Brancusi James Joyce tie". Burgess is colour-blind. Not knowing this at the time, I thought homage to the Emerald Isle was the point.

"I've read," he said, "Ellmann's *James Joyce* about twenty times." What, I wondered, did he make of my anatomising of himself for a big literary biographical study, called *The Paper Man*? "Shouldn't you wait until I'm dead? I do though, and who wouldn't, enjoy being written about. Great fun. But I don't want actively to be involved or influence you in any way. I offer you this, and you mustn't make anything of it: Joyce told Gorman he could do a biography, but he, Joyce, had to come over as a saint whose life was one long martyrdom."

We all laughed at this, and went in to enjoy the opera – a surrealistic production, set, for some reason, in a decrepit 1930s cinema. The librettist was alarmed. "Was that a boo?" he asked loudly at the conclusion. "I hope so. Rossini was booed!"

"I yam what I yam and that's all that I yam.
I'm Fleet Admiral Hiram J. Gibertson, the sailor man."

MARIA AITKEN

JUNGLE BELLES

"There seemed to be an enormous number of people waiting to arrest me on the Bolivian border. On closer inspection they turned out to be money-changers and the high level of inflation meant that fifty dollars' worth of pesos completely filled my hold-all. In one currency at least I was a millionairess."

WHEN I was a child, Immigration officers invaded the couchette on the Swiss frontier and gave my mother a hard time. In my adolescence, Gibraltar Customs solemnly cut all my North African melons and avocados in half. By adulthood, a string of similar experiences had convinced me that getting in and out of other people's countries required patience and stamina. Now that I have travelled in South America, filming *Lizzie: An Amazon Adventure*, I would like to add extrasensory perception and an unlimited capacity for alcohol to the list of necessities for border crossing.

The mysterious bureaucratic reasons that prevented us leaving Peru could not be voiced, but manifested themselves in teeth-sucking, head-shaking and incredulous study of our mountain of luggage. The officials at Pucallpa airport were polite but inflexible: they just didn't want us to go away from them to Brazil. We were a bedraggled little film unit, lying across our baggage and paraphernalia like beached starfish, forlornly trying to protect it from the attentions of the curious, and desperate to carry on with our filming schedule.

Many humid hours passed, dozens of bottles of beer were consumed, several dollars changed hands and eventually the airport guards sprawled with us among the cases. Out of this new intimacy emerged the root of the problem: the BBC luggage labels. Dyslexic – or possibly inebriate – confusion had led them to believe that the initials were not B.B.C. but P.B.C. (standing for Pasta Basica de Cocaina, or raw cocaine) and that we were the frankest smugglers ever to pass through Pucallpa Customs.

With this little misunderstanding smoothed away, we proceeded to Guajaramirim in Brazil, the most sophisticated town we had seen for weeks. The starfish revived: there were stranged cries of joy at the sight of a goodish hotel with fans whirring in the bedrooms; there was even a clothes shop where we could replace our Amazon-impregnated T-shirts, and, best of all, there were restaurants that served dishes other than river fish and manioc root. Fortified by *cachaça* (a sublime drink of cane liquor and lime juice that refreshes parts of you that you didn't even know you had), the unit faced the next border crossing with equanimity. At the end of the street ran the Mamoré river and across it lay the twin town of Guayaramirim in

darkest Bolivia. But the substitution of the "y" for the "j" gives no clue to the differences between these two places separated only by a few hundred yards of fast-flowing water.

"No one will believe this is an important border," said the producer, gloomily surveying the tiny port. "I think we had better beef it up for the camera." So I found myself round the corner hailing a truck with the stentorian instruction *"La frontera, por favor."* I was depressed to note that my best Berlitz had a definite undertow of "Harrods, please" and not entirely surprised when the driver took me out of camera range and dumped me. "I suppose it's useful footage to *have*," said the producer doubtfully. With *cachaça* coursing comfortingly through my veins, I saw no difficulties. The heavens opened in a tropical storm but I slithered down the port steps to hail a boat to Bolivia.

"Action," yelled the producer.

The boatman refused to take me. Intrepid women explorers are supposed to get everywhere they want to, so it was something of an embarrassment. "Cut," said the producer resignedly. By the time I'd finished my altercation with the boatman, the drenched film crew were under cover consuming consolatory *cachaças*. Trying to extract what dignity I could from the situation, I described my exchange with him as "a valuable piece of research". This was an idiosyncratic little border.

"He's a Brazilian boatman and he can only bring passengers from Bolivia to Brazil – he has to go over there empty. We need a Bolivian boatman to take us over and then *he* comes back empty."

The producer was very cheered by the Alice-in Wonderland evidence that this was indeed a

"As a matter of interest, what did you do with that second chance I gave you?"

"He's always done his best to protect the company
from adverse publicity."

proper border, and she and the cameraman and I piled into a little Bolivian boat, its engine roaring against the strong current. We concluded that this discreet frontier must be an obvious crossing-point for drug-smugglers and tried fruitlessly to spread our anatomies over the obstinately adhesive BBC labels. Hanks of weed and debris floating past us looked uncannily like the victims of summary execution, and by the time Guayaramirim was upon us, I had psyched myself into a life sentence in a Bolivian gaol.

The harbour buildings were under water – a recurring feature of South America is the fact that the annual rains seem to take builders by surprise – so I scrambled ashore across stepping-stones and up a red mud bank.

There were an enormous number of people waiting to arrest me.

On closer inspection they turned out to be money-changers, full of charm, their fingers flicking like lizards through bundles of pristine notes. The incomprehensibly high level of inflation meant that fifty dollars' worth of pesos completely filled my hold-all. The money-changing was an arcane ritual to one who failed O-level maths, but I savoured the knowledge that in one currency at least I was a millionairess.

It was difficult to see anything of Guayaramirim at first: the local young bloods churn up the red earth on their motorbikes into a permanent dust-storm like a William Blake vision of hell. Through the murk appeared white-clad convent schoolgirls like angels and clouds of yellow butterflies in great ethereal smudges. Later I noticed the schoolgirls were ogling the bike-boys and the butterflies were attracted by the smelliest mud-patches, but at the time it was extremely uplifting.

Then I caught sight of a semi-submerged building marked "Immigration" and experienced a sudden convert's urge to Do The Right Thing at a border. Squeezing past a woman selling toothy, prognathous fish on the verandah, I waded across the threshold, only to be stopped in my tracks by warning shouts. Our Mr Fixit, a former journalist who bore a startling resemblance to an emaciated W. C. Fields, splashed up behind me.

"On no account," he yelled, "are you to confuse the issue by going in *there*."

"But we've got permission," I said, waving the relevant papers, "and here's my visa," holding up an expensive sea of orange stamps.

"No!" he screamed and propelled me back towards the camera.

My passport shows no evidence that I have ever been in Bolivia. There was a football match on television when we returned to the Mamoré river a week later after filming in the time-warp that is the Beni region. No official was to be seen in Bolivian Guayaramirim or Brazilian Guajaramirim. After that, something snapped. All my reverence for frontiers evaporated.

That evening I popped back to Bolivia for a nightcap. The following day, we had breakfast in Brazil and elevenses in Bolivia. Dangling BBC labels from every extremity, we were nevertheless without a qualm, for we were habitues of the Mamoré river, the ultimate in border sophisticates.

Michael Heath
THE PAPER CHASE

Turn your back and Fleet Street starts another new paper…

"Room for one more inside."

"No, I'm only the editor – that's the owner over there."

"Bring it back, won't you? It's the only one we've got."

"Surely we can't all have the same scoop!"

"Thanks to new technology, you're the Agony Aunt, Crossword Compiler, Sports Editor and Pocket Cartoonist."

HOLTE
Among My Souvenirs

"Mind you, it's not what it used to be – even the unspoilt tribes of New Guinea are out to make a fast buck these days."

"They're permanently on the look-out for ivory smugglers – so how Arthur got this piece out I'll never know."

"You press this little button here – and he sings 'O Sole Mio' and makes a grab for your cornetto."

"We bought this lovely wallet in one of the back stree[ts]. Mind you, we had a little difficulty convincing th[e] Iranian authorities that it was paid for."

"Actually, they import the mechanism from the Swiss – but the concept is typically Haitian."

"Norman spent a lot of time down on the quay, watching the fishermen mending their nets. Until one day, they presented him with this lovely jersey."

"Right, the scene is set ... release the mosquitos, Bernard."

IS YOUR MEMORY HERE?

Up and down the country, pensioners are being pestered to record their reminiscences for posterity.
To save wear and tear on the memory, this handy checklist has been drawn up for issue to senior citizens.
It is believed to contain 95% of all likely recollections.

1. Was your earliest memory:
A voice telling your mother, "They often look funny at first" ( )
Ella the maid being turned out on to the street ( )
Your mother apparently driving hat-pins through her head ( )
Surprising your parents that day in their bedroom ( )
Men laying straw in the street when Grandfather was ill ( )
Standing in the corner in a dunce's hat ( )
The smell of horse dung everywhere ( )
Your father's face when he said, "Mummy has bolted" ( )

2. Did you ever catch a glimpse of:
The muffin man ( )
The hangman ( )
The man in the pub who bit the heads off live mice ( )
Lord Kitchener, either before or after his "death" ( )
Harold Wilson in bare feet ( )

3. Did you have any memorable experiences behind:
Bicycle sheds ( )
Cricket pavilions ( )
Gravestones ( )
Filing cabinets ( )
Sofas or ottomans ( )

4. What was the first thing you remember reading:
"Glaxo Builds Bonny Babies" ( )
Rainbow comic ( )
Your big sister's secret diary ( )
Das Kapital ( )

5. When you were young, was it a fact that:
Postmen looked like postmen, not scruffy day-trippers ( )
Children left school knowing the alphabet ( )
Mothers' skirts were long enough for a child to clutch ( )
Things did not fall out of trouser-pockets all the time ( )
You could sew on a trouser-button for nothing ( )
instead of paying a fiver for a new zip
Grannies were not put in homes, but made to pull their ( )
weight in the family
Men always wore hats, so that they could raise them to ( )
ladies, or cenotaphs

6. But was it not also a fact that:
People's false teeth flew out more often ( )
There were men with wooden legs everywhere ( )
The life expectation of gas mantles and ( )
subalterns was three weeks
Shepherds wore things like nighties ( )
It was so cold that crows froze to death in the air ( )
and crashed through greenhouse roofs

7. Did you ever see in the sky:
The Angel of Mons ( )
A Zeppelin in flames ( )
A doodlebug heading straight for you ( )
The Finger of God ( )
Halley's Comet ( )
The words "Bile Beans" in smoke-writing ( )

8. What did you do in the last war:
Volunteered for the Poor Bloody Infantry ( )
Went lecturing in America ( )
Served with a lot of failed novelists in Intelligence ( )
Built the bridge over the River Kwai ( )
Looked for parachutists disguised as nuns ( )
Rode a unicycle for ENSA ( )

9. Did you definitely not win the war so that:
People could be free to drop take-away rubbish in your garden ( )
Pregnant school-leavers could go straight into council houses ( )
Unmarried mothers could draw a dozen double-damask ( )
dinner napkins from Social Security
The population could be wiped out by evil men practising ( )
Abominations unto the Lord

10. In the days when "people made their own entertainment", did you:
Spin a top in the road ( )
Rattle a stick along the railings ( )
Recite temperance monologues ( )
Practise doing a "Flying Angel" on your bike ( )
Take up serious shin-kicking, Lancashire fashion ( )
Read the Works of Jane Austen in Pitman's Shorthand ( )
Sit around waiting for television to be invented ( )

11. Did you ever get a smart clip over the ear-hole from:
The local copper, for smoking in the street ( )
The park-keeper, for smoking in the park ( )
The squire, for not tugging your forelock/curtsying ( )
Your teacher, for dipping girls' hair in inkwells ( )
The farmer, for bird's nesting ( )
The vicar, for grave robbing ( )
Your mother, for ruining your new sailor suit/ ( )
clean new pinafore

12. Did your father ever:
Tie your loose tooth to a door-knob, slam the door ( )
and give you threepence
Cut your hair with a pudding basin ( )
Take you for a sniff at the gasworks to cure your cold ( )
Act the Fascist and dose you with castor oil ( )

13. Did your first romance blossom:
At the palais de danse ( )
In the back stalls of a flea-pit ( )
In the back seats of a charabanc ( )
On the Clapham omnibus ( )
In any of the locations listed in Question 3 ( )

14. Do you remember the siren voices of:
The sirens ( )
The BBC nightingale, coaxed by a cello ( )
The first Welsh Windbag, that fellow who won ( )
World War One
The Radio Doctor ( )
Lord Haw-Haw ( )

15. Where did you first see a red flag:
Carried in front of an early motor-car ( )
Waved by Shinwell in Glasgow in 1919 ( )
Hoisted everywhere in the General Strike in 1926 ( )
Flying from London town halls in the 1980s ( )

16. Were you ever disillusioned as the result of:
Praying devoutly for a Hornby train set and ( )
getting a wooden monkey-on-a-stick
Finding that the lower level of a chocolate box ( )
was only half-filled
Finding that a promised "scrumptious pudding" ( )
was tapioca
Seeing the King ride by with his face made up ( )
Seeing a chorus girl with sticking plaster on her thigh ( )

If you have any recollections over and above the foregoing, please write them here in not more than 50 words ....
....

CITIZEN STAN

"PSST!" a voice, male, but whether Caucasian or non-Caucasian I could not tell, came from a poison sumac bush. "Pssst!" the bush appeared to say, "Hey, you!"

A gigantic male personage in frock-coat, wing collar and tall silk hat with a dollar sign, $, printed on it, stepped out from behind the bush, followed by Arlene Dahl in a flowing gown of bimbo pink which permitted light and vision to pass through. So, I thought, that is the meaning of diaphanous.

The large man extended his hand in a friendly manner.

Like everyone else, I had seen the photographs in the daily press. I had seen the newsreels and the television. I immediately recognised Cyrus P. Hun, the billionaire newspaper magnate, standing before me.

"Son!" he said.

In that instant it became clear to me. Of course! It could be no other way. I had been kidnapped by the gipsies and sold to that old couple, a humble, lower middle-class pair, with some most amusing pretensions, quite laughable yearnings, really, for things above their station.

"Dad!" I said to Mr Hun.

"Name it," said Cyrus P. Hun, "and it is yours."

"I am only a humble, ordinary person, sir," I said, "but the humble folk who raised me – I speak of the old bore and his mate – taught me that might is not right. I wish, sir, to fight crime and corruption and crusade, through the pages of a fighting journal, for the rights and dignity of the little people, the common folk, God's poor."

"Say, honey," said Arlene Dahl to Mr Hun, "crime 'n' corruption, the same as you."

"Belt up, we're talking," said Mr Hun.

"Sir," I said, indicating Miss Dahl, "is this delightful female personage my Mom?"

"No, dummy, this," Mr Hun said, "is Dream Rabbit, your personal person."

"A bit old-fashioned, is she not?" I said. "She looks like Arlene Dahl."

"Arlene Dahl is *playing* her."

With a wave of his Havana-laden hand, before me was conjured up an empire of newspapers, paper mills, factories, chemical plants, radio stations, an army of industrious workers and Miss Dahl, Dream Rabbit, by my side, being very kind.

Then, towering above us, all glass and steel and shimmering onyx, was the *Morning Stan*, mighty organ of opinion. I stood in the centre of the newsroom and addressed my staff. They trembled before me. I had never felt more myself than at this moment.

"What's your name, boy?" I enquired of a likely-looking lad.

"Evans, sir." He shook. God! What fear!

"Max," I cried, "throw him out of here. And when you find the rest of him, toss that out too. And limp that other sneak over here and I'll toss him out myself." Sometimes one must be cruel to be kind. "And Max..."

"Sir?"

"Throw yourself out while you're at it."

I had often read, while studying the lives of great men, that it was lonely at the top. "What's your name, son?" I asked, "and don't cringe like that. It will only create in me an overwhelming desire to physically assault you."

"Andreas, sir."

"What are you, some kind of a goddam Greek? You got something against tit, boy? I don't see no tit in your pages. Look at Murdoch. Murdoch, for Christ's sake, I'm talking to you, you're not up Perth harassing the goddam sheep for Christ's sake. Murdoch likes tit. You like GREAT BIG BULGERS, don't you, Murdoch? And for God's sake stand up straight when I'm talking to you."

"Yes, sir."

"Speak up, or I'll have you torn apart limb from limb." A firm hand is needed.

"YES SIR!!"

"That's better. And how do you like your tit, ▶

McLACHLAN

LET'S PARLER FRANÇLAIS!

Lesson Trois-cent-soixante-quinze
Le Jeu de Monopoly

Papa: C'est ton tour, chérie.

Maman: Mon go? Sorry. Mon mind était elsewhere. Huit. 1…2…3…4…etc. Ah, Northumberland Avenue. Je vais l'acheter.

John: Tu l'as acheté sur ton dernier go round.

Maman: Dommage. Je n'ai pas beaucoup de property.

Janet: Tu as seulement Northumberland Avenue. Il faut concentrer, Maman!

Papa: OK, mon go. Ah, j'ai fait un landing sur Go!

John: Voilà. £200.

Papa: Non, c'est £400 pour un direct hit sur Go. C'est dans les rules.

John: Montre-moi la rule qui dit: £400 pour un landing sur Go.

Papa: Nous avons perdu les Monopoly rules. C'est la No. 1 rule de Monopoly — le rule-sheet est toujours perdu first. Mais nous avons toujours joué la £400 sur Go rule.

John: OK, OK. Maintenant c'est mon go, mais first je veux acheter des hôtels pour Bond Street et Regent Street.

Janet: God, tu es un mean capitaliste! Je déteste tes hotels.

John: Et maintenant, c'est mon go. Hmm. OK, Mayfair. OK, Janet, ton go.

Janet: Enfin! Ah — un six … Hold on un instant. Mayfair est à moi. Tu me dois du rent!

John: Non, c'est trop tard. Il faut dire: Rent, avant le next go. Otherwise, c'est null et void.

Janet: Ah, ce n'est pas fair! Tu m'as forcé à faire un go! Donne-moi le rent!

John: Non.

Janet: Eh bien, je ne vais pas jouer.

Papa: Oh, for God's sake, donne-lui le rent, John. Sois flexible.

Maman: Il est curieux, l'idée de construire des hôtels dans Fleet Street. Qui voudrait passer une nuit en Fleet Street?

Papa: C'est curieux, la présence de Fleet Street. Il devrait être Wapping nowadays.

John: Maman, c'est ton go.

Janet: Non! Je n'ai pas encore fait mon go!

John: Well, look sharp, petite soeur.

Janet: Ne sois pas patronisant … Ah, Chance. "Allez en prison". Damn.

Maman: Moi, maintenant. 1…2…3…4…5… Mayfair.

Janet: Rent!

John: Tu ne peux pas demander le rent pendant un sojourn en chokey.

Janet: Pourquoi pas?

John: C'est dans les rules.

Maman: Je n'ai aucune objection de payer du rent à un prisonnier. Voilà, chérie.

John: Ah, non, ce n'est pas juste! On brise les rules pour Janet, parce qu'elle est une fille!

Papa: Look, je n'ai pas eu un go pour yonks!

(Etc, etc. Le jeu continue until a) Janet a un crying fit b) John inflige le bankruptcy sur everyone c) Papa fait l'opting out pour le World Cup d) Maman resigne sa position pour aller dans le kitchen. C'est la grande unwritten rule de Monopoly.)

Murdoch?"

"Nice big ones, sir?"

"And one on each side, eh, Murdoch?" Sometimes one must share a joke with the men.

"Ho ho ho, sir."

"Knock off the sycophancy, Murdoch. Why am I surrounded by yes-men? I *am* surrounded by yes-men, ain't I, Max?"

"Yes, sir."

"Trelford? Where's Trelford? Max, find Trelford. What do you mean, you can't find him? Look under the desks, Max. Look in the desk drawers. Look in Tiny's pocket. How many places can a midget hide?" The workers do what they call "swinging the lead". Absenteeism is rife.

"Rees-Mogg, you *call* this a cup of tea? Get Hetherington to show you how I like it. Preston?"

"Yes, sir?"

"Where are you, Preston?"

"Here, sir. Behind you."

"Stop sneaking up on me like that. Creep up on me like a man. Look at Neil. Look at Howard. When they creep up, they *creep up.* They don't creep up in that creepy fashion."

"Yes, sir."

"Stop rubbing your goddam hands together like Uriah Heep, for God's sake. What's on the front page?"

"OFFICIAL SECRETS GIRL SENT TO PRISON."

"Women in prison. I like it. She got tits?"

"I think so, sir."

"Think so? Think so! Didn't they teach you no biology at Oxford?"

"Ho ho ho. Ha ha ha."

"Shut up!"

"Yes, sir."

One must keep a certain distance.

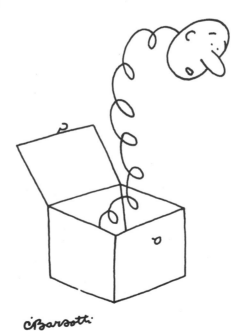

"My God, I'm a Jack-in-the-box."

"They taught Murdoch about tits at Oxford, didn't they, Murdoch?"

"And sheep, they got six titties, chief."

"That's very interesting, Rupert. Now you go over there and try again to teach that Bohunk Maxwell what the difference is between a knife, a fork and a spoon. Preston."

"Yes, sir?"

"Lay off them Greenham Common bimbos, unless the ladies down there got … got what, Preston?"

"Big ones, sir?"

"Speak up! BIG WHAT?"

"Big titties, sir."

"Now, again, so you won't forget. GREAT BIG WHAT?"

"BULGERS, sir."

"That's better, ain't it, Murdoch?" One must reward and encourage. "Who the hell are they, over there? What are they?"

"Women, sir. That's the women's page."

"Women? Throw those broads the hell out of here. Women got no place in newspapers."

They tremble. Their faces grow pale. I see them doing sums on bits of paper, wondering if they can afford to go freelance and have nineteen sonsofbitches as bosses instead of just one great big sonofabitch. They also whisper. I can hear them whispering. "Uncivilised," they whisper. "A monster." "A bully." "A monstrous, bullying brute." "How uncouth he is, and I always thought he was just a two-dollar shit-heel; of course, I am his mother, I look on the bright side." There is treachery. Scandal. Gossip. They put it about that Arlene Dahl, the Dream Rabbit, is only a rubber lady that you blow up. It is all lies. I personally have searched Miss Dahl for a tell-tale valve or spigot for inflation. She possesses no such orifice.

Staffing is a continuing difficulty. A Mr Kafka, highly recommended, is even now covering some long-winded, interminable trial but hopes for a verdict soon. I am *not* prejudiced as to sex or class. I have brought – I am *not* ashamed to say – a Royal Princess on to the staff. She is doing amazingly well. Her "piece" on Christmas, "Yes, Virginia, There Is A Santa Claus," was a marvel. Her series on family life – "All happy families are the same but all unhappy families are unhappy in their own way" – is up for a major prize.

And yet I am not loved. The little people, whose interests I serve, do not love me. I am attacked in the gutter press. Their vans have been set on fire. Their newsboys have been beaten up. And yet they persist in their lies and half-truths. I am not connected with the Trust. The banks have no hold on me. I am not a shareholder in Universal Traction. We meet, merely, at the club. My son knows the daughter of the Trust. My youngest is at school with Universal Traction. There was *no* cover-up. He's a fine boy. And, after all, he only raped her once.

My conscience is untroubled. I am innocent. I meant to do right. But Dream Rabbit alone is trustworthy, and she seems to have developed some sort of slow leak. I am surrounded by traitors. Self-seekers, their loyalty to the highest bidder. I have an awesome vision. A terrible vision. In it Eddy, the commissionaire, rushes into my office to tell me Jesus is at the door, and He's armed!

FIVE GO TO HEAVEN

"I coveted all my neighbours' wives, but since I'm an Eskimo, apparently that was OK."

"I don't care how it looks, this has got to be hell!"

"Alfred The Great, you remember Peter The Great, Ferdinand The Great, Catherine The Great, Charles The Great and Frederick The Great, don't you?"

"Poor Nigel. I begged him not to convert to Hinduism."

RURALITANIA

THIS morning I ran over a snake. It was dark, old-bottle green, shiny as a beetle, flexible as a whip, and it went skimming across the dusty forest track like a liver fluke across the eyeball. I think I just nipped its flickering tail.

Most probably, it was a grass snake, but don't hold me to that. It wasn't an adder – I awoke once from an after-lunch sleep on a Cornish hillside to find an adder still dozing, its head on my sandshoe, and I have never forgotten what it looked like. I am also nearly certain it was not a slow-worm – I made my son keep one of those as a boy, much against his protests, to make up for me not having any interesting pets at his age. But who cares about nature notes on close encounters with *animalia chordata reptilia squamata*? The key revelation in that opening sentence has to be "ran over".

I suppose joggers could be said to do so, or pedal-cyclists. But usually, the term is reserved for those in charge of power-driven vehicles. What can this mean? Have I betrayed *all* my life-long principles, succumbed to those temptations I have so often sworn would never tempt me? Already, I have at last finished a novel, so becoming a kind of Grandpa Moses of the typewriter ... retreated to live rough in the country ... am I now giving my blessing to the newfangled internal combustion engine and starting to pilot a car?

No. My career as a pawn of the road may not endure long. So I want it to be clearly understood that I am sitting tall in the saddle of a motorbike, not lolling on the throne of an automobile. And whatever may be later alleged for, or against, the machine, in hospital wards or coroners' courts, I would like you all to know it cost only £60. And this from a garage proprietor across the hill whose cheapest petrol-run lawn-mower was £160, second-hand.

"Only one old lady user," he assured me (about the lawnmower). "Kept in a shed all autumn and winter. Can't have been taken out more than half-a-dozen times, and then only to the bottom of the garden."

So, if I am ever found embedded head-first in a haystack, a banger in mash; or plastered, legs and arms akimbo, around a tree through which I was attempting a short-cut; or left spread out, like a Rorschach test of ogre's vomit, across the gravel of a dangerous corner, I would like my mates to know how it must have happened. And it was not through losing control of some bulbous, flaming, twin-exhaust belching monster, like those scarlet and silver, blue and gold parodies bolted on fairground rides.

Indeed, as an example of up-to-the-minute engineering design, my motorbike is not much deeper into the present century, anyway the post-war world, than my oil-caked, heavy-breathing, Meccano-classic, electricity generator that resides in a converted (though not much) thunder-box at the rear of the premises. Furthermore, were you to mount the generator on wheels, and launch it downhill, I doubt whether the occasional pedestrians coming in the opposite direction would be able to tell one from the other after they picked themselves out of the ditch.

Certainly, at rest and safely rooted, both seem to have very similar roll-calls of valves, pins, switches, levers and buttons to be opened, closed, pressed in, pulled out, pushed forward, pushed back in a prescribed order. I see now that I have been protected these many years, by a city-swelling, non-motoring, mains-supply, automatic-control, gardenless existence, from any naked, full-frontage confrontation with the beast in the machine. I thought the elves, or

little folk, did it all while we slept.

In London, I never had to enter in my diary any domestic reminders, even to order coal. My diary contained only social reminders. Mainly to attend all sorts of festive, free-loading, publicity thrashes, where I could meet my friends to eat and drink without any cost to us, but which I only noticed half an hour after the event was over. Here, it is like the last 24 hours aboard a scuttled submarine or an explorer's camp adrift on an Arctic ice-floe. Everything is always threatening to run low – diesel, petrol, Scotch, anthracite, water, bog-paper, fire-lighters. Captain Oates is always about to leave the tent, and who shall blame him? I'm surprised he stuck it out so long.

If I had not understood about self-supporting, circular-feeding eco-systems while in the metropolis, where they worked without most of us noticing, I should quickly have identified them out here in the sticks where everything depends on everything, and it is your fault if *anything* goes wrong. The difference is, Nature can afford limitless amounts of waste. We can't. So there is plenty of pacing of the poop-deck, like Bligh of *The Bounty*, when it becomes apparent that a multiple stove resembling the fire-box of the *Flying Scot* must be deployed, not to boil or simmer, not to roast or bake, not to prepare baths, not for dish-washing or clothes-cleaning, but solely to warm up one radiator in a top bedroom. Meanwhile a generator that could power a skiff from Charing Cross to Hampton Court and back continues spinning, not to keep the place ablaze with light, not to support vacuum cleaners, one-bar fires, radios or mixers, but only to service the pump which forces up the same water to that same radiator.

It may be that, like King Lear, I have taken

too little thought of this. Perhaps every macho male already knows these vast empires of mechanics where Murphy still rules. But it came as a surprise to me that most machines, anyway those produced since 1950, do not necessarily operate just because you carry out all the moves in the right order. Often, if I may plunge into the metaphysics of elemental technology, I find I am asking a Wittgensteinian question – if I had not known I have followed the prescribed procedure to the last detail, how would I have known I had done anything? The question is necessary because so frequently, after obeying all the instructions, *nothing happens!*

However, if you cock up the instructions, missing out this move, transposing these two routines, forgetting later to cancel some earlier initiative, why is it the machine nevertheless invariably starts?

In my simple, unscientific, arty-farty way, I should have expected obedience to result in at least some cheering purr; inefficiency in an instant freeze, possibly followed by an alarm bell or a hooter. Instead, machines are deliberately designed to fool you into thinking the wrong approach is right. They only seize up, or puff out black smoke, when you are out of reach of help or have just settled down, happy it is all ticking over nicely.

My motorbike is not exactly a sight to inspire instant confidence, which is what I like about it. Written all over it is the message: You have been warned! Here is a form of transport for those who like doing things the hard way! This writing is metaphorical. But the writing that appears literally all over it also signals the same warning. *Up On, Down Off, Back First, Level Neutral, Forward Second Third, Start Choke Right, Petrol Left.* These are not instructions supplied by the makers. They were written on the metal flanges (flanges?) with a felt pen by the garage proprietor, after delivery. Yesterday, they were bright and unmistakable, ballooned inside shields besieged by arrows, a miniature Bayeux tapestry. Today, not only the colour, but even the calligraphy, has suffered swift, terminal decay. They creep, like grey ivy, around bulges a trifle too low for me to examine and are now indecipherable. Still, I remember all the instructions, don't I?

These turn out like seaweed – clear and precise underwater (i.e. when the seller is around) confused and confusing on the sand (i.e. when he has left). The kick-start rips into a roar under his eye (though I now recall that was always downhill) despite me thinking it a rather obsolete device like a wind-up handle for a gramophone.

It is not quite the same today coming back up the gulley on which we live. I am too timid, so far, to take the sudden humpbacks at a pace which will roll me over, and I stall frequently. Am I becoming that person I have always hated to imagine I could ever be, who sweats and swears in the sunshine, swears and slithers in the rain, trying to manhandle a bike too heavy for him by the roadside? There is already too much of this. But when the bike goes, it *goes*. I have experienced nothing like it since I crashed a Tiger Moth in June 1943.

And this morning I almost ran over a snake.

"A classic case of governmental overspending. It sleeps one!"

"Not to worry, sir, most people get a little nervous the first time they crash."

171

KENNETH ROBINSON
Not Many People Read That

I'M an absent-minded collector of non-books – the sort that are packed with entirely random information. If you don't ever dip into this kind of thing, you cannot hope to know that it takes an average of one hundred years for a tin can to disintegrate; or that giraffes are able to lick their own ears, or that the Queen uses black blotting-paper to hide her secrets.

It's all a bit worrying because we've just been warned by Dr Mortimer, the psychiatrist-author of books on brain-power, that too many ill-assorted facts of this kind (they're from Michael Caine's *Almanac of Amazing Information*, Coronet, £1.95) can make our minds unhealthy.

The trouble is that I can't resist all the non-books that flood the paperback shelves. They're always to be found under the heading of "Humour", and this is pretty insulting to genuine jokers. There's nothing at all funny, for instance, about Dave Dutton's *Book of Famous Oddballs* (Arrow, £1.95), with its stories of the poignant tragedies of great men.

Or are you, in fact, *amused* to learn that Wordsworth couldn't smell the flowers he wrote about; that Swinburne grilled and ate his pet monkey, and that Tennyson, who didn't have a pet of any kind, often impersonated a bird on a twig as a party trick?

Even less funny was Beethoven's habit of bumping carelessly into chairs and tables, and Whistler's desperate attempts to replace his furniture, as the bailiffs removed it, by painting its likenesses on to the walls and floor.

It wasn't even very funny for Mussolini when he decided that he must give up his bowler hat, after seeing Laurel and Hardy for the first time.

I suppose this is all information that Dr Mortimer would deplore as unhealthy. And just as bad for the mind, I'm sure, is the more recent *Things You Thought You Thought You Knew*, by Graeme Donald (Unwin, £1.95), which shows that nothing happens in the way we've always supposed.

It seems that cows don't, in fact, lie down when it's about to rain; that no one gets gout from drinking port, and that no plane has ever hit an air-pocket, because there isn't such a thing. When you also consider that oxtail soup doesn't come from an ox; that rabbits should not be picked up by their ears, and that Sarah Bernhardt never had a wooden leg, you begin to see why Mr Mortimer warns us about abusing our minds.

Michael Caine's book is especially debilitating, with its revelations that Boadicea had no knives on her chariot; air crashes cause fewer deaths than kicks from donkeys, and Nero didn't fiddle while Rome burned.

How does Michael Caine *know* about Nero? Because, he says, the violin had not been invented in Nero's time.

Not that personalities like Michael Caine are always the actual authors of books of this kind that bear their names. Not so long ago I was flattered to see on a publisher's list *Kenneth Robinson's Book of Funny Facts*.

"Sorry, Mr Robinson," said the publisher, when I enquired about the book I didn't know I'd written. "We meant to tell you about it earlier, but we thought you'd be certain to accept a large fee simply for the use of your name and picture."

I *did* agree, but the book's contents turned out to be too filthy to have my name on it.

"Sorry again, Mr Robinson," said the publisher. "We'll get the boys to research it once more. Unless, of course, you'd like to write the book yourself."

Me write a non-book? I did, in fact, toy with the customary dishonest idea of pinching material that had been published elsewhere. I thought I might lift chunks of the out-of-print *Hamlyn Book of Amazing Information*, which I always keep beside my bed in readiness for any sudden need to learn.

But I wanted to improve on it by showing how all those unhealthy facts could be marshalled into conversational form. I pictured the possible dialogue between two readers enjoying the excitement of what Americans call Knowledge Gained.

"*Did you know that George Washington soaked his dentures in port to improve their flavour?*"

"*No, but I do know that crushed strawberries are good for cleaning the teeth. Have some coffee?*"

"*Thank you. I must say I'm not as bad as Voltaire, with his fifty cups a day.*"

"*Bune.*"

"*I beg your pardon?*"

"*Bune. Coffee was called bune when it was first drunk in AD 1000. It was for medicinal purposes only, of course.*"

"*Funny you should say that, because cocoa was used by the Aztecs as an aphrodisiac.*"

"*Cha?*"

"*Bless you. You seem to have acute nasopharyngitis, which is, of course, the scientific name for the common cold.*"

"*No. Cha is a cup of tea, from the Chinese.*"

"*Not to be confused with Chang, I suppose – the surname belonging to eighty million people.*"

"*Talking of statistics, it seems that nine million British families eat custard every day.*"

As you see, it is not easy to sustain a logical conversation based on the unending stream of facts from non-books. "These facts," says Dr Mortimer, "force us to make assessments and interpretations."

But *do* they, I wonder? As I browse through my enormous collection of non-books, I don't think I would ever try to assess and interpret the fact that George Formby won the Lenin award in 1936; that Mozart could never carve meat without cutting his fingers, and that none of us can sneeze while keeping the eyes open, or breathe and swallow simultaneously.

Anyway, there's nothing wrong with *my* mind, thank you very much, except that I can't easily forget that Hedy Lamarr could look passionate only if a pin was stuck into her rear; Marie Antoinette did *not* say, "Let them eat cake"; Christians have *never* been thrown to the lions; and budgerigar casserole is eaten with the bones of the birds intact, like sardines.

Incidentally, how does anybody *know* that the average life of a tin can is one hundred years? It's bad enough having so many facts to cope with, but if we suspected they might be wrong we couldn't feel the same about Shelley having a remarkably small head, the Ancient Romans dining off dormice, and Lichtenstein being a major exporter of false teeth.

I was wondering if Dr Mortimer was right to say we should halt this torrent of information. "Only then will you feel rested and relaxed." I was just about to stop the habit when I found, in Michael Caine's book, that "Eastbourne will be the safest place in a nuclear attack." For occasional news like that it seems well worth carrying on dipping.

Did you know that crocodiles can't stick out their tongues; that Prince Philip hides a transistor radio in his top hat; that there are half a million rivets in Wembley Stadium...?

"We used to get two collections a day before they privatised it."

BARGEPOLE

WALKING up Whitefriars Street yesterday I paused to curse the snivelling boors who have "refurbished" a thoroughly beastly building which will now be let to financial people, hundreds and hundreds of greedy whores and thieves dedicated to the immeasurable impoverishment of the country upon which they batten to suck.

Middle managers are worse, though. There is a rotten "club" near here where I go to drink myself sozzled at lunch-time. It used to be quite jolly, with newspapermen in there and a feeling of camaraderie, but now it is just middle managers, terrible grey vainglorious dullards in suits, jockeying for position, boasting and snobbing and swilling and playing the fruit machine which gibbers and whiffles.

I cannot understand the allure of the fruit machine. There is a particular middle manager in a grey suit with a pipe who stands there for hours, feeding its slot and pressing its buttons as it plays its demented symphonies at him. Perhaps he is trapped between two cultures; the obsessive gambling and the desire for free money mark him as a Eurobond broker *manqué*; yet the continual prodding and tooth-sucking and fiddling at his stupid machine perhaps calls ineluctably to some more ancient industrial streak, passed down the Northern genes to pool and stagnate in the pallid veins of this backwater of a man. Perhaps the poor sap is still stuck in some 19th-century industrial dream, working away, pushing the buttons, watching the cogs spin, just like Grandad.

While I was sitting there being culturally raped by my cold Budweiser I became aware of "beer" trickling down my chin. It was because my mouth had fallen open. Closer examination indicated that I was also staring like a sick myopic ape at a definitely gorgeous bimbo (sorry, that's the Budweiser talking) who had walked in wearing a jacket of the sort of infernal inflammatory scarlet which you can only wear if you have that wild black Irish hair and the white skin and pale blue eyes. And the man I was with said, Oh yes, she's called Jane and works for the *Daily Telegraph* and used to go out with a chap called ...

And so forth, until I knew what I needed to know, which was that this female was bereft and in need of a sympathetic friend, if you follow what I mean, somebody with style and sophistication who would not be aggressively *macho* but could take her around and distract her a bit and you could go to France, perhaps, and it would be foggy in the Channel so you'd have to stay the night ...

And then I pottered up Whitefriars Street, as I was saying, and who should I see but the immensely distinguished humorist Oliver Pritchett, debonair and point-devise as always, shambling towards Aldwych like a bag of spuds. And we nodded and waved and I thought, *Can't last.* Might be the very last time I see someone I recognise in Fleet Street, before long it will be fund managers dressed in shirts above their station, and sclerotic onanists from finance houses, and all the abysmal clotted albumenous blobbies which are making England what it is today.

And their dwarfish chums and dim henchmen are driving us out, to Wapping and Battersea and places only fit for Yuppies to live in; because the intellectual Porgies and those who get off on balance sheets and miserable foolish "trading statements" cannot see beyond the next annual exercise in deception and bullshit, the AGM, and fail to realise that there are some trades which need a clear geographical nexus.

I was reminded of this again this morning when I passed the new British Library which they are building from discreditable and ugly 1960s plans next to St Pancras Station. Perhaps the only valid argument for this monstrous piece of municipal perversity is that it will be so ugly and unappealing and sterile that no future Marx will ever be able to void his corrupt intellect in its intolerable surroundings.

At one stage I used to believe that the best thing was to be a conservative. True, one was not allowed to duff up old women or taunt madmen with peeled bananas, but it was worth it for the achievement of stasis.

Now I have changed my mind. We all have to become reactionaries. I shall be standing for Parliament at the next election and my intention will be to form the nucleus of a Government committed to dismantling all the hideous mesh of "progress" which has engulfed us since the last war. All modern buildings will be knocked down, the death penalty will be restored and made mandatory for things I do not like, left-wing councillors will be made criminal bankrupts, Mrs Shirley Williams will be publicly flogged in Smithfield before being deported in a Hulk, and Mrs Thatcher will be retired to Dulwich where Avon ladies will call on her every hour throughout the week; on Sundays it will be Mormon missionaries. (Q: What's the Missionary Position? A: You wedge the door shut with your shoulder and shout "We're Catholics!" through the gap.) As for the financiers and bores in suits and pushy Eurocurrency traders, hanging's too good for them, as they say, but it will just have to do.

"Electricity Board? There's no power behind my throne."

173

JAMES WHITE'S CAMPUS

IN THE SIXTIES, EVERYBODY KNEW WHAT A STUDENT WAS.
They had long hair, engaged in protest marches and went for long periods without contact with
soap and water. These days it seems that only bank managers can spot a student at forty yards;
they're the ones with the ever-increasing overdrafts and the ever-less-plausible excuses.
In the post-modernist 80s, students divide into as myriad groups as can be found in the outside or,
as it's sometimes called, the real world. For the purposes of research we have prepared 16
computer-extrapolated, campus-generated, hand-tooled questions in an attempt to pinpoint some
of the major breeds. Put yourself to the test today; complete our quiz and find out which group of
today's students you can call your own . . .

LIFESTYLE

*On a fact-finding tour of your college, Kenneth Baker is invited
by the Vice-Chancellor to inspect your room as a typical example of student accommodation. What reading matter does he
find casually scattered on your coffee-table?*
a) The *Daily Telegraph, The Spectator* and Evelyn Waugh.
b) The *Guardian, The Face* and Martin Amis.
c) The *Mirror, Kerrang* and Mickey Spillane.
d) *The Wall Street Journal, Campaign* and *101 Uses of an
   MBA*.

What's your proudest extra-curricular achievement?
a) Being elected president of a dining club established in
   1899 and named after some obscure woofter no one's
   ever heard of.
b) Setting up an arts magazine with pretentious articles
   about the colour of people's socks, a gossip column called
   "In the Gutter" and a circulation of 12.
c) Having your stomach pumped after drinking 18 pints in
   one evening in the Union Bar.
d) Getting a job with a starting salary package of over £10K.

Is your overdraft . . . ?
a) Chronicled in correspondence from your bank manager
   which you've framed and hung over the loo.
b) Pushing four figures.
c) £27.38p.
d) Mind your own business, I manage to mind mine quite
   successfully.

During the vacations, what do you do?
a) Stay on and arrange next year's dining club calendar.
b) Travel through South America. You did China last year
   and India's strictly for the year off.
c) Sign on.
d) Go on a marketing course run by Proctor and Gamble
   before snatching two weeks in the Algarve.

*At a dinner party someone strikes up intelligent conversation.
What do you do?*
a) Throw food at them.
b) Steer the conversation towards something less pretentious, like a discussion of your latest creative project.
c) You never get invited to dinner parties.
d) Return the conversation to a more interesting subject
   which all the guests can follow, like what jobs everyone's
   going to get.

*During some late-night high jinks, a fire-extinguisher is
emptied and the alarms set off. What's your attitude?*
a) It's pathetic. In my father's day they did this sort of thing
   properly; like the time they roasted the Dean on a spit over
   a huge furniture bonfire they'd built in the quad.
b) Well, if this is the kids' bag, that's their problem.
c) Better keep my head down until the flak's died down.
d) It's pathetic. We're all meant to be consenting adults here.
   It's so bloody thoughtless. They woke me up and I've got
   an interview tomorrow.

FASHION

Are your shoes . . . ?
a) Church's brogues (bequeathed by your grandfather).
b) Purple espadrilles.
c) Adidas Samba trainers.
d) Tassled Bass Weejuns.

*Lapel badges make a sudden come-back. What brand are
yours?*
a) "Will Power" (a picture of Shakespeare), "Nuclear Power –
   Yes Please" and "Hang Nelson Mandela".
b) A discreet enamel pin with a picture of the battleship
   Potempkin, bought in Red Square.
c) Dozens of funny little in-jokes like "Chemists do it in
   phials" and "Ignore me, I'm pissed".
d) J Walter Thompson's recruitment drive sherry reception
   identification badge (with your name on it) that you've forgotten to take off.

*Which programme do you fight for a seat in the TV lounge to
watch?*
a) *Brideshead Revisited.*
b) *The Tube.*
c) *Spitting Image.*
d) *The Money Programme.*

SEX

Are you . . . ?
a) Celibate.
b) Promiscuous.
c) Frustrated.
d) Monogamous (to a partner of equal earning potential).

At the end of term disco, what's your chat-up line?
a) I wouldn't normally be seen dead at a function like this, but
   I have a very valid excuse, as I imagine you must have.
b) Hi, I'm involved in shooting a low-budget, 35-mill movie
   and we're looking for cheekbones like yours. Fancy pop-
   ping back to my place for a screen test?
c) What subject do you do?
d) Didn't I see you at the sherry reception before J Walter
   Thompson's recruitment presentation?

DRUGS

What's your stand?
a) In my father's day it was all about slipping an aspirin into
   somebody's claret.
b) Don't mind if I do. What have you got?
c) Well, I tried pot once and I can honestly say it had no effect
   whatsoever.
d) Well, frankly, the Olivia Channon types are the only ones
   who can afford it.

CREDIBILITY TEST

ROCK 'N' ROLL

Your granny gives you a record token for your birthday. You rush out and buy albums by which three artists?
a) Brahms, Wagner and the collected speeches of Churchill.
b) Hipsway, Furniture and Big Audio Dynamite.
c) Ossie Osborne, Iron Maiden and Marillion.
d) Sade, Dire Straits and Alison Moyet.

POLITICS

Are you…?
a) Closet Tory.
b) AAA, CND, SWP and Bar.
c) Don't know.
d) A believer in the free market because that's the only way to create real wealth, but with a caring face; moderate but with a radical eye; keen for change but aware of the need to preserve continuity; SDP but not prepared to admit it.

STUDY

The local bookshop foolishly allows credit. You run up a £500 bill almost immediately. On what?
a) Gold-tooled, leather-bound copies of the letters of Benjamin Disraeli.
b) A host of semi-pornographic/glossy arts photography/coffee-table numbers.
c) All your course books.
d) Books on interview technique and how to write the perfect CV.

The Library introduces an electronic screening system to stop book theft. During an essay crisis, how do you ensure you get hold of the appropriate books?
a) Tear out the relevant pages and take them home to copy.
b) Library?
c) Arrive there first.
d) Photocopy the relevant pages and take them home to consult.

Now check your answers against our quadrangle-level, sociologically analysed role models.

Mostly A

Young Fogey
You wear green wellington boots and suits that old men have died in. You smoke a pipe and regret the general decline in standards. You take a sensible course like Law or Land Economy. You see university as a useful apprenticeship for your adult social life and you go to a lot of drinks and dinner parties, a substantial proportion of which you're obliged to wear black tie to. You often get whelping drunk with your chums, indulge in high-spirited vandalism and bag lectures the next morning with a frightful hangover. Rather than joining societies, you think it's more important to learn how to mix Pimm's in the proper proportions. You think your fellow students probably went to state school.

Mostly B

Too Smooth to Move
You like to see yourself as a modern Renaissance figure. Whilst your fellow students are plunging into a premature rat-race, you are broadening your mind. You dress flamboyantly to distance yourself from the jeans-and-tweeds style of your contemporaries, and eschew existing societies in favour of exciting projects of your own; low-budget movies, new magazines and producing platform theatre productions. You leave college accommodation after one week ("it's so depressingly institutional") and set up a Bohemian flat in a fashionable part of town, from where you start rumours about your wild lifestyle. At the end of three years, despite all your apparent creative zeal, you will succumb to the well-documented fact that last year ten per cent of all Durham University students became accountants.

Mostly C

Northern Chemist
You're one of the 85 per cent of students no one ever sees between the freshers photo on day one and the graduation snap at the end of finals. You live for three years in college accommodation and you decorate your room with posters of Sam Fox and a tea-towel explaining the rules of cricket to a foreigner. Sometimes you manage to save a little bit from your grant at the end of term. You're insanely jealous of the college socialites with their pretty partners and you cling to the fervent hope that, whilst your honest endeavours will see you through, they'll get their come-uppance when the UGC cuts the History of Art department. With the current vogue for an emphasis on the needs of industry, it is a universal truth of the Thatcher years that Northern Chemists will inherit the earth, for is she herself not one of them?

Mostly D

Curriculum Developer
You regard university as a wearisome qualification for your ultimate goal – getting a good job. Bed sores are no longer a student's most sought-after social medals; in the 1980s you pass social muster by flourishing a contract of employment from a corporation everyone has heard of. A well-rounded CV is your aim and, however regrettable it may seem, no CV is sufficiently rounded without a reasonable degree. Thus there is no social stigma attached to working; after all, you'll have to get into the habit for those long meetings in the City. Good CVs also include a generous sprinkling of extra curricular activity. Your involvement in societies, however, tends to end with getting your name on the letterhead.

James White is probably on holiday.

DONEGAN

"We've been trying to move to the country for years, but Boris won't sell."

"I _had_ to let him in. He's from Customs and Excise."

"…And stay out!"

BEWARE OF THE DOG!

"It flatters him like mad, of course – but then his self-portraits always do."

LETTER TO A DUKE

To His Grace the Duke of Rutland

"*If you can't control him, put him on a lead!*"

Dear Duke,

I dropped in at one of your seats the other day and was chagrined to find that the film crews were once again giving you the run-around.

Of course, I know how it is. We have had them in our road, making what is called a situation comedy. They sent round a letter asking for our co-operation, saying they would let us get our cars out of the lock-ups if we chose a suitable time and kept a civil tongue in our heads, or words to that effect.

It was on arriving at your elegant mediaeval pad of Haddon Hall that I was again asked by a film company for my co-operation. "Co-operation" this time meant not raising objections to a very clever fake turret built on one corner of the Hall, a camera tower raised above the terraced rose gardens and some tarting up of a four-poster bridal bed. My first thought was: what is the Duke of Rutland doing, letting people build additional turrets on Haddon Hall? Collecting £1,000 a day was my immediate guess, and I hope I am right. It is not so long, I gather, since the Hall was used in the film *Lady Jane* and now there is to be this new "major motion picture" (did anyone ever make a minor one?) called *The Princess Bride*. Not much of a title, if you ask me.

If I know anything about film-making, the location scouts searching for a fine old Tudor house first combed Europe and came up with a shortlist consisting of Mad Ludwig's Neuschwanstein, the château of Azay le Rideau and the Blue Mosque at Istanbul. Then, having stumbled across your Haddon Hall and found it ideally suitable, they sought your permission to add a few improvements. I gather they also erected some rather fine hardboard stables, but these had been removed before I arrived. I noticed a mass of scaffolding poles on a rather lovely stretch of the River Wye and these, I imagine, were for building an East Wing, if the producer felt he needed one.

I would like your guidance, my dear Duke, on the degree of co-operation to be expected of a visitor who finds that Haddon Hall has sprouted a false tower. Should he give an amused shrug of toleration? Is mere apathetic acquiescence in order? Or should he rejoice at getting more for his money? If he asked for his money back, would he get it? My feeling, if I may be so bold, is that you should have warned me at the gate that all was not quite as it appears in the engravings on the biscuit-tins. I have not yet been to your other seat, Belvoir Castle, where the advertisements say *Little Lord Fauntleroy* was filmed. How do I know the grounds will not contain a hardboard mausoleum erected by Hammer Films? Or that the ballroom will not be given over to promoting a cigar called Macbeth? Whichever it is, the car-park is sure to be chock-a-block with stately vehicles labelled "Wardrobe" and "Canteen: Film Crews Only". (Did you ever try to scrounge a chicken leg from a film company on location? You should be so lucky.)

Suddenly I remembered that it was you, my dear Duke, who threatened to lie down before an excavator if the Coal Board dared to desecrate the Vale of Belvoir. Obviously a bit of passing desecration of one's own stately home is relatively unimportant. I am sure you will never allow the film-makers to affix permanent plaques to your walls, like the one I saw — excuse me, while I consult my notes — in the Bavarian town of Rothenburg: "Photographed in this beautiful town: *The Wonderful World of the Brothers Grimm*: a George Pal Metro-Goldwyn-Mayer production, 1961". A bit much that, wouldn't you agree?

I am confident you will take the foregoing in good part. I like to think of you regaling your friends with spirited tales of the indolence and overmanning which are inseparable from these occasions. Soak them hard is what I say, and the best of luck!

Yours sincerely,

E. S. TURNER

PS: I hope you have been able to put up your television aerials again.

Know Your Everyday Countryfolk

**KEVIN PILLEY's
guide to rustics today**

OI be Honest John an' a-while back oi be a-panking it off bold as a bull-otter to them wetlands o' Whit' all to ear-ache ol' Maggie. Cows give if they be sung to. So oi want in an' thur she wur lookin' at me like a gassed badger. "What you warn't?" she axed. "Oi be Honest John," oi sed. "F.U." "Beg pardon?" she sed, white as som battery sow. "Farmers' Union," I tell'd her, elongatin' the fust syllabubs like a good 'un an' versoon we were a-yappeting on an' she be sayin',

"Indaid. Indaid," when oi sed oi might be a slommacky bacca-reekin', catkin-pickin' thick 'a' swill we-be-a-shearing-come-Monday oink an' cider sop with the catch-on o' a peewit egg but oi al so be a tax-payin' charp an' as Blue as a shepherd's tranklements on a winter mornin'.

I wur gwain 'ansom oi woz as ne'er avoor. Oi sed we be sick 'an turd o' 'er an' the way she do a-treat uz. I sed come wind, come weather hill-farm folk beant afeard o' work nary on a us. I sed

oi a-sin thin's oi can't a-bear an' the world be a-far safer place if there be more chair-turning folk than politicians. I tell'd her, "T'aint right," an' sed, as true as God's in Gloucestershire, she better treat uz better or com zummer we might a-be a bit mor' particuler in our votin'. She know'd what oi myums. I tell'd her. That's the sartin truth. Oi be a man who be a-puttin' his cards on the table. Speakin' me mind. Allus have done, honest-to-goodness.

WE'RE the self-sufficient Sixties couple. We dig everything. We live in a converted haystack and get high on the cool beauty of the local stone. We've opted out of the twentieth century. We'd rather soak lentils than condone despotism and plutocracy. We didn't want to be the wage-slaves of industrialism. We wanted to be on the dole. It's cool and has great karma. D. H. Lawrence is our spiritual father. We believe in what he said about the emotional paralysis caused by urbanisation. We're not sure about the phallic insouciance of the daffodil. Angie believes heavily in the unreasoning Me.

We are expecting our first child. We're hoping it will be a vegan. Stock-cubes are bad news. We enjoy our life-style and country-life but my Dad says we can squat in his huge house in Holland Park once he's had it redecorated. We have a lot to do in the meantime. Carrying on with our photo essay of the natural landscape and liberating stuffed trouts from glass cabinets in pubs. We make everything ourselves. Even our own babies. We are wholly self-sufficient. We are nature-worshippers. We've made a lot of friends like Basil and Rosemary. They live in the herb nursery.

I'M jolly glad to say the Women's Institute i flourishing and continuing to help its member overcome those familiar problems of countr living – boredom, loneliness and rampan

alist and bowled me over with his huge collection of botanical terms. He was the first man I ever showed my paw-marks chart to. We go walking all the time. Even when we walked down the aisle after being pronounced man and wife we stopped halfway, got out a packed lunch and had a breather. My mother couldn't stop crying. She said I looked so lovely in my cagoule. Robin and myself are born conservationists. I was conceived in a portable hide and he spent the first six months of his life on a bat watch. We are members of the Green Party and spent our honeymoon redirecting sewers. We are very anti-nuclear war. It would alter the whole balance of Nature. Hedgerows would disappear and there would be nowhere to go at weekends.

LIVE a healthy, outdoor life. I love things like mudflats, becks, brecks, tors, fells, gorse-grown commons, open hilly ground, lush downland pastures, piled moraines, rocky boulder-strewn localities, alderholts, fen drains, peat bogs, copses and combes. I love rambling. My first husband, Bartholomew (named after a great grandmother who read maps), proposed to me along Offa's Dyke. He ran off with another woman as soon as the mist lifted.

I'm now married to Robin. He's a keen natur-

THERE has been an old boy sitting on this seat watching the world go by for centuries. The last one did it for forty years. Surely there isn't a more enduring or endearing sight in British country life than the smelly old bore with trousers up to his nipples? I am one of the few surviving examples of a vanishing way of life. I'm a landmark and historic monument to a bygone age. My hip has just been lovingly restored and my teeth (circa 1972) are back to their former glory.

I believe it essential that traditional country crafts and customs are kept alive in an age when so much is being threatened by progress. So I sit here looking all olde-worlde saying stupid things like "Raw morning," "The church be worth a-looksy," and "Hardly believe New York is only five thousand miles away it's so peaceful." I pour my soul into these fatuous remarks as old codgers have done since time immemorial. We don't like it but tradition is such a sacred thing. I'll continue boring passers-by till I drop. I love to tell the kids about Tobruk. The wife, bless her, died of decimalisation a long time ago but I don't mind the solitary life. I love isolated places like Dartmoor. I feel they're the sort of place I really belong.

---

asparagus cutters. Today's countrywomen live in constant fear of agricultural labourers and rural craftsmen with their funny-shaped tools, loving handicraft and desperate desire to pass on their skills to a new generation. Uncouth peasants, the lot of them!

That's why more and more ladies are joining our self-defence classes and learning the most effective way to overpower a sex-mad wheelwright or a spoon-carver with designs. "Stay calm and cover your chutney," is the advice we give them and "Never open your door to anyone unless they have a National Trust card." Our mini-markets are popular too. The local environmental safety officer has, however, limited them to one a month because of the inordinately high and potentially lethal levels of marzipan.

The WI has an important role to play in preserving our heritage. The onus is on us to protect the countryside from the growing numbers of watercolourists and etchers. They are ruining the countryside and must be culled. Stalking them is fun and we select the worse specimens and hang them from tea-shop walls. It's not very pleasant but it has to be done. The nicest thing about the WI is the corporate spirit. Everyone works together. Like when poor Mrs Wheatcroft's husband Donald fell into the baling machine. The sewing circle rallied round and Donald was soon back on his feet again. We're tightly-knit people. The WI is always looking for new members regardless of profession, class or politics. All you have to have are ostentatious tweeds.

BEING the village bobby is hard work, make no mistake. Stile-stealing and orchard vandalism is on the up. We had a spate of murders here recently. It was the gamekeeper. He was very clever but not quite clever enough. He left one clue that gave him away. All the victims were professionally skinned. We had a bank robbery, too, but I was out chasing speeding sheep-drovers and by the time I got to the scene of the crime the robbers had gone and most of the witnesses retired. We had the nasty business of the Wetherby boy. He was found behind an ancient burial mound with the verger. He said he was only researching an evocative account of a country childhood. A likely story.

Then that hang-glider got shot and we caught the lock-keeper dressed as a woman. He said he was going to a fancy-dress party as Flora Thompson. Another likely story. Then we had the rape and that got harvested and made into little cattle-cakes. And of course Drabblemania hit town. The women went barmy when Mr Drabble came to talk to the WI. Speaking of which, I had to arrest Mrs Hobbs for causing unnecessary suffering to animals when she gave a very informative talk on moths to the young farmers. It's a busy life being a village bobby. Make no mistake about that.

"Frankly, there weren't a lot of new identities to choose from."

THE SNOW MUST GO ON

"He makes £85,000 a year just for doing that?"

"He's much earlier than we thought. His trousers have got fly-buttons."

"Look out! Here comes another one."

"I'm mad about forgetting my snooker cue."

"It's OK, we're just browsing."

HALDANE

"And don't forget – Rufus has his chocolate finger at two o'clock every afternoon."

"Listen, mate, you think I enjoy being lumbered with the tequila promotion?"

NEAL ANTHONY
KNOW YOUR AMERICANA

TEST PAPER

1 Who said, "Call me Ishmael" – was it: *Melville; Ahab; Starbuck; Queequeg; Pequod; Queequod; Pequeg; Starbod; Larbod; Ishmael; somebody else?*

2 Comment on the genealogy of: *Uncle Sam; Grandma Moses; Brer Rabbit; Babe Ruth; Uncle Remus; Uncle Tom; Ma Barker; The Godfather; Billy The Kid; The Man From UNCLE.*

3 Have you ever had The American Dream?

4 At what point did you wake up?

5 Spell the following: *Nook-yuller; Missl; Progg-ram; Ink-wurries; Labber-turry.*

6 Revere in order of importance to the maintenance of Democracy and World Peace: *God; Motherhood; Apple Pie; Paul Revere.*

7 Denounce in order of threat to the American Way Of Life: *Misfits; Loony Toons; Squalid Criminals; Pointy-Headed Liberals; Bleeding-Heart Do-Gooders; Lousy Pinko Faggots; Socialists.*

8 Who said, "Go ahead – make my day!" – was it: *Dirty Harry; Tricky Dicky; Lucky Luciano; Rocky Graziano; Wild Bill Hickock; Crazy Horse; Johnny Friendly; Elmer Fudd?*

9 Write down the only thing you know about the War of 1812.

10 Estimate the average speed of: *Fast food; fast women; fast thinking; a fast buck; Speedy Gonzales; the Deadwood Stage; American Express.*

11 What did George Washington cross: *The Delaware; the Mississippi; the Rubicon; the floor of the House of Representatives; the sitting-room; a sheep with a goat?*

12 Concede categorically that the First World War lasted from 1917 to 1918.

13 Accept unreservedly that the Second World War lasted from 1941 to 1945.

14 Remember the Alamo.

15 Who said, "There's one born every minute" – was it: *Phineas T. Barnum; Darryl F. Zanuck; Louis B. Mayer; Cecil B. De Mille; Otis B. Driftwood; Rufus T. Firefly; Richard M. Nixon?*

16 At what point in the play was Abraham Lincoln assassinated by John Wilkes Box while sitting in a booth at the theatre? Were the reviews good?

17 Who would have made the best President: *Jesse Jackson; Jesse Owens; Jesse James; Walter Mondale; Walter Kronkite; Walter Pidgeon; Walter Mitty; Walt Disney; Douglas MacArthur; Joe McCarthy; Charlie McCarthy?*

18 Explain the Monroe Doctrine, and analyse how it helped make her a star.

19 Buddy, can you spare a: *dime; nickel; quarter; greenback; ten-spot; C-note; grand?*

20 Tote that barge.

21 Lift that bale.

22 Which bird do you particularly identify with the United States: *Bald Eagle; Thanksgiving Turkey; Bald Turkey; Dead Mockingbird; 1965 Thunderbird; Roadrunner; Woody Woodpecker; Tweetie-Pie?*

23 Draw a map of the United States, showing the locations of the following: *The Deep South; The Mid-West; The Old West; North By North-West; West Point; Mae West; The Big Apple; Teapot Dome; The Yellow Brick Road; Sunset Boulevard; Moon River; Old Man River; Veronica Lake; John Ford.*

24 How come you never learnt to distinguish between Haldeman and Ehrlichman? Does it matter?

25 Note these, The Ten Truly Memorable American Quotations:

"History is bunk."
"What's up, Doc?"
"The British are coming!!"
"Beulah, peel me a grape!"
"There can be no whitewash at the White House."
"Top of the world, Ma!!!"
"The buck stops here."
"Fascinating, Captain."
"I'll make him an offer he can't refuse."
"SHAZAM!!!"

PAUL JENNINGS

Riley – Ace of Vets

THE fact is we have all been underrating vets. Why do we place them beneath doctors, just because they "only" deal with animals? A moment's thought will show that this places them intellectually *above* doctors. A vet's brass plate simply says J. CRUMPSON (or whatever his name is), MRCVS; it doesn't say in brackets *horses*, or *dogs*, or *birds*, let alone *elephants* or *snakes*. Yet we automatically assume he knows about the infinite range of animals. A doctor only has to know about people.

In the days when we had dogs, from a Sealyham that ate chair legs to a spaniel which thought all telephone calls were from the devil and set up an unearthly howl every time the bell rang, we had a vet who never arrived without an extraordinary tale of some quite different animal. "Had to shoot an Alsatian through the letter-box today" was one of his more prosaic cases. Once, asked what had caused the huge scar on his forehead, he said, interrupted in his description of some divinely obscure opera, "you'll never believe this, but I've been bitten by a bittern." He took a client's budgerigar, suffering from the bird equivalent of alopecia, to his own house, treating it with cortisone to make its feathers grow again; no doubt he would have got into the text-books if it worked, but the bird just sat there morosely, as well it might, looking like a tiny vulture. He never gave up hope for it, though.

Like presumably all vets, if you rang him up to say your snake had pneumonia or your elephant's liver was enlarged he would at least know if a snake has lungs to have pneumonia *with*, and what size a normal elephant's liver should be. And, in a rural area, he obviously had to deal with everything from poultry (which can get such diseases as Gapes and Bumblefoot) and sheep (Braxy, Bradsot, Quarter-ill or Evil, the Jumps, Orf, Outburst, Swayback, Wool on the Stomach etc) to cattle (Scour, Apoplexy, would you believe it, if they get too much nitrogenous linseed cake, and God knows what other ills – after all, they have four stomachs, to begin with).

I'm ready to bet that this story about Mr Cahalane is only the tip of the iceberg, the bit of the story that is publicly known anyway, so they might as well print it. Vets are, must be, pretty well up in exotic chemistry. Even an urban ignoramus like me knows that a good remedy for Scour is "Compound tincture of morphia and chloroform, 4 dr; liquid bismuth, 4 dr; oil of cloves, 1 dr; cooled linseed tea, 7 oz; the dose being a tablespoonful every eight hours" (just try that on a man, with his mere one stomach). If I know this, from quite a small encyclopaedia, what must a vet know?

And these are *Irish* vets, mythic figures in a wild Atlantic countryside of mountain, bog, misty smallholdings and, of course, illicit stills. "'Tis sorry I am to be callin' ye out at this time o' night, R.-R.," says Aeioun O'Clahomagh, "but I looked at me little bit of a recipe here for the Scour, that I had from me Da, an' his Da before him, an' I ses to meself, the dear knows where I'd be gettin' some liquid bismuth, for isn't your bismuth some kind of a little white powder, now?"

This vet's actual name is Riley, but he is always addressed as R.-R., for Riley-Riley, since the day thirty years ago when he arrived fresh from college and asked a local the way to "Bridgebridge", having had some difficulty reading the small print in which Bridebridge (a few miles south of Fermoy) appeared on the map for which he has had no need these last 28 or so. He has been to attend a case of parturient apoplexy in a cow owned by Danny Shenanigan, over Kilmurry way, and well entertained by a Danny elated at his two fine new calves.

This evening, in the long, rainy, still, rose-tinted twilight, R.-R. stares at O'Clahomagh as a strange harmony resounds from the rough mountainy pasture outside. "If I'd not had a day busy to the world's end, and meself too much leppin' from one call to another to have time for even a drop of the creature, Aeioun, I'd swear those cows of yours haven't the Scour at all; 'tis drunk they are, and happy with it. Can you not hear? They are mooing in parallel thirds, the way you'd think they were trying to do a sort of cows' barbershop."

O'Clahomagh comes to the doorway of his lonely cabin to join R.-R. "By the great Standin' Stones of Clonakilty, 'tis the God's truth I believe ye're speakin', R.-R. 'Tis that ould divil

"Can you do anything to stop him chasing ambulances?"

Professor O'Baumgartner, with his..."

"Did ye say O'Baumgartner?" Well may R.-R. sound excited, for this name had been on the tongues of all his fellow-students at the Royal Hibernian Veterinary Institute all those years ago: a brilliant scholar, son of a German father and Irish mother, while still in his twenties he had won world fame for pioneering research into alcoholism in cattle, and had left Dublin at the height of his fame to do what he described tersely as "further research". There had been various vague reports of his brief stays in laboratories in California, Germany, Mexico and India; and now these persistent rumours that he had been seen in remote villages in the Boggerach mountains in Cork – just such a one as Carriganimmy, where Danny lives.

"Wirra, 'tis the very same, R.-R. And here's the thing of it now. Ye'll not need for me to tell yez there's no fences nor walls at all on the Boggerach; them cows knew which was their own patch and 'twas there they'd stay all hours of the day. And then didn't your man put up a kind of a trough just below his grand house there, with the carpets and the pianola and the grand furnishin's of it, and didn't all the cows on the mountain – not mine alone, but Jimmy Teague's and J. J. Murphy's an' – but sure ye'll not need a grocer's list of us all here – didn't they all go up to drink from it? And isn't *drink* the word for it? Did they not all come back roarin' and singin' – a sort of cow-singin' the like of which ye never heard till tonight? The way a mortal immortal man with a true livin' soul would sound when he'd the potheen on him?

"And didn't those same cows start goin' down to the towns – Macroom an' Mallow an' the city o' Cork itself, an' them bellowin' an' roarin' outside the pubs, till the Gardai come out here in their military veehicles to see who'd been makin' the creature – and then th'ould divil had nothin' only water in his trough?"

Later, the Professor receives his ex-pupil, Riley, with every appearance of friendliness, the more apparent in the mixed German-Irish unchanged from R.-R.'s memories of thirty years ago.

"Ach, me boy, 'tis good to see ye, and me after wanderin' the world to find ze pot of gold zat is waitink for me here in the County Cork, nicht wahr? Did ye hear zem talk of O'Baumgartner and his fool's search for Cold Distillation when I vos after leavink Dublin? I've found it, me bhoy. Glory be to Gott, I've found it. Ze fools, zey were after thinkin' that distillation, turnin' a solid or liquid into gaseous form, could only by heat achieved be. But 'tis meself has discovered a formula that will feed your cereal into the cow's first stomach till the omasum –"

"– that's the third stomach of a ruminant."

"Well, God be praised, me teachin' after all wasted wasn't, the third stomach it is, and what should come out of th'ould udder only pure potheen itself, 80% proof, an' 'tis well I've done out of it, as ye can see. But I vill haf to stop zese demmed cows getting dronk on zeir own product. The Gardai are getting suspicious, though zey can prove nozzings. D'ye think ye might help me in the lab, make it unpalatable to cows?"

Making it unpalatable to humans comes later. *Much* later. Even to vets. ☙

184

HOLTE
RISING ZAP

"Oh, look, Norman – the first snowdrop!"

"It's spring all right – the tortoise is awake!"

"Mean-machine to Red Leader…am returning to base…"

"We're winning, Margaret! We're winning! There's not a bug to be seen out here…"

"Amazin' stuff! Can't understand why they took it off the market – I mean, just look at the size of those Brassicas!"

IS YOUR TRENDY NAME HERE?

Is your name Toni, Viki, Jaci, Jenni, Judi, Debbi, Ceri or Patti?

If you are known by any of these names, you are the victim of an unwholesome compulsion akin to the dancing manias of the Middle Ages. Teams of onomasticians are trying to discover how the fashion arose of ending names with "i" instead of "y" or "ie", in order that they may drop bags of lead and sand on those responsible. Meanwhile, if you have such a name, avoid over-excitement and go to bed early, preferably alone.

As it is unlikely that such a name was bestowed on you at the font, you must have picked it up somewhere, possibly from a Page Three girl or a party of tourists from California. You might even have caught the infection from one of those little name-plates employed by female bank tellers to facilitate getting off with customers. Or it is possible that you have seen such names in by-lines in the financial pages of the *Sunday Telegraph*.

The only acceptable girl's name ending in "i" is Fifi, which has a long and honourable tradition, especially in French farce. It is surely of some significance that the British Prime Minister does not yet sign herself Maggi, though this may be to avoid giving publicity to a well-known range of soups.

Not the least risk incurred by having a name ending in "i" is that of attracting men called Jimi or Freddi, not to mention Ali, Eli and Oli.

Is your name Kelly or Kerry?

As girls' names, these are strictly for yesterday, but you must try to live with them. On no account change to Kelli or Kerri.

Is your name JoAn, SuAn, DeeDee or NatWest?

If so, take a firm grip on yourself and decide how many people you are. It is sheer exhibitionism to insert capital letters into your name and you will only antagonise the powerful printing unions.

Is your name Winston, Leroy, Wayne or Caesar?

These are names to be borne with pride, but you will do well to keep a low profile when you see a police officer approaching.

Is your name Debra, Barbra or Evonne?

Evidently your parents thought so little of you that they could not be bothered to spell your name properly. Try not to let their thoughtlessness cloud your future. Remember, they might have called you Sherree or LooLoo.

Is your name Ranulph?

If so, it is because your surname is almost certain to be Twistleton-Wykeham-Fiennes. Be grateful for "Ranulph". You would look a proper fool if they had christened you Baz.

Is your name Debo, Bobo, Decca or Farve?

You probably have Mitford blood in your veins. See your General Practitioner at once.

Is your name Ringo?

If it is, you will soon be an old-age pensioner and it need not worry you much longer. The name derives not from "ringworm" but from "gringo", meaning anyone who does not speak Spanish; also an idle busker.

Is your name Chas., Geo. or Jno.?

It is likely that you are descended from a long line of fruiterers or family butchers. The abbreviation "Jno." for John, now increasingly rare, was probably dreamed up by an illiterate signwriter who ran out of space.

Is your name Wally?

No doubt you were christened Walter or Wallis and you were not to know that the name would attract hatred, ridicule and contempt. In the exceptional circumstances you have permission to call yourself Walli.

Is your name Madonna or Yasmin?

Your best course is to put your head in a bucket of water three times and take it out twice.

"A bit of judicious editing, and you've got a copy of The Sun there."

DRYING OUT TIME

> **"Augustus John would be banned today and so would all the authors, poets, writers, painters and musickers of my lifetimes – I've had at least three lifetimes, one with each girl, two more with wives."**

I HAVE been banned from four pubs in the last nine weeks, mostly in this Milton Keynes area but from one in Harpenden. I don't drink, so it doesn't bother me that much. When I go into a pub it's because there is a nice girl there. What I do there is unimportant. I keep buying packets of nuts that I smuggle into ashtrays in little heaps.

"What can I get you?" the girl says.

The reply is metaphysical. Your requirements are so fundamental and even unknown (in their more poetic elements) to yourself that you are lost. My eyes range desperately around the bottles and tins and those baffling pump-handles and I cry out some little liquid menu that rests on top of the head.

"Small beer and a large scotch, please." Then they say what beer and I ask *them* to choose – it all becomes involved. If the place is all right and the girl friendly, remaining there is difficult. You can't drink any more if you're driving and if you're not it's even more important to stay in command.

"I'll drive you home if you like," Lincoln offered. Lincoln is very pretty and seems to like me, so I drink a bit more in order to stay. I have been waiting for someone like Lincoln to say that, make that offer, to me of all people in the White Hart, waiting for it for nearly 50 years – predictably, I gave the wrong answer.

"But then how will *you* get home?"

Watchers of Jack Trevor Story have since told me that what she said was quiet and promising, but my reply was loud and deep and passionate, making a big deal and letting the whole bar know that Lincoln wasn't bothered about getting home. What an idiot I am.

She quickly moved away to a more mature chap. So that was the fourth banning. I mean, they don't ban me, I ban myself. Sometimes it's not my ignorant behaviour but politics. I tirade.

"The first time you say your four-letter word, I know I have to get you out," says Bill Johnson. He is my best mate for the past 30 years – I have written several novels inspired by Bill as central character. You saw him perhaps on the Paul Daniels show, riding his bicycle with the reverse steering. He has always done things like that and I suppose it explains his choice of friends.

Bill has been with me and contained my exuberance many times but now we are separated – by geography and circumstances. He is now the father of a demanding teenage daughter and I have lost my teenage wives – just recently, since the banning started. Elaine always contained me by being more over-the-top than I am. She taught me to swear but finally rescinded – I think that's the word – and went to university. Although she showed me how to yodel, as it were, I embarrassed her at low table at Oxford and she did not intend to let me turn up too many times at Lucy Cavendish in Cambridge.

"*Quietly*," she said, for a few months, like a ventriloquist.

That was my first banning, really. And the worst. I cried only last night, looking down into her dark garden, now lit only by the late white blossom of her plum-tree, shining above her daffodils. I saw her squatting down there in her dungarees, weeding the beds with a table knife, patiently, or combing Queenie's fur, that mangy dog on her back with her eyes closed and her paws in the air, but now dead.

"You're always on your own these days, Jack," said Moura at the Plough at Easter. What embarrassment. It's that obvious, is it? And what a danger. Middle-aged men start talking to one. The danger is to everybody present. Because, if I detect any blandness in their political or social thinking, or if I detect apathy or worse – if I detect laughter or funny jokes reserved for people like me (the greatest put-down surely) – I use my first four-letter word of the evening on them. Moura, of course, I shall never see again – banned.

The artist in English society today has been banned. Yes, it is a fact and it is what I am saying tonight, Saturday night and stuck here. Augustus John would be banned today and so would all the authors, poets, writers, painters and musickers of my lifetimes – I've had at least three (lifetimes), one with each girl, two more with wives. I married Elaine recently, which was probably an error. She took me into ecstasies for many years with her marmalade and preserves, wines, chutneys and delicious cakes and pastries and Greek dishes.

"And now I'm going to re-appraise Joyce Cary," she announced, taking off her Habitat apron. It was about five years after we had moved from Hampstead to take up this wretched Arts Council job in Milton Keynes. And it was, of course, the beginning of the end – *Dwarf Goes To Oxford* is my new book about it.

But I am not here to advertise. I want to point out, just after spending a weekend in Tunbridge Wells, that Thatcher or what she stands for has taken the colour out of life in this country.

▶

"I said, I'm thinking of calling it a telephone."

▶ JACK TREVOR STORY

"Dad, what were you doing to Jane in the back of the car going home?" asked Caroline, my daughter. It was the last straw in a pretty strawy weekend – Sussex is like going back 50 years.

"Now look here, Caroline," said I to her, quite fed-up. We were sitting in a small but over-priced country pub in a place called Sale Green, I think, and I had recognised the chap in the window as Harry Andrews, the actor. "Now listen, daughter, last night we went through the whole evening, chat, drinks, darts, without my swearing once – right?"

"Wrong, Dad," she said.

She then destroyed my halcyon memories of conforming to Tunbridge Wells. The first time she and Rohan had taken me to their local, which was in middle-March, I had apparently, *apparently*, passed out and been put outside in the Range Rover for an hour, then brought in again and normalised. But this time I had purposely, of course, watched myself pretty closely.

Well, somehow I had got away.

But is it so terribly terrible? Does it mean that a person, regardless of his talent or lack of it, shall not be allowed mad-drunks any more? If so, the quality of mercy is not being very selective these days. I've seen Peter O'Toole fighting and covered in blood and laughing, watched John Hurt creep up behind me in the mirror at the Coach NW3 and grab me by the neck, heard from his chauffeur, Gustave, about Dicky Burton doing things heroic and dangerous which would have sent ordinary people to jail.

Take the case of Colin the jazz drummer, top in his class, Ronny Scott's and The Stables and The Hundred and everywhere; he has stopped drinking altogether. It can be done. Drink fruit juice. Tea.

"I'll have a double-tea!"

Well, not tea – that's slang for potleaf, isn't it? Colin and I discussed it many months ago, this pub-banning in England. In that wildly discursive manner we mad-drunks adopt. The discussion of related issues. Art, the liberal arts, of which drinking or drugging or girl-watching and man-watching are a somewhat pleasant part, innocent in all its facets, is not banned in Paris or New York or anywhere where art is still part of the colour of the nation. My most fervent hope for Labour is that they will see this in the nick of time and get rid of that red – let's have a few pastels, another George Brown, some scandal, discover a corrupt son or daughter on the game.

"What do you actually do, Colin?" I asked, during discussion.

"I hit people," said the drummer.

Ah, that is a problem. Unless they are related to you.

Still, now I've got his particular mad-drunk crime in print, it doesn't seem too bad at all and you may like to know that his real name is Bryan Spring and our connection is his greatest rimshot and mine, Rosie Dalziel, whose father is a doctor and who reads for Cape, writes for *Tribune* and was Maggie's and my favourite flat-sharer at 18 East Heath Road, 1965-1977. Now I think of it, that was probably the *fin de siècle* of the mad-drunk age. One night my Dwarf, pre-emptively I see now, pushed me into a six-foot sewer trench in Canon Place and left me for dead.

About the present, as Doctor Faustus was heard to remark, the only time the golden past comes to Milton Keynes is when Goodtime George Melly rides in. But this is the optimum place when one writes one's long-awaited auto-biography. Nothing is likely to top it or distract you. Old letters, in the archiving, old columns and tear-sheets and books give me names like John Heath Stubbs, the poet, and the night he was banned in Bloomsbury and eight of us crossed the street in ritual protest keeping our glasses – Ian Hendry, John Watson, Byron Rogers, Maureen Pryor, Rosie and me and Fred – a cat-burglar who had just done John Watson's block but had a special no-go arrangement with friends.

And that's us, you know, at the far end of the Museum Tavern, Maureen with her waggish shine, fresh out of *Ladies In Retirement*, John Ingram being beastly to dinosaur publishers and nobody waiting long for the first four-letter word. That is the colour, the missing colour, nobody getting burgled, nobody getting pissed except in some fruitful way. ☙

"You were warned not to muscle in on the expanded polystyrene market!"

A Wok in the Sun

NAVIGATING the public parks of Peking at the moment is a somewhat delicate exercise, especially if you happen to be of a prim nature.

Eyes have to be carefully averted as bushes, or the many crumbling wooden benches, are approached. For summer provides a chance for the young to catch up on opportunities missed for romance, during the five months from November throughout which they have worn four sets of long-johns under the padded Mao suit, sometimes day and night, to keep the frost out.

Often sex, or in most cases a Chinese form of heavy petting, is also seasonal. Few, apart from the offspring of the powerful, have their own places, and certainly no quiet spot in the maze of Hutong alleys and cramped family homes, in which to snatch even a few moments of passion. In addition, the Marxist rulers frown on such establishments as the discreet "love" hotels of Tokyo or Manila, where rooms are rented by the hour.

Privacy is a luxury that only the powerful can afford or command. For the masses, life, if you're young, is spent waiting, and longing, for the summertime.

So, come the warm weather – and at present the days steam by in furnace-like heat – the Chinese are out in the open air, doing what comes naturally.

A poignant sight can be glimpsed as dusk falls on the Forbidden City. Between the high walls and the moat, there is a narrow road and a tall hèdge. Here, bicycles – all black and usually of the Shanghai "Phoenix" or "Flying Pigeon" variety – are parked in pairs, with their front wheels carefully positioned together and rear wheels facing out in opposite directions.

This is a sign for strollers to keep on walking. Couples are nearby and have no wish to be disturbed. Usually, with the trysting being so close to the heavily-patrolled Tian An Men square, the activities are innocent. While some may risk erotic games, most of the youths simply sit and talk quietly together. All they want is to be left alone for a little while.

Unlike in other capitals, there is no compulsive mowing of lawns by the residents, who, bereft of gardens, like to spend their leisure time wandering around the streets. Hundreds sit on the edge of highways until late in the evening, watching the traffic which has more than quadrupled in the three years I have lived here.

The audience includes many mothers, who sit with arms around their beloved offspring (the one-child family rule is rigidly imposed in Peking), right on the edge of the road in the "waiting-for-the-bus" crouch adopted by all Chinese from infancy. They can dawdle for hours in this seemingly excruciating and awkward position – legs bent and arms forward, with the chin almost resting on the knees.

The pose is necessary if you've ever waited for a bus in China. A play that was eventually banned by the authorities showed a bunch of would-be commuters waiting anxiously at a bus-stop. As they persevered, the men grew beards, the women became grey-haired. Eventually, after ten years, according to the script, a bus arrived. But it was packed to the doors, and the driver passed on without a pause.

For Pekingers, watching the world go by until late into the night is always enlivened by the guessing game of who is concealed by the heavy curtains in the red-flag limousines that swish by. The cars (which also include Volkswagen Polos, status symbols of the military) hog the highway, and are often escorted by outriders – in a country that is supposed to adhere to the rights of the proletariat, the class struggle and the slogan of the late Mao Tsc-Tung, who himsclf always rodc about in these veritable mastodons of the road.

As for the foreigners who live in the city, we, who have privileges way beyond the ken of the masses – constant hot water in the awful winter, together with stifling central-heating – find summer as magical as the rest of the inmates.

We live in our compounds, which resemble Glasgow tenements, and complain mightily about the dust which swirls in from the Gobi Desert to mix with the pollution for a choking daily cocktail. All of us have *ai yis*, literally "aunties" or maids, who clean the flats in the morning, only to find by evening a thin layer of fine dirt covering everything from stereo to Chinese chandelier.

But we love the summer, if only because it is a time of little pain. Everybody perks up. The blues, the coughs and the migraines – the most common complaints among the Peking expatriates, especially the women – vanish with the sun, and Sunday is picnic time at the Ming Tombs, or, for a group of British diplomats, a day for windsurfing on the Mi Yun reservoir, much to the puzzlement of peasants.

The most lively lot of foreigners are the students. They tend to accept the fine films of coal-dust that settle over their university dormitories

LET'S PARLER FRANGLAIS!

Lesson Trois-cent-soixante-dix-huit
Sur le Pick-Your-Own Farm de Fruits

Client: Excusez-moi, vous êtes ouvert?
Farmer: Oui.
Client: Bon. Je cherche les raspberries.
Farmer: Ah, non. Les raspberries sont finis.
Client: Les strawberries?
Farmer: Likewise.
Client: Les loganberries?
Farmer: Pas un loganberry, pour amour ni argent. La saison de soft-fruit est terminée.
Client: Ah. Et la saison de hard-fruit?
Farmer: Pas encore commenceé.
Client: Merde. Je fais une 30-minute drive, pour rien!
Farmer: Ah, mais non, mais non. Nous sommes maintenant un Pick-Your-Own-Round-The-Year Farm!
Client: Vraiment? Un P-Y-O-R-T-Y farm?
Farmer: Oui. Ou, non. En July et August nous sommes un Catch-Your-Own-Fish Farm. C-Y-O-F-F.
Client: Le self-catch poisson? C'est une joke, ou quoi?
Farmer: Absolument pas. Vous voyez le grand shed là-bas? Eh bien, dans de grand shed il y a beaucoup de tanks, et dans les tanks il y a beaucoup de sea-food. Vous faîtes votre selection, vous payez, vous allez en hot pursuit de votre sea-prey.
Client: Blimey. Well, OK. Qu'avez-vous?
Farmer: Nous avons un grand tank de oysters. Pour ça, vous payez £10 et vous prenez un wet-suit, un cylindre d'oxygène et un petit rowing-boat.
Client: Un *rowing-boat*?
Farmer: C'est un très grand tank. Ou bien, vous aimez les trouts?
Client: Oui, bien sûr.
Farmer: Eh bien, pour £20 vous avez un fishing-rod, une paire de gum-boots et un ghilly nommé Angus, qui ne parle pas anglais.
Client: Hmm. Avez-vous quelque chose de plus tranquille?
Farmer: Les limpets. Vous prenez les gum-boots et un paquet de hand-grenades.
Client: Hand-grenades? Ils sont tranquilles, les hand-grenades?
Farmer: Non, mais les limpets sont tranquilles, après! Et nous avons un peu de squid.
Client: Squid, eh?
Farmer: Oui. Nous vous donnons un fighting-knife, et puis c'est mortal combat entre vous et le giant squid.
Client: Blimey. N'avez-vous pas quelque chose de simple, comme un kipper?
Farmer: Un kipper? Oui, si vous attrapez le herring — puis on vous donne un smoking kit.
Client: Non, merci. Je vais revenir pour la saison de hard-fruit.
Farmer: Up to vous, squire. See you en septembre.

190

---

in the winter, plus the lack of much good food.

Banned from the weekly "Thank God it's Friday" parties, held in rotation by the embassies, they are setting the pace again this season with an activity that has never before been seen in the Middle Kingdom.

This is the Toga Party. The other night, 150 students, more than half of them Chinese, gathered on an island in the middle of a lake at Peking's old summer palace, which was sacked by the British in 1860. At sundown, a ceremony occurred at a traditional red-columned tea pavilion, to the bewilderment (and, one suspects, secret delight) of the local inhabitants, who spend evenings staring at each other waiting for the cool of midnight.

Participants gathered, clutching Chinese bedsheets which, unlike most of those in the West, are rarely white, but striped, plaid or flowered.

There was a one-minute silence. Then togas were donned over jeans and tee-shirts, and the theme music from *Animal House* was broadcast.

According to one of the revellers, the Chinese were even wilder than their overseas counterparts. A group of them performed a mad-cap jig, shaking bottles of Chingdao beer and spraying the assorted company with a gentle foam.

Inevitably, officers of the Gong An Ju, the bureau in charge of internal security, arrived on the scene, took one look at what was going on and issued orders. Candles which had been placed around the island were snuffed out, and the music was toned down. The party was over. But for some Chinese at least, these are days of true reform in the Communist state, and a far cry from the "Bitter Sea of Life" endured during Mao's Cultural Revolution. People are beginning to have fun.

"Pay no attention – it's just another of our weekly fire-drills."

WHAT, AGAIN?

The Most Oft-Seen Movies On The Box

ZENDA, The Prisoner Of (1937): Ronald Colman as Rudolf Rathbone stands in at his coronation before rescuing himself from the clutches of Raymond Chandler and Rupert of Henreid, insanely jealous because they cannot all have top billing. C. Aubrey Smith is Colonel Sapt with an *S*.

ZENDA, The Prisoner Of (1952): James Stewart Granger stands in for Ronald Reagan as Rudolf Valentino before rescuing both of him from Rupert Bear and Robert van Heflin. Louis Calhern is Zapt with a *Z*.

WORLDS, The War Of The (1953): Updated version of Orson Wells' radio play first broadcast in the 1890s, causing widespread panic throughout Pinewood and Shepperton. Everyone in sight is Zapped with a heat-ray.

CASABLANCA (1942): Rick (Humphrey Bogarde) resents the reappearance of the woman from his past (Ingmar Bergman), finally packing her off in a plane with Paul Hentzau. He then walks happily into the distance with Claude Colbert, commenting, "Louis, I think this is the beginning of a beautiful friendship." Oddly enough, this classic is never actually billed as a gay movie.

SOUP, Duck (1933): The three Marx Brothers (five, with Zeppo, but four without Gummo) take over the running of Freedonia and throw fruit at Louis Calhoun. Harpo Marx appears in a non-speaking role; Margaret Dumont is ably supported by an all-singing cast and an outsize girdle.

KANE, Citizen (1941): Story of newspaper magnate Charles Orson Kart, not really based on William Rosebud Hearst, who really didn't like it anyway, whether or not it was really written by H.G. Welles.

CAESAR, Julius (1953): Marvin Brando as Marx Anthony delivers the funeral oration after Perry Mason as Brutus has got the knives into Rory Calhern, as if being pelted by the Marx Brothers wasn't enough.

LOVE, From Russia With (19007): Lotte Lenya and Bertolt Brecht conspire to get Sean Connery in revenge for their not having been cast as James Bond and Honeychile in *Dr No*. He gets garrotted, Lotte gets shotte, and Connery gets to make *Goldfinger*.

SEVEN, The Magnificent (1960): One superstar and six hopefuls take on spaghetti heavy Eli Walbrook and his forty stunt-riding extras to boost their careers. Only Yul Brynner makes it to the sequel, and nobody can remember the name of the Seventh Gunman, played by…played by…Anyone who still doesn't know this film was based on *Seven Samurai* must have been dead already by 1959.

DRACULA (1931): Vampire casts amnesic spell over movie audience: result, everybody remembers Bela Lugosi, nobody remembers anyone else. Well – can *you* name any other member of the cast?

OZ, The Wizard Of (1939): Judy Garfield is swept out of tatty, run-down, black-and-white Kansas farmland into stunningly-coloured, fun-filled, thrill-a-minute Oz, and for some reason can think only of getting back to Kansas. Strange child.

LARGE, Doctor At (1957): Starring Dirk Bogart. James Robertson does full Justice to his role.

ADVENTURE, The Poseidon (1972): Ocean-liner is turned upside-down so audience can play "Which star will get it next?" Gene Kelly leads handful of cast towards the thinnest part of the plot, hoping thereby to escape to better movies.

"Be positive! At least now we know that being able to fly has got nothing to do with having a pointy head!"

"To be honest, Miriam, I'd never realised I was this important."